The
Earth
in Her
Hands

The Earth in Her Hands

75 Extraordinary Women Working in the World of Plants

JENNIFER JEWELL

TIMBER PRESS
PORTLAND, OREGON

Published in 2020 by Timber Press, Inc.
The Haseltine Building
133 S.W. Second Avenue, Suite 450
Portland, Oregon 97204-3527
timberpress.com

Printed in China
Text and cover design by Kim Thwaits
Cover illustrations by Lara Harwood

ISBN 978-1-60469-902-9

Catalog records for this book are available from the Library of Congress and
the British Library.

To the memory of my mother, Sheila Balding Jewell, you were my first landscape and the gardener who grew me; and, to my father, Samuel Rea Jewell, my first trail guide, your lifelong curiosity kindled my own love of learning.

We shall be known by the company we keep
By the ones who circle round to tend these fires
We shall be known by the ones who sow and reap
The seeds of change alive from deep within the Earth

It is time now
It is time now that we thrive
It is time we lead ourselves into the well
It is time now
And what a time to be alive
In this "Great Turning" we shall learn to lead in love
In this "Great Turning" we shall learn to lead in love.

LYRICS AND SONG BY MAMUSE, "WE SHALL BE KNOWN,"
FROM *PRAYERS FOR FREEDOM* (2018)

Contents

Introduction

Women have been sowers of seeds and tenders of seedlings for a very, very long time. For much of that time these women didn't have the time or the means to document their history. There is no telling the whole story of women making their lives with plants or women broadening the field of plant knowledge and practice. I can't even superficially acknowledge all the women in plants who've cultivated this territory before us, except to say the compost-rich soil they left behind is what germinated the seeds that grew the vibrant women I'm writing about today.

What does it even mean to be a woman in plants? For the purposes of this book, it's not exactly being a plantswoman, though many of these women are that to be sure. Compiling this list has felt akin to mapping mycelia pathways between collaborating organisms in the soil of a forest. They are distinct individuals, and yet in connection and communication: learning from each other, riffing off each other, reacting and responding to one another. While writing, I was determined to focus on the diverse ways horticulture intersects with our everyday world and on women whose work has enriched and expanded these intersections in the last twenty-five years.

I'm interested in how the plant world is improved by not only greater representation of women generally but also by diversity among those women. I want to explore the ways this field is a more viable and creative career path for women than ever before and how the plant-work world is demonstrating greater social and environmental responsibility, in large part due to women's contributions.

Our human engagement with plants connects us to the natural world, to our communities, and to ourselves on powerful intellectual, physical, and spiritual levels. My own fifty-three-plus years of digging in the dirt, tending plants, and finding life there has been complemented by a simultaneous observing, questioning, interviewing, and learning from other people on the same journey—resulting in a sort of meta- or quantum-gardening. These profiles of women doing current and innovative work in all fields I count as horticultural—botany, environmental science, landscape design/architecture, floriculture, agriculture, social justice, plant hunting and breeding, seed science, gardening, garden writing and garden photography, public garden administration, research, and public policy—often represent larger issues or shifts in our world. Their work illustrates how the many challenges of our world can be met through cultivating an interdependence with plants. It is a rebirth in many sectors. And like all birthings, this one is being sung, screamed, crooned, whispered, hummed, and rocked into existence by distinctly *female* voices.

In many cultures women are socialized to collaborate, nurture, and think holistically—we tend to employ systems thinking, which is related to a multi-tasking mentality. These seventy-five women are smart enough to be wary of the constraints of binary thinking and reverse bias. They hope that more women of all kinds, in all fields of study, will forge greater balance in how we approach life's challenges as a *community*.

One of the most compelling, sometimes uncomfortable, and always energizing missions in my own work has been

what I've come to refer to as "Decolonize Your Garden." For centuries now the most visible representations of horticulture have been images of middle-aged and middle-class or affluent white people. But horticulture is a human impulse, in all cultures, in all times, practiced, codified, ritualized, and valued across any and all social boundaries. I find it eye-opening to interrogate myself about my own biases, while striving to never inappropriately use or appropriate others' cultural ways of being and knowing. These are tricky, winding pathways, but important to navigate with humility, openness, respect, and acknowledgment.

A note on other biases: I am a white, middle-class, middle-aged, cisgendered woman who loves this planet, her plants, landscapes, gardens, and all her people, but especially her plant-loving people. While I've chosen for the sake of simplicity to use the standard pronouns she/he/they, I embrace and applaud a wide, inclusive view of gender and sentient life. Our physiological ranks include all beautiful manner of non-binary beings, and I aim to advance and celebrate a feminine principle while encouraging ever-greater balance and broader diversity in all fields.

The hardest part of writing this book was choosing the women to include. For every woman here, there are many more who could be. But constraints are both necessary and useful. I limited the geographic scope to the world I know best, with representatives from the United States, England, Ireland, Wales, Canada, Australia, India, and Japan. They range beautifully across race, ethnicity, socioeconomic and religious backgrounds, sexual orientation, and age. Of each, I asked them to note either women who preceded and inspired them or women coming up in the field whom they thought the world should know about. You'll find these names listed at the end of each profile—they create a beautiful, often overlapping web of women in the plant world. Sometimes they're very personal choices—mothers, aunts, grandmothers—sometimes they're simply identified by name and occupation, and sometimes the profiled woman has written a bit about how and why they're important. I hope you're intrigued and follow these connections, helping make the network of women in plants more visible.

This book is an extension of my ten years in public radio and podcasting with my program *Cultivating Place*. Through interviews with plant people and organizations from around the world, *Cultivating Place* explores the relationships between our plants and gardens, the natural history of the places in our lives, and their importance to our cultural and environmental literacy, our broader communities, and our individual well-being. I've gardened my entire life, lived in many places around the world while doing so, and have been a professional garden communicator for the past twenty years. I believe gardens and gardeners are powerful, intersectional spaces and agents of betterment in our world. I see hope and value in a self-sustaining cycle of living with plants, loving plants, learning plants, growing plants, knowing plants, interpreting plants, and educating and engaging upcoming plantspeople and the public through communication and interpretation.

My hope is that this collection is informative and inspiring for *all* readers. There are so many ways we engage in and grow from the cultivation of our plant places. Enjoy the cultivation of *your* places while you enjoy the beautiful stories of how these seventy-five extraordinary women cultivate theirs—one handful of plant-rich earth at a time.

—JENNIFER JEWELL

Leslie Bennett

HER WORK Owner and founder, Pine House Edible Gardens; founder, Black Sanctuary Gardens, Oakland, California

HER PLANT "The passionflower. It's vibrant, beautiful, strong, medicinal, visually inspiring, delicious. I just love it and all the different forms it comes in. Plus it was one of the first plants I learned about when I lived in Jamaica. I love that it's tough and grows rampantly, and that it's so healing."

HER PLANT JOURNEY Leslie designs, installs, and maintains edible landscapes, "landscapes that are both beautiful *and* productive, including plants that can be harvested for food, medicine, and beauty." More and more, specifically through her work on Black Sanctuary Gardens, Leslie's work and advocacy speak directly to the value of cultural heritage in gardening.

Born in 1978, Leslie came to her life's work as the daughter of a white English mother and a black Jamaican father. Her mother read Beatrix Potter aloud, instilled a love of gardening and stewed rhubarb over ice cream, and taught her the native plant names of Leslie's childhood home in Palo Alto, California. Her father would make lemongrass tea (known as fever grass in Jamaica) to comfort her through cough and fever. She graduated from Harvard College with a degree in environmental science with a specific focus in how environmentalism interfaces with social justice. She achieved her law degree from Columbia University and then her master's in law from University College London, where she focused on issues of cultural property and landscape preservation. "I wanted to bring these lenses into the garden. I did and do find it really interesting to consider how people's collective heritage and collective identity affect how their landscapes look—how they treat, use, and value their landscapes—public and private."

In England, Leslie worked for the USDA's foreign agricultural service and took on volunteer positions as a WWOOFer (Willing Workers On Organic Farms).

> Expanding the collective horti-cultural imagination

While working on a permaculture course at a Herefordshire apple orchard, Leslie realized she wanted to make living on farms and working for food her life. But she had some family traditions to reckon with first.

On the Jamaican side of Leslie's family, working as a gardener or land-based person wasn't a source of pride. It didn't represent "progress as a people, as a family." She recalls, "To leave law and become a farmer/gardener I had to question a lot of things. 'What is happiness? What is success? What is important to me?'" After several years of a self-directed farm, garden, and growing education in the form of apprenticeships in Jamaica and Nevada County, California, her career moved quickly. She founded her first business, Star Apple Edible Gardens, cowrote her first book, *The Beautiful Edible Garden* (2013), and moved on to founding her second business, Pine House Edible Gardens.

Early Victorians used the term "pine house" for conservatories, which were often built to grow pineapples—a plant the colonial plant-hunting, turn-of-the-eighteenth-century English adored and coveted. "This was a moment where Jamaica and England met in the horticultural world, and while there are a lot of layers to that story, I chose the name anyway, because I continue to find that moment where cultures come together around plants to be really interesting. It is complex—there is cruelty, pain, and exploitation—and there is also rich exchange."

One of the more exciting explorations in Leslie's work—dating back to her early legal academic life—is wrapped up in her interest in "cultural property," things like national parks, state trees or flowers, skylines, coastlines, and concepts that are "owned" by whole cultures. "What and who is a gardener and who are gardens for?" Leslie muses. "Gardening in the United States is highly racialized—assigned as a value, activity, and identity for white, middle-class culture—not so much people of color—and yet, we all garden! Unsaid cultural tags get assigned—whose cultural property is this and who decided this? As I've worked in this field, it's become apparent to me how important it is to reframe edible gardening (and gardening generally)."

Since 2014, Leslie's work has consciously included creating garden spaces that center on people of color, building on their cultural backgrounds and lives to guide the shape of a garden space, and "using plants that provide food, flowers, and medicine relevant to their specific experiences. In other words, in my garden design work I am trying to literally *make space* for people of color in the landscape of American gardening."

Leslie and her collaborators, Seven Asefaha and Elizabeth D. Foggie, on the first Black Sanctuary Garden at the Alena Museum in West Oakland.

Leslie puts her name, face, and voice out there in the world as a model of what a black woman gardener, designer, and businesswoman looks like and can accomplish. She works to embody her mission in all aspects of her business, from hiring to training and supporting her employees: "I try to hire a diverse team, to provide the support needed for employees of color to thrive in a white-dominated industry, and to celebrate and shine light on the contributions of all members of my team."

Her "space-making" includes creating gardens of beauty and meaning for clients of diverse cultural backgrounds. And her designs benefit not only her clients but also their neighbors, impacting the look and feel, or "garden literacy," of the shared outdoor living space.

In 2018, Leslie, with the help of two collaborators, Elizabeth D. Foggie and Seven Asefaha, was awarded funding for the first in a proposed series of "Black Sanctuary Gardens—gardens that provide physical/ spiritual sanctuary and sustenance for black people, especially black women." Leslie sees women "as keepers of culture, in our families, in our communities, and in the plant world too." They bring "communication and intuition and so many of the skills and histories and practices that don't usually get written in books but that we all rely on to know who we are and where we come from. Specifically, women are often the food and medicine makers in families, which is the source of many of our closest human relationships to plants."

Leslie and her collaborators broke ground on the first Black Sanctuary Garden space at Oakland's Alena Museum in 2019, concurrent with her own home garden, which she shares with husband Linval Owens and their two small children. "I think that having a relationship with plants has made me a happier and more supported person, and I'd wish that for other little black and brown girls too."

Leslie designed this garden for a family of Chinese American heritage. In it, she's layered traditional Asian edible plants, including loquat, guava, edible bamboo, and persimmon, with drought-tolerant, climate-adapted native plants of California, such as manzanita and spring-blooming poppies.

OTHER INSPIRING WOMEN

- All black women who were enslaved here in the United States and tended gardens, grew and made food, and held/made black and American culture what it is today
- Rue Mapp, founder and executive director of Outdoor Afro Network—Where Black People & Nature Meet
- Kristyn Leach, founder and farmer, Namu Farm, "growing predominantly crops of the Asian diaspora," based in Northern California

Erin Benzakein

HER WORK Owner and founder, Floret Flower Farm, Skagit Valley, Washington

HER PLANT "Sweet peas are what started me down this beautiful flower-filled journey. Their scent reminds me of my great-grandmother and brings back happy memories of my time spent with her."

HER PLANT JOURNEY A flower-farming revolution has been sweeping across the world these past few years, and one of the leading US-based names associated with this revolution is Erin Benzakein. In 2008, Erin and her husband, Chris, began a very seedling-sized version of what is now the well-known Floret—self-described as "a family-run flower farm specializing in growing unique, uncommon, and heirloom flowers. Our thriving research and education farm is dedicated to giving flower lovers the tools and information they need to grow the gardens of their dreams."

Based in a fertile and historic flower-growing region, Floret is at the heart of encouraging and educating budding and established flower farmers and farmer-florists on the whens, whys, and hows of getting started and making a go of a farm-based floral business.

Erin was introduced to the wonder and love of flowers and plants by her beloved great-grandmother. Having started her cut-flower farm and business serving florists, event planners, and retail businesses, she expanded Floret in 2013 to include a series of educational workshops held several times a year on the farm and aimed at introducing beginning flower farmers and florists to the work. "Through our workshops, flower lovers not only learned about flowers but also had the opportunity to find their flower tribe." As the workshops grew in number

and popularity, the press they received helped spread the word about local, seasonal flowers and the rise of creative female entrepreneurs combining their love of flowers with business.

Out of more than 500 people who attended the in-person workshops in the four years they were held, about 95 percent of them were women looking to build community-based, creative, flexible, and soul-feeding work for themselves and their families. "I've watched hundreds of amazing women uncover their passions and learn how to grow businesses that not only light them up and make a difference in the world, but also generate a viable source of income. This new generation of flower growers and consumers is much more in tune with nature and committed to cultivating beauty without the use of harmful chemicals. They are much more aware of their choices and how they will impact their children, their communities, and the environment." The Floret team gets hundreds of emails every month from flower lovers all over the world sharing how "flowers have changed their lives." And, "nothing," says Erin, "makes me happier than knowing our work has such a profound impact."

Erin's first book, *Floret Farm's Cut Flower Garden* (2017), aimed at new flower growers, is centered on Erin's actual farm—from planning and seed selection to sourcing, planting, harvesting, and arranging blooms.

Although Erin started with cut flowers for weddings, markets, and grocery stores, she was always trying new things. "In the fringe hours, I was always working on a new project. Most of them revolved around variety trials and writing. Two of my favorite things to do. I love farming, but even more, I love to do research and share what I've learned with others. As the business has evolved, our focus has shifted to education. I know how difficult it can be to grow a flower business, and I wanted to make the process easier for the next generation of flower farmers and farmer-florists than it was for me."

While writing her book, it became clear to Erin how limited home gardeners really were when it came to sourcing specialty cut-flower seeds. In order to make her favorite flowers available to others, she realized she would have to start a seed company of her own. "We're heading into our fourth year selling seeds, and I'm blown away by the level of interest and demand. It has far surpassed my wildest dreams. If you would have told me a decade ago that all of my obsessive trials and note-taking would have led to this, I never would have believed you. It's truly a dream come true."

In 2017, Erin and Chris bought an adjacent twenty-five-acre farm in order to expand Floret once more—this time moving more fully into specialty flower seed production, trials, and research. She wants to encourage aspiring flower farmers, florists, and other creatives to "follow their dreams and live their passion." She

Arranging cut roses, peonies, and campanula as well as farm-foraged foliage for a photo shoot.

hopes her work—her blog, website, books, and online flower-farming course—will help others "avoid the costly and discouraging mistakes" she made and "get pointed in the right direction" growing flowers of their own.

Erin's second book, *A Year in Flowers*, is due out in the spring of 2020.

OTHER INSPIRING WOMEN

- Ariella Chezar, American floral designer and flower farmer. "Discovering the work of Ariella completely changed my life. Learning from her was a huge turning point in my career. She showed me how to work with seasonal flowers and create gorgeous natural arrangements and designs. Her work has inspired an entire generation of floral designers seeking to connect more closely with nature and tie their work to the seasons."

- Sarah Raven, British garden designer and flower farmer. "One of the most amazing things about Sarah is her ability to take intimidating concepts and explain them in a very approachable, easy-to-understand way. She has inspired countless gardeners, farmers, and designers all over the world. Her books were the training wheels I used to learn to grow flowers, and I am forever grateful for her generosity and sharing."

Eliza Blank

> "Americans spend nearly 90 percent of our lives indoors, so bring plants indoors"

HER WORK Founder and CEO, The Sill, New York City

HER PLANT "I love a *Philodendron cordatum*—basic, maybe, but I love it for that very reason. It doesn't take much to make it happy, and it grows quickly, constantly unfurling new heart-shaped leaves. A reminder to be resilient, resourceful, and open to growth."

HER PLANT JOURNEY "I didn't know what a nature-connected person I was until I moved to New York City. My friend and I would cross the city from our NYU dorm just to sit on the grass in Central Park."

Frederick Law Olmsted and other Industrial Age urban park planners of his time knew how important safe and welcoming green spaces were to city dwellers' quality of life. And, though young and newly urban, Eliza understood this need intuitively as well. She was born and raised in the relatively rural town of Northampton, Massachusetts, to an American father and a Filipino mother, who tended a healthy home garden and many, many tropical indoor plants.

It wasn't until 2007, when she had graduated with her degree in communications, gotten her first job in the city, and rented her first "closet-sized" sixth-floor walk-up with a window facing a brick wall, that Eliza began to comprehend how challenging it can be for urbanites to incorporate living green plants into their lives.

In order to buy some houseplants for her new apartment, Eliza made the trek to Midtown Manhattan's Home Depot—the only source she could find to buy a living plant, a pot, and a largish bag of potting soil. After carrying the bag of soil up the six flights of stairs and wrestling with the pot and plant, dirt was effectively spread across her small living space.

She knew there had to be a better way, and she felt her skills and both business and personal ambitions converge. "I wanted a life in the company of plant companions, and someone needed to create a consumer brand to sell me the things I wanted, in a way that I (urban twentysomething) wanted to buy (online and shipped direct to my doorstep)."

Fast-forward six years, during which Eliza worked as a brand strategist in New York City, married her husband, Steve, and spent four years in Boston working with beauty start-up Living Proof. In those years, she "essentially earned an honorary MBA," and, at the age of twenty-six, Eliza and Steve returned to New York City, where she had the tools she needed to start her direct-to-consumer specialty houseplant company—The Sill.

Eliza firmly believes "we need plants in the spaces we occupy like we need clean air, sunlight, or a jacket on a cold day. Americans spend nearly ninety percent of our lives indoors—so I made it The Sill's mission to encourage others to bring the outdoors in by making it more accessible, compelling." Her vision for The Sill revolutionized the way city-dwellers, especially younger ones, find, buy, can be successful with, and enrich their lives with a diversity of long-lived indoor foliage plants. At The Sill, customers can buy healthy potted plants, in appropriately sized, aesthetically appealing ceramic containers, and have them delivered to their doorstep. By 2017, she had opened two retail shops in the city.

As of 2018, The Sill had scaled up from Eliza's tiny apartment to a 12,000-square-foot facility in New Jersey. From plants to pots and soil, "ninety percent of the supply chain is domestically sourced, which improves our sustainability and is something I love about this sector of the industry." In 2019, The Sill opened its first physical location outside of New York City—in Los Angeles.

From the beginning, Eliza chose team members she could learn from. Currently, half the team has a

Eliza, with some of her favorite bold foliage.

horticultural background. When the greenhouse and shipping facility moved to New Jersey (the business offices are in Chinatown), Eliza made a valuable connection with Rutgers University—New Jersey's land-grant university. Since then, seven Rutgers grads, with backgrounds in everything from plant science to agriculture, environmental science, and horticulture have contributed to the team, which has "upped the game in terms of managing a commercial greenhouse in a unique setting as well as in building out the educational components."

"Starting a business is really hard—a roller coaster every day. If it wasn't for plants, I couldn't do it. Just walking into our greenhouse is calming—you can't step into it without smiling. It has an amazing impact on your mood and outlook. That has helped me to be as dedicated to the business as possible."

Eliza can't step into The Sill's New Jersey greenhouse without smiling— happy in the company of plants.

Eliza believes every plant they send out has a positive impact in someone's life, and she summarizes where she is in her work now with this: "I'm proud of the mistakes I've made and that I show up every day. Ultimately, when I think about what The Sill can be as it grows up—it's even more than just about plants. In the world that we're moving toward—becoming more and more disconnected from nature—to be a reason for people to put their phones down and water their plant, for them to be in the present moment and focus on something outside themselves, I hope we are contributing to that in some way."

OTHER INSPIRING WOMEN

◆ Tovah Martin, American gardener and garden writer. "Martin's classic book, *Once Upon a Windowsill: A History of Indoor Plants* (2009), might have inspired the name for The Sill."

◆ Katherine Aul Cervoni, founder and principal of Staghorn NYC, a landscape design, construction, and maintenance firm

◆ Shanti Nagel, principal and founding partner of Design Wild, a landscape design firm in New York City

Jinny Blom

HER WORK Principal and founder, Jinny Blom Ltd., Clerkenwell, London

HER PLANT "The grapevine—it is so generous and lives long on very little. It even improves its gift in hard and uncompromising soils!"

HER PLANT JOURNEY "On the face of it, I'm designing and building gardens. It draws together all the things I care most about: people, landscape, plants, social confluences, architecture, quality of life, and the long-term view of our culture and cultural deposit on the earth."

Jinny Blom was born in Leamington Spa, Warwickshire, to an English/ Scandinavian self-taught engineer father and a musical French mother who was a keen gardener. Invention, engineering, artistry, music, and to some degree gardening go back generations in her family, and Jinny was an inquisitive plant-and-soil person from the start. "As a small girl, I was obsessed with mud—I had a little bucket that I would pull around on a string so I could fill it with soil and water at the drop of a hat. I would spend a lot of time stirring it and analyzing its constituent parts." Her father called her Mrs. Mud, due to this deep interest and affection.

Jinny took a circuitous route to her current profession, becoming a transpersonal psychologist and practicing for many years in the public sector. "The transpersonal approach understands that sometimes 'you have to break down to break through.'"

By her mid-thirties, she was overwhelmed with challenges. "In the 1990s, I was running a charity that cared for men with severe mental illness such as psychosis, and AIDS was epidemic in our cities. Four of my closest friends, one of whom was living with us, were very, very sick, and it was a heavy load and had an effect on me. I was manifesting more and more gardening at work with the

> "We're building temples—if you're going to move the earth around, you have to put something good on it"

guys at the charity as way to help them and myself. I'd always loved gardening but never thought it was a job."

"Then, all four of my friends died within six months of one another, and all four of my pets died. Which was an awful lot of death. I took a break to Picos de Europa National Park in Spain and sat up a mountain for days, 'til a little voice in my head literally said, 'Be a gardener, be a gardener. . .' It's as simple as that. You know, change starts with something quite pivotal but quite small. I was thirty-six."

She started working with residential gardens and apprenticed with the designer Dan Pearson for four years. She continues to study plants and design at every chance. "Fear is a great motivator," Jinny says wryly of her job, "and there's no magic. Get up early and really work hard, show up on time, be nice, don't overcharge, get a client and look after them. Be enthusiastic. You have to be knowledgeable—I've given myself a challenging education—I am open to other people's thoughts, and I ask questions. I remain deeply grateful for all the people who have generously shared their knowledge and allowed me to learn from them. I try to repay this generosity every chance I get."

In 2000, Jinny opened her own design studio. Things moved rapidly and she gained a lot of large-scale projects quite fast. In 2002, His Royal Highness (HRH) the Prince of Wales chose Jinny to codesign a healing garden for the Royal Horticultural Society (RHS) Chelsea Flower Show. This opportunity gave her sudden visibility, and new projects flowed in. She designed subsequent Chelsea gardens for Laurent-Perrier Champagne in 2006 and 2007, which focused symbolically on "the journey of life" and took gold. In 2013, she worked for Prince Harry (now HRH the Duke of Sussex) and his charity, Sentebale, on a garden to raise awareness about the HIV health crisis in Lesotho.

The Thoughtful Gardener (2017) is Jinny's first book, and it summarizes her diverse aesthetic—lush, romantic plantings and large-scale work around the globe— while it insightfully and humorously walks readers through her particular design process, which starts with "seeing" and ends with "liberating." It is in the early "seeing" aspect that the ecological, geological, and cultural appropriateness and sensitivity of her work is made clear. Speaking of the

One of Jinny's lushly layered and floriferous garden designs, featuring mature grapevines as pathway intersection/threshold sentinels. Her designs are characterized by brilliant spatial demarcation and a sense of age and establishment, even in newly planted gardens.

book's success (it's a bestseller), she reflects that her work "touches a chord that lies somewhere in the balance between the natural world, our gardens, our health, and our lives generally."

Ecological and cultural health weigh on her, and this sense of responsibility is regularly reflected in her work. She sits on the advisory board of the Therapeutic Landscapes Network, an organization founded by Naomi Sachs, ASLA, EDAC, in 1999, in order to expand global awareness of evidence-based therapeutic benefits of landscape design across a broad spectrum of populations, from cancer patients to those experiencing PTSD or memory loss issues, and well beyond.

Of her studio, which includes designers and landscape architects, the majority of whom are women, she says, "We are collectively idealistic and share enthusiasm for creating a healthy culture and good environments for people. Increasingly, our clients want to champion a pastoral ideal where nature and mankind are harmonized. In the contemporary world this is fraught with challenges: overpopulation, disease, neglect of land, and overuse of land. I plant a very great number of trees—trees are the future—and hedges and revert as much garden space to natural landscape as I can."

"My team and I are working on a number of significant commissions both public and private, gently and firmly pushing the boundaries of creativity and intelligent design. This sensitivity to places and people allows us to respond thoughtfully to commissions. The work we produce tends to have a uniqueness that challenges a definable style. Commissioning a landscape is no different to commissioning a work of art or a piece of music—it is a sensitive, erudite process, not a commodity."

OTHER INSPIRING WOMEN

- Constance Spry (1886–1960), British floral designer and writer. "She cooked and 'did the flowers.' My childhood was very 'Spry'; her knowledge was much deeper than her epoch allowed her to express."
- Elizabeth David (1913–1992), British cook and food writer. "For her ease and brilliance with food."
- Beth Chatto (1923–2018), British plantswoman, garden designer, and author. "Of course."
- Jane Grigson (1928–1990), British cookbook author and food writer. "Her fruit and veg books are richly anthropological and utterly fascinating."
- Mrs. M. Grieve (1858–1941), British plantswoman, herbalist, and writer. "Her magnificent herbal encyclopedia, *A Modern Herbal* (1931), covers everything from medicine and folklore to botany and cultural anecdotes."

Carol Bornstein

HER WORK Horticulturist, garden designer, writer; director, the Nature Gardens and Live Animal Program, Natural History Museum of Los Angeles County, Los Angeles, California

HER LANDSCAPE "Old-growth chaparral with gnarled manzanitas, dimpled bigpod ceanothus, and buckwheats. But I also love the desert."

HER PLANT JOURNEY In the past twenty-five years, the branch of the plant world focused on native plants has been particularly vigorous. In an increasingly urban world, as well as one of ever-more degraded, fragmented, or lost natural habitats, native plant experts and advocates are points of connection addressing—consciously or not—multiple urgencies on both human and environmental fronts.

Carol Bornstein is one of California's most highly respected native plant experts, and the state, with its highly diverse flora, is a global center for native plant research and education. Carol has devoted much of her career to lauding California's native plants and the benefits of designing gardens to work with the realities of their natural environments. Native plants provide beauty, a sense of place, and essential habitat support for wildlife. Native plants are also well adapted to the soils and climates of their own region, so their informed/thoughtful/appropriate use in the landscape reduces the amount of supplemental water, fertilizer, and pesticides needed for healthy growth.

As interest in landscaping with native plants has increased, obstacles have emerged—or emerged again. Carol explains, "There were several earlier efforts by horticulturists in California to heighten awareness and appreciation of and access to native plants in the cultivated landscape. So while the subject wasn't new to me, certainly the time was right to run the message up the flagpole again. Obstacles to landscaping with natives include the limited availability of

> Discovering garden-worthy plants from the wild or in cultivated landscapes is a joy

native plants in the nursery trade and getting reliable information on how best to grow natives successfully in a garden setting—which can be tricky."

One of Carol's earliest industry jobs was at the Santa Barbara Botanic Garden as plant propagator. She worked at SBBG for twenty-eight years, moving into the position of director of horticulture, where she oversaw the living collections, retail nursery, and plant introduction programs. Her love of grasses inspired her "to transform the garden's iconic meadow into a centerpiece for native bunch-grasses and wildflowers." She also worked on the design and construction of the Home Demonstration Garden, Southern California's first water-conserving, public-demonstration, residential landscape featuring native plants. Under her leadership, the botanic garden's retail nursery became the premier source of California native plants on the central coast. Several of Carol's introductions from this time have since become popular cultivars, such as *Verbena lilacina* 'De La Mina', *Corethrogyne filaginifolia* 'Silver Carpet', and *Salvia* 'Pacific Blue'.

A colorful and evocative chalk-board sign welcomes visitors to the Nature Gardens. Similar interpretive signs throughout set a tone of creative, informative, and participatory engagement for visitors to the urban oasis.

A notable drought hit California in the late 1980s and early 1990s, impacting how garden staff interpreted the garden and worked together—they began really focusing on communicating the positive impact of gardening with native plants. "I worked very closely with the director of education on developing interpretations for new living displays, crafting and coordinating several landscape design symposia, and writing articles and pamphlets about gardening with natives."

The concept of aesthetically *and* environmentally valuable native plantings was new to this generation of the plant-loving public and really opened people's eyes and minds to the possibilities of plants that met their aesthetic standards, provided for native wildlife, and used far fewer inputs of water, fertilizer, and maintenance when appropriately sited in gardens. In the two game-changing native plant gardening books she coauthored with Bart O'Brien and David Fross, *California Native Plants for the Garden* (2005) and *Reimagining the California Lawn* (2011), Carol helps expand the palette of native plants for gardeners and landscape designers to consider and provides detailed information on how to keep these plants happy and looking beautiful in a variety of settings.

In 2012, Carol shifted and expanded her perspective once more, taking the position of director of the nature gardens and live animal program at the Natural History Museum of Los Angeles County—a truly urban environment. The 3.5 acres of "urban nature," created in large part out of former museum parking lots, were still under construction when Carol arrived. The master plan for the multimillion-dollar project had been developed over several years with museum staff and the designers at Mia Lehrer + Associates (now Studio-MLA), an award-winning urban landscape architecture firm known for thoughtful and culturally resonant landscape solutions and designs in the LA area—including some seminal regreening of the LA River.

Carol sharing her enthusiasm for and knowledge of California's native plants with visitors at the Nature Gardens.

"With almost one million visitors a year, these still-new gardens introduce so many people to nature, many of whom have little to no experience with the natural world. The gardens are a much-needed example of the complex relationships and interdependencies between plants and animals, as well as a model for how to create a garden that respects and reflects sense of place and how to tend it responsibly."

Carol has—she noted with humor—started taking a lot more pictures of birds and insects under the influence of her more animal-centric Natural History Museum colleagues. But she hasn't been tempted away from plants yet. She continues to seek out exceptional California garden plants and to share her knowledge through writing, teaching, and public speaking. Her latest cultivar introduction—*Encelia californica* 'Paleo Yellow', an unusually pale bush sunflower—exemplifies the easy-to-grow, attractive, and habitat-supportive characteristics she espouses. "Such garden-worthy selections make the act of gardening rewarding for the gardener and, better still, for the planet as a whole."

OTHER INSPIRING WOMEN

◆ Beatrix Farrand (1872–1959), American landscape architect

◆ Gertrude Jekyll (1843–1932), British plantswoman, garden designer, and writer

◆ Mary Carroll, botanist, horticultural historian, and writer, Santa Barbara Botanic Garden, Santa Barbara, California

◆ Isabelle Greene, landscape architect, Isabelle Greene & Associates, Santa Barbara, California

◆ Naomi Fraga, director of conservation, Rancho Santa Ana Botanic Garden, Claremont, California

◆ Pamela Berstler, executive director, Pacific Horticulture Society; cofounder of G3, Green Gardens Group, Los Angeles, California

Marion Brenner

HER WORK Photographer of landscape architecture, Berkeley, California

HER PLANT "Any plant that someone I love or have worked with has given to me. Garden people are very generous. My garden is a plant collection keeping alive the memory of those other gardens and gardeners. I love to walk through my garden and say, oh, that plant came from so-and-so. I *love* that."

HER PLANT JOURNEY Photographers help us to see space. Garden photographers help us to see gardens and plants. Through a directed, curated, framed view, they make completely still a fleeting moment in the living, breathing, dynamic life cycles of plants, gardens, and gardeners. Sometimes in seeing plants or gardens through the eyes of a gifted photographer, we see and understand something completely new about these other living beings. Garden photography can act as elegant and poignant storytelling of a very particular perspective, a valuable asset to the intersection of plants and people.

Photographer of landscape architecture Marion Brenner has been at her craft for more than twenty years, shooting gardens and landscape architecture around the world for magazines, publishers, garden designers, landscape architects, and architects. "Most of my photography involves the built landscape. Although I love plants, I am more interested in how people design exterior space, what they consider beautiful, how a landscape functions."

"I like all gardens—I like plant-y gardens and chaos gardens. I learned to photograph in chaos gardens that have no logical organization, but a logic of their own. I think my least favorite gardens are the formal-style gardens that almost require you to stand in a

> "It's fascinating and political—gardens are cultural statements. My job is to make sense of the space and reveal it in two dimensions"

certain place to photograph them—they control your vision. I like when experiencing a garden space is a process of discovery: How do you find the logic of a garden? How do you tell this story? Well-designed gardens—chaos gardens or not—have their own inherent logic."

Born and raised in Mount Vernon, New York, Marion graduated from Wellesley College, where she studied art history, and went on to study at the Pennsylvania Academy of Fine Arts. She took her first photography class at the Boston Museum School in the late 1960s. "My father owned a camera shop, so I took a photography class."

After moving to California, Marion found work photographing architecture. In 1991, a large fire swept through Oakland and Berkeley, missing her house by a very close margin. She began taking photos of her neighborhood, wandering all over the burned areas and documenting the loss. Editor Zahid Sardar, then at the *San Francisco Chronicle*, ran Marion's fire photos in the paper's magazine, cover shot and all. "It was really the first thing I had published. And after that he asked me to photograph gardens for the magazine."

She began photographing gardens and planted spaces in relation to the built environment, collaborating with writers like Diana Ketcham, author of *Le Désert de Retz: A Late Eighteenth-Century French Folly Garden, the Artful Landscape of Monsieur de Monville* (1994), and landscape architects like Andrea Cochran and Topher Delaney, with whom she created a series of botanical photographs documenting plants used in the treatment of cancer.

"I realized afterward that taking photos of the fire was a way of making order out of a chaotic experience. It helped me deal with the vagaries of life. I was interested in space all along; I'm interested in how people create space. It's fascinating and political—gardens are cultural statements. My job is to

Marion frames her views with great thought and care. Here, a path leads the eye to the offset focal point of the vine-covered arbor. The trees in the distance set this private Bay Area garden in context to its environment.

make sense of the space and reveal it in two dimensions. I compose my photographs within the full rectangle [of the camera's viewfinder] and from the outside edges in, working quite tightly."

Her characteristic way with light was honed with the directional insights of editor Senga Mortimer, while working on projects for *House & Garden* in the mid- to late 1990s. "We were photographing a garden in Napa Valley. We worked long hours—starting very early and ending after sunset. We were sitting at lunch one day and Senga said, 'Ok, the light is good now, we can go now.' The seminal thing was: you don't photograph unless the light is *right*. The key to my education in garden photography for the past twenty years has been learning how to see light and understand how it's going to look in two dimensions; how in those two dimensions you can define space and make clarity out of whatever the design."

Described as "peerless" in garden photography by the *New York Times*, Marion's many books include *New Garden Design: Inspiring Private Paradises* (2008); *In and Out of Paris: Gardens of Secret Delights* (2014); *Outstanding American Gardens: A Celebration: 25 Years of the Garden Conservancy* (2015); *The Bold Dry Garden* (2016); and *Private Gardens of the Bay Area* (2017). Of her work, she says, "The plant world encourages humility. It is a transient, unpredictable world, with plants growing and blossoms lasting for a brief moment. You have to be able to embrace a lack of control."

OTHER INSPIRING WOMEN

- Senga Mortimer, editor at large, *Elle Decor* and *House Beautiful*, New York, New York
- Annie Hayes, nurserywomen and owner, Annie's Annuals & Perennials, Richmond, California
- Flora Grubb, nurserywoman and co-owner, Flora Grubb Gardens, San Francisco, California
- Caitlin Atkinson, garden photographer

A serene and beautifully framed image of a landscape design by Christine Ten Eyck, in which the plantings—old and new—and the built human space are seamlessly interwoven.

Cynthia (Cindy) Ann Brown

HER WORK Manager, Horticulture Collections and Education, Smithsonian Gardens, Smithsonian Institution, Washington, DC

HER PLANT "Dandelion, once described by a friend as the perfect perennial. It pops up in the spring with cheery exuberance, blooms a long time, nurtures fauna with pollen, has reliable returns year after year, boasts edible leaves and roots, disturbs monocultures, and adapts to many climates. It can be a pest to those who don't appreciate its attributes, but brings smiles to those who appreciate common beauty."

HER PLANT JOURNEY Public gardens are often a primary interface between horticulture and the general public. What people encounter in a public garden affects cultural understanding of and relationships to plants and the importance—or lack thereof—of horticulture to the world at large.

This might be especially true of Smithsonian Gardens, which comprises the gardens encircling each of the nineteen Smithsonian museums, as well as interiorscapes and horticulture-related collections and exhibits. People don't necessarily go to Smithsonian Gardens with the idea of visiting a garden. Rather, many—especially first-time visitors—find themselves in these gardens on their way to a museum. In 2017, the museums of the Smithsonian documented 11.4 million visits, so these public gardens have a unique horticultural reach into a large population of people.

Smithsonian Gardens became an official branch of the Smithsonian Institution in Washington, DC, in 1972 when S. Dillon Ripley, the eighth Secretary of the Smithsonian (1964–1984), determined the "outside of the museums of the Smithsonian should be as engaging as the insides of them." Cynthia (known as Cindy) Brown has been the manager of the Horticulture Collections and Education of the Smithsonian Gardens since 2010.

Of her job, Cindy says, "Horticulture is a field with great depth. I don't think its complexity is always understood or appreciated by the general public. My job is to show people how gardens and green spaces affect our lives and our communities. Gardens are an expression of our social, cultural, artistic, and environmental values—the beliefs we hold, scientific innovation, foodways, and cultural and community traditions are reflected back at us in the why and how of our gardens. Gardens sustain us and keep our communities healthy. They are so much more than a pretty space, although being a beautiful, restful space is vital."

Cindy was born in Williamsport, Pennsylvania, but moved around during her childhood. Moving around was "awesome" in Cindy's estimation, allowing her to experience all kinds of people, food, and culture. Her father would often take her and her four sisters to public gardens and nature centers.

Her career actually started with an education in sociology and gerontology (years later she would joke that she is very good with "old plants that have a chemical dependency"), and her nomadic existence continued into the role of Navy wife. When her family eventually settled in the Washington, DC, area, she went back to work, following up on a help-wanted sign at a local nursery. "I had always gardened, but till then it had been a hobby. At some point, I 'saw' the beauty of plants—their colors, textures, and fragrances." From there she became a Master Gardener, started a landscape design business with a partner, and in time, went for her degree in horticulture.

> "The beliefs we hold, scientific innovation, foodways, and cultural and community traditions are reflected back at us in the why and how of our gardens"

"The experience that most nurtured my chlorophytic side was my first public garden job at Green Spring Gardens, a public garden in Fairfax County, Virginia. The site, the employees, the visitors engrossed me to my core. I worked with plants, I talked about plants, I delivered programs on plants, we went on botanizing trips. The experience was exhilarating, and I thrived. The motivation and drive incubated in me there continues."

In 2010, Cindy joined the team and mission of the Smithsonian Gardens, an accredited museum through the American Association of Museums—but one without ceilings or walls. "The Smithsonian Gardens are a museum in their own right, capturing history, art, and science—modern conversations, modern challenges."

Cindy's work includes educating the educators and overseeing garden outreach and communication programs. Annually, she organizes staff education and professional development events for ongoing educational credit, in the form of lecture series from professionals around the world that are offered to all staff (employee, student, and volunteer) at all the public gardens of DC.

In her experience, public horticulture in the last twenty-five years has had to "reconsider its value and best practices and integrate into communal conversations about needs and concerns, not just focus on plants on display. Horticulture by way of gardening is a way to get people engaged in the bigger pictures and the world around them—in other words, to care." Public gardens, she believes, "can demonstrate the nuances of big concepts," from environmental concerns like climate change or pollinator declines, to faith, race, and other large cultural issues.

At work, engaging and informing visitors to the Smithsonian Gardens.

One of her favorite jobs is overseeing the Smithsonian Gardens' digital archive, Community of Gardens. It's a complement to the Smithsonian's Archives of American Gardens, which is a collection of garden images that "tell an American gardening story from the late 1800s to now," and documents history through garden design, plants, garden labor, and gardening trends. But, as Cindy notes, the Archives of American Gardens tend to highlight gardens of the wealthy and elite—Community of Gardens is a collection of stories that document and collect vernacular garden stories of everyday gardeners. "These are garden stories like those of my own grandmothers' during the Depression. This collection lets us listen to what America thinks is important about their gardens, which to me is so wonderful. I know what a garden means to me—I know how important gardening is, and I can see it in the faces of people who visit our gardens. And I can hear it through the voices of all kinds of gardeners in this forum."

OTHER INSPIRING WOMEN

- Martha Stewart, lifestyle leader. "Her presentation of and love for making beautiful gardens, for growing and cooking beautiful food, are still inspirational to me."
- Rosalind Creasy, edible garden designer and author
- Kathleen Socolofsky, assistant vice chancellor, director of UC Davis Arboretum and Public Garden, Davis, California
- Kathleen Wolf, research social scientist, University of Washington, College of the Environment, Seattle, Washington
- Randee Humphrey, director of education, Lewis Ginter Botanical Garden, Richmond, Virginia

Yolanda Burrell

HER WORK Owner and founder, Pollinate Farm & Garden, Oakland, California

HER PLANT "A fig tree—is there anything more beautiful or generous in the world?"

HER PLANT JOURNEY We've all heard of the concept of a food desert—places so remote (for example, poverty-stricken rural counties) or so marginalized (for instance, low-income urban neighborhoods) that basic foodstuffs aren't available—and their cousin issue, food swamps, regions which are not only low on grocery stores but also have an overabundance of fast food and gas station–type food marts. To borrow the metaphor, more and more of us are living in plant- and gardening-supply deserts. Shopping options are increasingly limited to big box stores and online sources that offer very little variety or knowledge. If we consider plants an essential element of a quality life, then we need to ensure we have access to a diverse and high-quality selection of seeds/plants, tools, and knowledge.

Yolanda Burrell wants to do this for her hometown of Oakland, California. Her mission—sharing the joys of urban agriculture—represents a recent trend in the world of plants that's demystifying gardening and connecting a whole new generation to its possibilities.

Born in South Central Los Angeles in an Air Force family, Yolanda grew up in a variety of places around the globe, including Northern and Southern California, Texas, Arizona, and Japan. Wherever they lived, her family always gardened. She remembers climbing the giant

> If you step back one or two generations, we've all gardened and grown food—our mothers, grandmothers, aunties, or *tías*. Giving others *access* to the resources and knowledge to grow their own food is really about teaching them *not to forget how*

Urban farm life in
the garden.

peach tree in her grandmother's garden and eating the juicy fruit when she
and her family returned to Los Angeles for summer visits. When her father
retired, her family settled on one acre in Santa Rosa, California, where she and
her brothers would tend to their weekend gardening chores in order to support
their favorite sport—eating.

Every place she's lived in adulthood, Yolanda has gardened, planting "a little
of this and a little of that." After she and her husband bought a home in Oakland,
Yolanda became active in a loosely knit group of mostly women called the East
Bay Urban Agriculture Alliance. "It was kind of a skill-sharing group, and we'd
meet once a month. The interest centered mainly around food—some women
had chickens, some goats, some women made cheese—and we were all experience levels. There was a person in the group from the Oakland Food Policy

Council, which promotes healthy eating for everyone—to make sure everyone had access to good, healthy food."

"Knowledge and availability of supplies were challenges for everyone. There'd be conversations like: How can we share our knowledge with others? I live over here, where do you live? What grows well there? What do you use for fertilizer? Where do you buy your Agribon row covers? I made this widget from some odds and ends I put together from the hardware store."

Yolanda found herself thinking: "Wouldn't it be great to have all these locally relevant resources, goods, and knowledge under one roof and available all the time?" So she started a business plan to aggregate resources and help people avoid going to the four winds for their plants, seeds, supplies, and community.

After many years of dreaming and two years of active business planning with the help of a SCORE (Service Corps of Retired Executives) mentor, one day Yolanda was browsing Oakland commercial real estate availability and noticed a building on a double lot (which for over forty years was a carpet and linoleum store) in the neighborhood known as Fruitvale. Finding the right space in town, with easy access for other city dwellers, had been one of her biggest challenges. "I took my lunch hour in the middle of a rainstorm to look at it and knew it was *just* what I wanted (the adjoining lot had an old fruit tree orchard that was completely hidden from the street!). I signed the lease and hosted lots of pizza and beer work parties to get the site in shape. We opened six weeks later, on the first day of spring."

Pollinate Farm & Garden opened in 2013, an edible plant nursery and urban homestead emporium specializing in "DIY food." It includes supplies, resources, and educational programming on topics like urban farming, edible landscapes, food forests, backyard chickens, beekeeping, and food preserving.

"Our motto is Grow Raise Preserve. We supply the essentials for seed-to-table organic farming and gardening, food preserving, small-scale livestock raising, and beekeeping. We offer a speaker series of authors and experts, as well as hands-on workshops and cooking classes in our community meeting/learning space. We teach the hows and whys of DIY food."

With Georgie.

Yolanda admits that getting Pollinate up and running was hard work, and, like all plant-passion efforts, it's always 24/7/365. "Getting people in the door was a challenge in the beginning. Pollinate was in a really depressed part of town—so people who didn't live there didn't want to go there, and the people who did live there didn't understand *why* we were there."

"Now that we are five years old and established, the neighborhood loves us. I'm most proud of the community we've built—from the lovely hodgepodge in the Urban Ag Alliance to now. We're in this very economically, ethnically, and age-diverse area; the thing that brings us together is that we all eat and we all deserve fresh and healthy food. No matter if you're a recent immigrant or have been here on this land for a long time, Pollinate tries to remind you of what you once knew."

At Pollinate's fifth anniversary, a customer brought Yolanda a jar of honey from their home hive and a card, which read, "Thank you for having gotten us started on this journey. I would never have taken on caring for bees or growing a garden without you."

In the shop at Pollinate Farm & Garden.

OTHER INSPIRING WOMEN

- "My grandmother, lover of gladiolus, elephant ears, St. Augustine grass, petunias, impatiens, hydrangeas, bougainvillea, Shasta daisies, and houseplants of all kinds—scissors at the ready, always ready to talk plants and forever on the hunt for a 'propagation opportunity.'"
- Christine Hwang, environmental activist/hobby horticulturalist/beekeeper. "With a very analytical day job, she never does anything halfway. Chris has an encyclopedic knowledge of California natives, rare tropical plants, and edibles (she knows her food, too!)—they've overgrown their yard with specimen plants and have taken over their neighbor's yard."
- Laura Nicoletti, horticulturist and landscape designer; owner of For a Greener Living, Mill Valley, California. "Laura integrates natives with edibles—she likes to grow what she likes to eat and used to be a chef. She's a seed advocate and generous steward of the land."
- Marion Brenner, photographer of landscape architecture. "She sees what others don't see."
- Shirley Watts, landscape designer and sculptor. "Her work focuses on the symbiosis of art and plants in shared environments."

Ava Bynum

HER WORK Founder, Hudson Valley Seed education program, New York

HER PLANT "I love trees, especially aspen trees for their underground connections. I have also always loved watercress, since its growth demonstrates the presence of clean water."

HER PLANT JOURNEY Interest in and support of school gardens has waxed and waned throughout the history of American schools, mirroring cultural interests and urgencies. In the current era, school gardens are experiencing a resurgence as a means of meeting critical needs for physical activity, hands-on engagement, outdoor time, and nutritional education.

Ava Bynum believes we can do even better and even more. At age twenty, she founded Hudson Valley Seed, a school garden project in New York inspired not by traditional school garden programs—which were developed through the lens and bias of mainstream, white, European culture—but "driven by the agricultural history of the country," especially as it relates to communities that have been disenfranchised based on their cultural backgrounds or economic standing. Her focus is on communities whose lands, cultures, languages, traditions, and values have been erased, marginalized, and subsumed.

Hudson Valley Seed works to intentionally and authentically partner with communities, based on those communities' histories and values. Ava hopes the program can be a model for other school garden programs across the country. It currently educates more than 4000 kindergarten through fifth-grade students. Students engage in the garden as an outdoor classroom, integrating Common Core standards in science, math, the arts, and many other interdisciplinary topics in the "real-world, hands-on setting of the garden."

Ava moved to the Hudson Valley at age five. Her Aunt Fay strongly influenced her political awareness and understanding. "When I was initially getting

very interested in local food and organic agriculture, she was quick to point out that I had better be trying to figure this out for everybody, and not just a wealthy elite."

"I've always loved plants, trees, and anything wild. I always feel most peaceful and alive in the woods, but I think my love for plants changed when I was around age eleven and got a job as a cashier at our local farmers market. I loved being an access point to bring people their food every week, and I especially loved building relationships with all the customers. That job bloomed into working on Four Winds Farm, something that I did every summer through high school and beyond and was the foundation of all of my food and farming experience."

"When I founded Hudson Valley Seed, I was excited about children learning to grow food and try new vegetables. While that is an extraordinary thing to experience with young people, I now understand nature, and particularly gardens, to be perfect containers for people of all backgrounds to learn emotional intelligence, teamwork, self-reflection, environmental stewardship, expansive and creative thinking, and more. Where my focus used to be exclusively on learning about plants, I now understand the outcomes of working with plants to be much more vast and long-lasting than I could have imagined." Ava is especially interested in gardening as a way to bridge socioeconomic and racial divides.

Early in her time running Hudson Valley Seed, Ava became a fellow at the Environmental Leadership Program, a national nonprofit with the goal of training a new generation of environmental leaders characterized by diversity, innovation, collaboration, and effective communications. During the training, a white woman made a racist comment that broke the group apart. The woman who had made the comment couldn't comprehend her offense, and Ava didn't feel she had the skills to intervene. Meanwhile, the incident made it impossible for the group to come together to discuss environmental issues. For Ava, as a young white woman and leader, this was transformative. "Where I had previously believed environmental destruction to be the root cause of unrest in the world, my understanding shifted to the belief that creating justice for people would, in the process, create justice for the planet."

In 2017, Ava cofacilitated a weeklong immersion for farmers bringing racial justice into their agricultural work. "During the entire grueling week, I felt hope. I recognize now that political work—along with wild spaces—keeps me learning and growing. When I think about the many injustices historically and currently handed to people of color, my LGBTQ community, poor and working-class folks, and other marginalized communities, there is no option but to follow my heart and move in whatever ways I can toward creating a more humane world for us all."

Ava handed Hudson Valley Seed off to a new executive director in early 2018. Through her new consultancy group, Omnymyst, she is directing her energies toward thinking deeply about how to take the kind of education that Hudson Valley Seed offers and make it accessible on an even broader scale.

"I'm taking the lessons from Hudson Valley Seed on how to build a great program in and with community members from the ground up, and on how to integrate radical education into public school systems and other organizations. I'm working as a consultant with mostly educational and food-related organizations, helping them listen for what students really need, growing food that resonates with our communities, and trying to not participate in the nonprofit industrial complex in its

> "Every time I walk into a Hudson Valley public school classroom and participate in garden time, my heart fills with joy to see the program alive, lighting up students and filling each young person with a sense of joy and wonder"

Hudson Valley Seed garden students and their freshly grown carrots.

extractive systems. So much of the food world (including those of us trying to fix it!) is very shaming and oppressive; my work with food has always been about nourishment in so many ways."

OTHER INSPIRING WOMEN

- All small-scale women farmers doing amazing work in their communities
- Dolores Huerta, Mexican American labor leader and civil rights activist. "She was the cofounder of the National Farmworkers Association with Cesar Chavez, which later became the United Farm Workers (UFW)."
- Michelle Obama, first lady of the United States, 2008–2016. "Michelle planted the most expansive vegetable garden the White House has ever had, this one created out of the lawn in 2009 in order to start a national conversation about health and well-being in our country."
- Carmen Goodyear, back-to-the-land farmer, filmmaker (*Women on the Land: Creating Conscious Community*), feminist, and queer leader
- Leah Penniman, founder of Soul Fire Farm, author of *Farming While Black: Soul Fire Farm's Practical Guide to Liberation on the Land* (2018)
- Dr. Vandana Shiva, founder of the Seed Sovereignty movement in India, international seed advocate

Ariella Chezar

HER WORK Floral designer, educator, author; co-owner, Ariella New York; flower farmer, Zonneveld Farm, New York

HER PLANT "Martagon lilies blow me away—they are so refined and subtle, botanical, exquisite, and quiet."

HER PLANT JOURNEY Ariella Chezar is widely credited as being the origin of a movement beginning in the mid-1990s away from what she calls the "contained, French chic, roundy-moundy" dense floral displays of the time. Her arrangements were more expansive, open, and richly layered naturalistic designs, characterized by dynamic and dimensional foraged branches, vines, fruits, and seeds intermingled with flowers in tonal color schemes— generous designs speaking of both season and place.

Born in New York City and raised in the Berkshires near Great Barrington, Massachusetts, Ariella learned discipline studying classical voice as a young woman. She describes herself as having been a plant person "since forever, courtesy of my parents"—American father, Howard Chezar, and Dutch mother, Famke Zonneveld. She also had early professional models in garden and floral designer Pamela Hardcastle and horticulturalist Barbara Bockbrader, co-owner (with husband Robin Norris) of the Campo de' Fiori garden shop. She describes Hardcastle as "precise and studied in her design process" and Bockbrader as "intuitive and spontaneous." Between these very different talents, the ethos and aesthetics of her childhood in the Berkshires, and travels to Holland, her path was seeded and her unique style germinated.

She started in New York, working with famed event and floral designer Robert Isabell, then made her way to San Francisco, where the local and natural

> "You find yourself working with the same things over and over again— and yet because of the seasons, these moments are brief and never boring. When the peonies are blooming, it is heavenly peony madness, which passes all too quickly and leads you into the next love affair. This seasonal rhythm allows for the opportunity to fall in love over and over again with old friends year after year"

foraged materials filling the San Francisco Flower Mart—"seasonal jasmine vines, passionflowers, fruits on branches, garden roses"—were just the materials she needed to begin crafting the wild, organic, field-and-farm and garden-to-vase style for which she would become known. Soon after, she wrote her first book, *Flowers for the Table* (2002).

Though widely recognized as the founder of the wild/foraged look, Ariella notes, "This is a look that has been alive and well forever before me, starting most particularly with Constance Spry. So I don't actually feel it's mine, I feel it's anyone's who gets out in nature and incorporates nature's wild splendor alongside cultivated beauties. Years ago my good friend Emily Thompson and I were talking about how we begin to design. As a former sculptor, she approaches the plant world as a sculptor would—with form and gesture as her starting place. I begin with color. Shape, season, place, all of these come into play of course, but my starting point, my love and my joy, is combining and layering colors and watching them sing. I was taught this language by my mother during my childhood, spent surrounded by her artist friends and the art they made."

One of the earliest well-known designers to host floral and event workshops in destination locations, Ariella has deepened her exploration of color—tied to season and place—as her career has flourished. "My appetite for different colors has gone a little more wild, a little more esoteric. In 2014, I was doing an event in Hawaii at the Haiku Mill—it was dripping with this little orange trumpet flower, *Pyrostegia venusta*. And I'd recently found this wallpaper by Scandinavian designer Camilla Meijer—this huge graphic floral in red with a marigold-orange center and then surrounded by powder blue! It really grabbed me—this color combination was a revelation. The whole event became centered on it, from table linens, vessels, and candles, to the floral designs—a vivid punch of color resting on a canvas of soft powder blue."

"I feel like I intuitively know what a space needs. Once, when I was designing a room for FlowerSchool New York in the south of France with Emily Thompson and Shane Connolly, the flowers that were ordered from Paris looked way too Parisian. The three of us knew we wanted to take it somewhere else—so we went out into the wild, to the meadows and the markets, to find what the room needed. We came back with branches of wild plums, clematis vines, melons, grasses and garlands, and finally, when the restaurant staff got a feel for what we were doing, we were allowed access to copper vessels and molds from the closet of treasures in the restaurant's storage." She describes the final result as "a grassy meadow garland by Emily, accented with

At Zonneveld, the flower farm she named for her mother, Ariella enjoys sharing her skills and love of flower arranging with workshop participants.

blue bachelor buttons, a glorious cornucopia of foraged and potted plants by Shane, and table arrangements made in copper molds consisting of fruit branches woven through with wild clematis." She reflects, "Keying into place, season, and color—those are the things I love and feel I'm good at." One of the many notable spaces Ariella has helped to dress in floral seasonality is the White House during the Obama administration.

In 2016, in part as a way to "begin to try to reconcile with the dark underbelly of this beautiful work—the often toxic (to people and land) growing practices, the carbon footprint, the waste," Ariella and her husband, stonemason Christopher Gregory, established their own growing farm, Zonneveld. Named for her mother and meaning "sunny field," this is where Ariella can trial, experiment, and source her own sustainably grown plants and flowers. "In many ways it's about bringing things (plants, resources, focus, energy) *home*—an impulse and intention I'm trying to incorporate into in my life and work." The farm staff consists of Ariella, her husband, and their kids—August Oak and Celeste Neva. They have ninety acres total, with two in cultivation.

One of Ariella's floral designs exploring subtle shades of pink, offset by seasonal branches budding out in fresh spring greens.

"I get three weeks of narcissus and tulips, hellebores and Solomon's seal, then there's a pause followed by ninebark, clematis, and glorious peonies before the annuals get going, and then the dahlias. Between August and October, I can cut just from the farm; I supplement at other times by foraging and gathering from farms around the Berkshires. I also source from local farmers and flower farmers, a resource that has really kicked into gear this last three to five years."

Early in her workshop experiences, Ariella realized a sense of joy and satisfaction in teaching and collaborating—mentoring and "watching others bloom." In 2016, her second book, *The Flower Workshop,* was published. In 2017, she joined FlowerSchool New York as artistic director and master designer. Her third book, *Seasonal Flower Arranging,* arrived in 2019.

OTHER INSPIRING WOMEN

- Famke Zonneveld, mother and artist
- Constance Spry (1886–1960), British floral designer and writer
- Pamela Hardcastle, floral designer
- Barbara Bockbrader, garden and floral designer, co-owner Campo de' Fiori
- Emily Thompson, floral designer
- Nicolette Owen, floral designer; owner, Nicolette Camille Floral; cofounder, Little Flower School, Brooklyn, New York

Marina Christopher

HER WORK Nurserywoman and owner, Phoenix Perennial Plants, Hampshire, England

HER PLANT "A spring woodlander, *Gillenia trifoliata* (also known as bowman's root or Indian physic) is a perfect plant—wonderful pink stems and early pink foliage, lovely white butterfly-like flowers with fantastic red calyces, and then really pretty little seed pods that look like bird's feet, then the whole thing goes red in autumn before dying down."

HER PLANT JOURNEY Since people first began living with plants, plant hunters and nursery propagators have worked to select and then collect plants from the wild or from other places around the world. People have long manipulated and moved plants around for food, medicine, and beauty. While the discovery and supply chain might be longer, more corporate, and perhaps even completed in labs more often now, plants still come to us by way of age-old methods—observing, collecting, trials, breeding, and introducing via catalogues, nurseries, and flower and garden shows.

Marina Christopher is one such plant hunter, as well as an educator and author in "the coldest bit" of Hampshire, England. For going on thirty-five years, she has "surreptitiously, in the background," introduced the gardening world to "new-to-you" plants. She is one of the minds behind many of the plants chosen, sourced, and grown for top designers and plant wholesalers. Marina also lectures and leads workshops across the United Kingdom, and is a regular instructor at Great Dixter House & Gardens.

Marina first recognized her fascination with animals, specifically pond life, in her primary school's nature study

> "I'm interested in the root. Because I am basically a botanist and scientist, I can't bring myself to grow a big blousy thing with all top and no roots. Many people don't understand that a lot of top is less valuable than a lot of bottom"

class. At Bangor University College of North Wales, she studied botany and marine biology, and it was there she realized she was a plantswoman: "We were on a field trip to Box Hill and Juniper Hill in Surrey, and I was lying on my back in the sun, my eyes closed—all I could hear was the incredible noise of the insects. When I opened my eyes, I saw lots of little blue butterflies and ants happily wobbling off into the thyme. What looked like just really short turf was so alive. I thought, 'This is fantastic, I love this.'" She went on to Bristol and then Oxford, studying symbiosis. After three years, she took her PhD and was "very specialized and completely unemployable."

But she found a use for her knowledge eventually. In 1984, after finding post-graduate fieldwork in the plant industry and specialist nurseries, Marina opened Wildflower Nursery, growing primarily pollen- and nectar-rich wildflowers, many of which were natives, from seed. From 1986 to 1990, she was owner of Firecrest Nursery in Southampton, and from 1990 to 2002, she partnered in Green Farm Plants with plantsman John Coke. "When I started, most people weren't yet interested in the naturalistic plantings, which came in the 1990s, but because I was trained in ecology, I was really interested in interactions between organisms and plants. I wanted to grow plants (without chemicals!) for the bees, butterflies, beetles, and flies."

Gold-medal-winning show gardens in the making. Marina consults with, acquires seed for, and custom grows thousands of plants each season for leading landscape architects and designers.

Over time, Marina experimented specifically with umbels, peas, and grasses, "because they're great larval food and shelter for adult moths and butterflies as well as helpful predators like violet ground beetles, which eat slugs and grasshoppers." She's also interested in American prairie plants, "which bloom so much later than most British plants."

On her forty-fifth birthday, Marina launched another nursery endeavor, Phoenix Perennial Plants, on 6.5 acres, with about 2 in cultivation, in Hampshire. At Phoenix, Marina has continued to source, grow, and introduce plants that expand the public awareness of and access to interesting plants. In 2015, she suggested the unusual *Papaver dubium* ssp. *lecoqii* var. *albiflorum* (also known as "Beth's Poppy" named for plantswoman Beth Chatto) for a Cleve West garden at Chelsea, and it took hold with the public. In 2016, her suggestion of a British native, "the lovely little annual, *Adonis annua*—like tiny red buttercups," again caught the public's attention. In 2018, she introduced at Chelsea

Trifolium willdenovii, a California native annual clover, and "an absolutely beautiful thing!" She grows many umbellifers—fifty-five different types currently—and has a book on umbels for the garden in the works.

Based on Marina's timely and skillful use of plants from around the world to extend the season of flowering interest, horticultural publisher Frances Lincoln invited her to write the book *Late Summer Flowers* (2006), and a new and expanded edition is set to come out by 2021. "It will include some new plants and will not include others, like the echinacea, which were a disappointment and just not well suited to the damp British climate."

Marina and her unusual offerings from Phoenix Perennial Plants.

Marina finds it interesting to observe changes in public taste, and she notes that it's just in the last decade that the wildlife and regional ecology-supporting plants she loves have really come to the fore.

Phoenix Perennial Plants is run and maintained solely by Marina, and she is one of the few grower/nurseries propagating all her own material, much of it from wild-collected seed and cuttings. She's concerned about the diminishing number of growers/nurserypeople training young people to come up. She currently spends close to 10 percent of her long work weeks teaching, and she emphasizes to students the wide variety of ways to have success in the garden, encouraging them to "challenge themselves and to try different ways and to see what works for them based on observation and experimentation."

In Marina's world, "rigid prescriptiveness squelches creativity, initiative, and innovation. Sharing knowledge and experience without prescriptiveness allows others to always do better."

OTHER INSPIRING WOMEN

- Marjorie Blamey, British botanical artist
- Miriam Rothschild (1908–2005), British natural scientist
- Beth Chatto (1923–2018), British plantswoman, garden designer, and author
- Derry Watkins, British seed grower and plantswoman
- Carol Klein, British gardener and gardening expert
- Sarah Price, British garden designer, plantswoman, and writer

Peggy Cornett

HER WORK Garden historian and curator of plants, Monticello, Charlottesville, Virginia

HER PLANT "Large, ancient, venerable trees—massive live oaks forming cathedral-like spaces or the type of giant tulip poplars that once flanked the West Front of Monticello."

HER PLANT JOURNEY Garden history is like all history—it's complicated. It's layered and rich in adventure, drama, and beauty. In the intrigue, tragedy, and comedy of the everyday and the extraordinary, it's as full of lives lost and gross injustice as it is of lives saved and redemption. Garden history is a prism shifting in time and across space—as ephemeral yet stubbornly resilient as plants and landscapes themselves.

Monticello, the plantation and main residence of Thomas Jefferson (1743–1826), third president of the United States (1801–1809), embodies this complicated history. At the age of twenty-six, Jefferson inherited the 5000-acre property in the Piedmont region of Virginia, along with hundreds of enslaved African American men, women, and children. He designed the house and developed the grounds. After Jefferson's death, his holdings, including 130 enslaved people, were auctioned to pay off debts. In 1923, the house and gardens became the property of the Thomas Jefferson Foundation, a private nonprofit historic organization. In 1987, UNESCO named Monticello a World Heritage Site.

Peggy Cornett has worked on the horticultural staff and in the gardens at Monticello since 1983. She currently serves as the curator of gardens on the now 2500-acre site, 8 to 10 acres of which are intensively cultivated in flower, fruit,

and vegetable gardens. Her work includes public education through lectures, writing and editing papers, staff training, public workshops and nature walks, and plant record keeping and research. She also provides internal consulting for garden staff and external consulting on advisory panels and boards of other public, nonprofit institutions.

Born in North Carolina, Peggy grew up in a town called Southern Pines. Her mother, Velma, was a dedicated, *Farmers' Almanac*-following gardener who "planted by the moon and built up the poor, sandy soil by adding food scraps, manure, composted leaves, rotting newspapers, and grass. She sowed rows of lettuce, collards, cabbages, and tomatoes. She mulched with pine straw." When Peggy was about thirteen, her mother shared with her "a collection of family pole beans passed down through generations [of her father's family in Hazard, Kentucky], nurtured in the rich mountain soil and preserved carefully year after year." Even at thirteen, Peggy understood that this passing of knowledge and heritage "was really significant. I just didn't know it would sort of launch my own life."

This inherited plant legacy eventually led her to study botany at the University of North Carolina, Chapel Hill, and from there to pursue a master's degree at the Longwood Graduate Program in Public Horticulture, where she focused her thesis on "the history of annual flowers in America" and fell in love with nineteenth-century seed catalogues, books, and periodicals. Dumbarton Oaks Research Library later published her paper, validating her view that she was "a combination of hands-on gardener and garden historian."

In 1983, Peggy was tapped by Peter Hatch, longtime director of gardens and grounds at Monticello, to join him as an assistant director. The Thomas Jefferson Foundation owns and manages Monticello as well as satellite properties that once belonged to the third US president, including nearby Tufton Farm, which is now the home of the Thomas Jefferson Center for Historic Plants, established in 1986. Peggy launched Monticello's first garden tour program—researching, developing the interpretive content, and training guides as well as overseeing Monticello's nursery and propagation of plants. She later served as the director of the Center for Historic Plants for seventeen years, from 1992 to 2009, overseeing the nursery as well as connecting period plant collections from

> " The reason I love plants and gardening is because, in my estimation, I'm touching a world beyond thought, beyond the bounds of time "

other historic sites. The Center is unique, she notes, in focusing on the value of ornamental plants rather than just edibles.

Through ongoing archival research (for instance Jefferson's private papers are still being found and made available), ongoing archaeological research, and a variety of annual events, such as the Historic Landscape Institute and the Heritage Harvest Festival, Peggy helps Monticello navigate the complex prism of historic preservation.

"We're trying to meet the complexities of a man and a built landscape inclusive of the paradox of slavery head on, not to run away or whitewash it." In 1993, Monticello launched Getting Word: The Monticello African American Oral History Project, which seeks out and interviews descendants of Monticello's enslaved people. Through it, they have shared stories of people such as Wormley Hughes, the enslaved lead gardener and stable manager at Monticello in Jefferson's lifetime. The twenty-fifth anniversary of the Getting Word project was in 2018; it featured exhibits dedicated to all the remarkable individuals whose stories it preserves.

The famous terraced, fenced vegetable garden is one of the most intensively gardened areas at Monticello.

The history of the site at Monticello dates back well before the time of Thomas Jefferson—native plants, topography, geology, and indigenous cultures formed the richness and diversity of the place. How to interpret and interweave the diverse human and non-human natural history into the story of a place is the joy and the challenge of historic preservation.

OTHER INSPIRING WOMEN

- Jean Skipwith (1748–1826), eighteenth-century Virginian gardener and diarist
- Elizabeth Lawrence (1904–1985), early twentieth-century Southern garden writer
- Flora Ann Bynum (1924–2006), horticulturalist, author, and historic landscape expert. "She articulated and spearheaded the restoration mission of Old Salem in Winston-Salem, North Carolina, and was instrumental in founding the Southern Garden History Society."

Philippa Craddock

HER WORK Owner and founder, Philippa Craddock, floral and event design, East Sussex, England

HER PLANT "I love anything that is wild and free and not contained. I love an orlaya—it's understated, works well with others, is delicate, serene, and beautiful in its own right, yet it lasts a long, long time in an arrangement."

HER PLANT JOURNEY Chances are, you will know floral designer Philippa Craddock's name as a result of her work on one of the sweetest and most romantic bridal bouquets of the past decade—that of standard-changing Meghan Markle, now Duchess of Sussex, in her 2018 wedding to Prince Harry, now Duke of Sussex. The posy-style bouquet was understated yet meaningful, featuring fragrant lily of the valley, astilbe (the larger inflorescences of which were hand separated into slimmer sections), astrantia, jasmine, and myrtle, as well as the late Princess Diana's favorite flowers: forget-me-nots. Philippa and her team likewise engineered the epic, bride-framing arches of white flowers and lush foliage throughout the wedding venue, Saint George's Chapel at Windsor Castle.

"I love greenery—how branches bend just so and create space"

The mastermind behind these historic displays is a mother, wife, businesswoman—and a relative newcomer to the world of floral design, having just started in 2009. She lives in East Sussex with her managing director husband, Tony, whom she credits as being the "level-headed one," and their three children, and she started on the path to floral immortality when she was unhappy at the prospect of going back to work outside the house after the birth of her first child. Instead, she started an online delivery service of beautiful and aesthetically packaged living green plants. "I loved the idea of beautiful plants given as gifts in lieu of cut flowers." When one of her houseplant clients styled her plants as wedding table centerpieces, another bride-to-be asked, "Do you do floral design as well?" She didn't. But she would.

After scanning top books on floral design for ideas and basic concepts, she began experimenting, and, as she describes with both a sense of happy gratitude and surprise, "I fell in love with flowers and foliage. I was really excited about creating designs with an abundance of greenery at a time when floristry seemed to focus on as many flowers as possible."

In her first career, Philippa worked in human resources, helping companies seek out top-level executives. She understands herself to be "a really good listener"—perhaps because of her job training, and perhaps because it's a trait encouraged in women. In any case, she credits good listening as part of why she's at ease with "interpreting and nailing a brief." From her first kitchen-table consultation to working with the royal couple, good listening helps her understand what her clients want and need, and allows her to provide it in her own style. She feels similarly about physical spaces and architecture. Rather than applying standard floral styles to any and all spaces, she observes and "listens" to the spaces in which she works, and strives to integrate her creativity with them.

In all her work—whether with individuals or with elite organizations such as Dior, Hermès, Jo Malone, and the Victoria and Albert Museum—Philippa sees herself as "tapping into a need for people to have flowers and plants." Through her love affair with flowers and the building of her business, she has stepped into her sense of self, creativity, and confident leadership, attributes which she tries to pay forward in the way she manages her creative team of twelve core women and up to sixty freelancers.

For example, all the floral displays she created for the royal wedding featured locally sourced flowers, and the now-famous bowers of greenery were gathered largely from the grounds of Windsor Great Park. Notably, the final creations were assembled without environmentally destructive floral foam or unnecessary plastic. At the end of the event, the flowers and greens were repurposed into bouquets that were distributed to hospice facilities and women's

Philippa's arranging often includes foraged and cultivated floral and foliage specimens from the site where she's working. Here, romantic hedgerow wildflowers—Queen Anne's lace and foxglove—pair with foraged oak and hornbeam branches.

shelters around London. While the concepts of locally sourced, sustainable, and foam-free floral designs are not new to the industry, these purposeful tenets gained global attention when Philippa and her team used the social media hashtags #foamfree, #floralfoamfree, and #britishgrown in this event seen around the world.

In 2018, Philippa began working with the Victoria and Albert Museum (V&A) on a collection of fabric flowers modeled on floral illustrations from the V&A's extensive archive. "It started with an exhibit I did with the V&A on Frida Kahlo using solely fabric flowers, which in hindsight was really brave—I'm always willing to try new ideas. I have used fabric flowers a lot, especially in interior jobs for companies such as Lancôme and Dior. We're not replicating, but are inspired by, fresh, wild flowers, and each fabric flower is a miniature work of botanical art, hand-painted individually by artisans. They're creative, lovely, useful, and far less expensive and wasteful in many circumstances."

Among other charity work, she serves as a patron for the Prince's Trust charity Women Supporting Women, launched in 2018, which works with marginalized women, providing entrepreneurial skills and guidance. In some ways, this work serves as a tribute to the people who encouraged her to believe in herself in her youth. "A year ago, I met one woman helped by this charity, and she now employs ten people. I would love to create a series of workshops and guides to help other women explore who they are and where their strengths lie."

Whether she's acting a floral designer, project manager, businesswoman, or role model and mentor, Philippa reminds us that "it doesn't matter who the clients are, the ethos is identical. I listen, I observe, I am creative *and* organized. My very first meeting with my first bride at my kitchen table received the same attention as my meetings with Christian Dior or the royal couple."

A Philippa Craddock plein air floral installation.

OTHER INSPIRING WOMEN

- Phoebe Philo, fashion designer, businesswoman
- Anya Hindmarch, fashion designer, businesswoman
- Willow Crossley, floral designer, author of *Flourish* (2016)
- Rose Uniacke, interior designer, businesswoman

Karen Daubmann

HER WORK Associate vice president for exhibitions and public engagement, New York Botanical Garden, The Bronx, New York

HER PLANT "I'm into all sorts of plants—dahlias, primulas, Korean mums, magnolias. I think I am into these plants because of the memories I have made with them. People who have given them to me. Stories told about them."

HER PLANT JOURNEY When sculptor and glass artist Dale Chihuly began, in 2001, to successfully exhibit his work created specifically to be displayed at gardens and conservatories, public gardens around the United States sat up and took notice. Chihuly's work demonstrated that large exhibits expanding on forms found in nature could draw a large, new audience. A new world opened for public gardens, institutions that have always been dedicated to informing and engaging people about the importance of plants in our lives.

The New York Botanical Garden (NYBG) hosted its first Chihuly exhibit in 2006. NYBG is an "iconic living museum, a major educational institution, and a renowned plant research and conservation organization. Founded in 1891 and now a National Historic Landmark that receives more than 1.3 million visitors per year, NYBG has a three-fold mission: to conduct research on the plants of the world with the goal of protecting and preserving them where they live in the wild; to maintain and improve the gardens and collections at the highest horticultural standard; and to use the garden itself as a venue for teaching the public about plant biology, horticulture, and the natural world generally."

Since 2007, Karen Daubmann has researched, planned, and installed more than fifty exhibitions at the garden. "I work to connect people to plants through a variety of lenses in the exhibitions, whether historical, scientific, or art-based; there are so many wonderful themes that help to draw people into plant life.

> "Looking to tell really great plant stories from around the world"

Exhibitions are planned over many years with the intent of bringing to life distant lands, influential people, interesting plants, rarely seen gardens, and fantastic landscapes."

When Karen and her team began to research Frida Kahlo for a 2015 exhibit, they "wanted to delve into the story of the woman who has been examined through her pain and suffering and depict her through the solace and inspiration she found in the natural world, through the view from her Mexico City studio into her garden—the fruit, flowers, and vegetables which were reflected in her art and informed the entertaining that kept her sane."

The Kahlo exhibit was the first large-scale exhibit at NYBG with bilingual Spanish-English interpretive materials throughout—from the labels to the audio guide to the signage. For a botanical garden embedded in a neighborhood with a large Spanish-speaking population, the bilingual exhibit was "like laying out a big welcome mat. The neighborhood surrounding NYBG attended in numbers we'd never seen. This exhibition appealed to them as never before."

Sharing a love for plants and being a "plant person" has been part of Karen's life for as long as she can remember. She still lives in Little Compton, Rhode Island, the town where she grew up and where, she recalls, "My grandmother was a fabulous gardener. She would send me home with little bits of sedum so I could have my own garden. In time, she moved me to dianthus and physostegia. Everything about plants made the calendar come to life for me. Everything became cyclical, something to look forward to."

These cycles would become part of her professional career. After double majoring in landscape architecture and urban horticulture at the University of Rhode Island, she went on to an internship at Walt Disney World, where theatricality, horticulture, and timing worked hand in hand. Here she learned "you don't need a class to learn plants—you need curiosity. If you pay attention, you'll pick up on the rhythms of horticulture."

After seven years of working on and studying "taxonomy, field botany, curation, plant-mapping software, board relations, and nonprofit fiscal responsibility," Karen brought her depth of skill in public garden horticulture programming to the exhibitions at New York Botanical Garden. She started in September 2007 as the only woman working under

Telling stories and having fun with plants at New York Botanical Garden.

the vice president of horticulture. Over the course of eleven years, she has stepped into leadership and grown her team to include five women (as of 2018) working on planning, researching, writing, and interpreting the exhibitions at the garden.

Their 2018 blockbuster exhibit, *Georgia O'Keeffe: Visions of Hawai'i*, explored the artist's 1939 immersion in the flora and landscapes of the Hawaiian Islands. The exhibit focused on O'Keeffe's paintings as well as "evocations of the Hawaiian gardens and landscapes that inspired her and galleries devoted to the complex history of Hawaii's plants and ecology."

"NYBG has been here for 127 years and until about 30 years ago there was no perimeter fence—people would drive their cars through the incredible tree collections/arboretum, sunbathe on the lawn, use it as a dog park. Now it is taken seriously as a cultural institution. I think the work that we do highlights this. We get visitors excited about horticulture through dynamic, engaging, and diverse voices."

In 2017, the garden's annual Orchid Show was a tribute to Thailand, and 2019's landmark exhibit focused on planthunting, conservation efforts, and the garden design of Brazil's Roberto Burle Marx. Such multicultural narratives open and change the horticultural conversation to include far more diverse voices and cultural histories/perspectives. "We're looking to other populations that we haven't yet had an opportunity to showcase to help us tell really great plant stories from around the world."

Inside the giant pumpkin, an annual favorite at the Garden.

OTHER INSPIRING WOMEN

- Lucinda Mays, gardener and garden correspondent. "For her hosting and being southern correspondent for *The Victory Garden* on PBS."
- Audrey Hepburn (1929–1993), actress. "For her narration of the *Gardens of the World* series."
- Gertrude Jekyll (1843–1932), British garden designer, plantswoman, and writer
- Florence Griswold (1850–1937), patron and nucleus of the Lyme Art Colony, Old Lyme, Connecticut

Andrea DeLong-Amaya

HER WORK Director of horticulture, Lady Bird Johnson Wildflower Center, Austin, Texas

HER LANDSCAPE "Enchanted Rock—a sculptural granite outcrop dome (geologically known as a batholith) in Texas with beautiful flora, creeks, and wide-open views."

HER PLANT JOURNEY The simply stated mission of the Lady Bird Johnson Wildflower Center is to "inspire the conservation of native plants." A fully self-funded part of the University of Texas at Austin, the Wildflower Center is one of the largest native plant research centers and gardens in the United States, welcoming about 185,000 guests annually. And it operates one of the largest native plant databases in the country, with online user visits numbering in the millions.

Andrea DeLong-Amaya has worked in nearly every garden on the 284-acre campus, approximately 9 acres of which is under garden cultivation—"meaning those areas have irrigation (although the irrigation is not always used). The 16-acre arboretum is also irrigated. I consider that a horticultural endeavor, but not a garden." She designed many of the gardens herself, including the Texas Mixed Border ("a Texas native plant riff on the classic English border"), the Botanist's Bed and stock tank displays in the Theme Garden, the naturalistic homeowner inspiration garden, and plantings for the 4.5-acre Luci and Ian Family Garden (Luci Baines Johnson is the daughter of Lady Bird and President Lyndon Johnson).

Andrea has worked at the Wildflower Center since 1998, and she is currently the director of horticulture and oversees the cultivated gardens, the native

> "Physiography and ecology inform the plants and botanical signature of a place"

plant propagation nursery, the arboretum, and the natural areas programs, which showcases more than 800 native plants of Texas. As an integral team member in the design and construction of the Family Garden and the 2005 master plan for the institution, Andrea has developed a love of teaching and sharing her passion for native plants and ecology. The relatively new Family Garden, "developed as a model of sustainable design and nature play," has "programming directed intelligently at the children (and their adults) at the core of our mission. Some families might never go camping or hiking, but they might come to the safe, interpreted, and controlled environment of a garden. We could be their only contact with nature or we could be the inspiration that empowers them to step out of their comfort zone in nature; maybe we'll help them feel a sense of familiarity and stewardship once they get there."

This familiarity and stewardship has come naturally to her throughout her life. "Even as a small child, I literally talked to the trees. One of my 'best friends' was a tree in my front yard. I spent a lot of time in the woods around my house, and remember convincing my dad (who inspired in me a deep appreciation for living things and natural phenomena) to let me keep a patch of dandelions that had invaded the lawn."

While Andrea's favorite place and moment in the garden is at the peak of bloom in autumn for the "luxurious native grasses" in the Central Gardens, conceptually, she loves the Taste of Place area, entirely filled with edible native plants. "There's no more direct way to link people with the natural world than through that very basic need to eat, and we're pretty far removed from that as a culture. It's fun to reconnect people with something as simple as using the wild onions growing in your yard in your scrambled eggs. A lot of native plants are edible and delicious, so just to preserve that information is important."

The beauty and diversity of the native plants of Texas—grasses, agave, and trees in fall color—highlighted at the Lady Bird Johnson Wildflower Center.

Its focus on the native plants of Texas, a geographic area that is vast and diverse in climates, soils, and plant communities, makes the Center a model for scientists and home gardeners around the world—in restoration ecology, fire ecology, native plant research, and sustainable gardening. Andrea sees profound importance in native plant research and climate-appropriate planting and education: "Part of it is understanding how plants fit into a bigger picture of local ecology. I remember seeing turk's cap (*Malvaviscus arboreus* var. *drummondii*), native to the southern and southeastern United States, in the greenbelt of Austin at the same time I was planting it at home in my garden, and it was an epiphany of connection. We all have friends, and we invite our friends to come over and visit—I like this analogy with native plant gardening—I'm inviting my region's native plants into my garden. Having them outside my kitchen door allows me to get to know them better—and visit them often."

Andrea oversees a staff of seventeen part-time, seasonal, and full-time employees across the Center, and these core people are supplemented by dozens of volunteers. The team develops and determines plant selection and management techniques. "Working with native plants in our region, we have few pest issues, don't need frost protection, and use little to no fertilizer due to climate and soil-adapted plant choices. We have beautiful areas of naturalistic design, and we incorporate so-called traditional garden techniques, such as an espaliered redbud on the seed silo, a topiary wax myrtle, and occasional native-plant bonsai displays. One of my goals is to expand people's understanding and vision of how to work with native plants."

Over her twenty years there, Andrea has helped grow the scope of the Center's work and reach. She reflects that "knowing I've been able to make decisions that have resulted in improvements with the hard work of the staff and volunteers is very satisfying." And she has more goals in mind, namely overcoming the "perception about and availability of good native plants in the trade."

Andrea's love for Texas's native plants is deepened by their coevolution and importance to native fauna. Here she shows students a *Hyalophora cecropia* or giant silk moth caterpillar, North America's largest native moth.

Toward that goal, the Center's two major plant sales, one in spring and one in fall, and their smaller tree and shrub sale each year, are major suppliers and introducers of native plants to the region. Andrea has also introduced several native plants into cultivation herself, including a popular globemallow (*Sphaeralcea incana*).

In 2017, the Center launched a new strategic plan in which they conservatively set an intention of introducing two new native plants a year to cultivation, though Andrea proudly admits, "In just the last spring plant sale, we introduced more than a dozen—we're too geeky to stick to just two."

OTHER INSPIRING WOMEN
- Claudia Alta Johnson (née Taylor) (1912–2007), aka Lady Bird Johnson, first lady of the United States, 1963–1969, cofounder of the National Wildflower Research Center in 1982 (renamed the Lady Bird Johnson Wildflower Center in 1995)
- Ganna Walska (1887–1984), American gardener, founder and creator of Lotusland botanic garden, Montecito, California

Sasha Duerr

HER WORK Artist, designer; professor, California College of the Arts, Oakland, California

HER LANDSCAPE "Honolii—the rocky, elemental, porous black-sand beach and river near where I grew up in Hilo, on the rainy side of the Big Island. It is a raw, gorgeous, spiritually moving, and ever-changing beach. I'm always inspired by the abundance of deep, soothing colors, especially the deep jade-greens of the jungle reflected in the river as it makes its movement toward the sea."

HER PLANT JOURNEY Our world—in the refracted light around us, the ocean's depths, the rocks, minerals, and soils of our geologic basis, and the vast world of plants that clothe the planet—is awash in color.

Since ancient times, humans have honed their knowledge and appreciation of color—how color in living systems has evolved to attract and repel other living things, and impart information. The colors vary by season and location, and they carry important information, including the health and point in life cycle of the colorful items in question. Animals (including humans) use the colors around them to make decisions. An inflorescence colored one way signals that its pollen is ripe, colored another way, that it's already pollinated; a forest of trees colored one way might indicate youth or health, another way indicates maturity or deprivation and disease.

Northern California–based Sasha Duerr is an artist and educator who directs the way her audience and students see and intersect with plants using a colorful lens. She applies this lens to conceiving a healthier and more just world.

Raised on Hawaii "by parents deeply connected to nature," her "creativity was nurtured by the jungle and the abundance of flowers and fruits that grew wild." Artistry and plantcraft run in her family. "My maternal grandmother, whom I never met, was a botanical garden postcard model in Florida in the 1940s. I have a beautiful image of her surrounded by floating hibiscus flowers. She cultivated blue ribbon–winning hibiscus flowers and left an artistic legacy of all the ways that she creatively engaged plants, from arranging them to painting and embroidery." The legacy of her family and her environment cultivated in Sasha a strong appreciation for plant and cultural biodiversity and "for a creative source centered in the plant world," which she brought to her subsequent career as an artist.

After studying art at Middlebury College in Vermont, she settled in San Francisco. She describes the Bay Area as "ripe with color—a rich, in-between place," where she was able to enjoy plants from both Maine and Hawaii, and she painted large-scale, "nature-based works focusing on transformational processes." Ironically, she came to realize the very materials she was exploring were also making her sick.

In an effort to move away from synthetic pigments and textiles, which are toxic and sometimes carcinogenic to those who work with them, Sasha experimented with making pigments herself. "It was difficult to find recipes or formulations for naturally derived colors, and many I did find were from the early twentieth century or older sources, which relied on equally toxic, if natural, elements," especially in the realm of mordants (or fixatives) and use of plants known to be toxic. "Natural does not necessarily equal good for you," she notes wryly.

As she explored the Bay Area's plants, she got familiar with the urban garden movement and gained a better understanding of modern food systems. She realized "fashion and textiles were suffering from the very same issues as food"—they were controlled by large corporate entities and disconnected from health, place, and the people who grew or crafted the products. "Knowing where you were, being connected to place and being able to tell the story of your place through the plants and agriculture there—had been lost." She returned to school to get her master of fine arts degree at California College of the Arts and simultaneously worked in the Berkeley public school system to develop curriculum for the Edible Schoolyard program. "I found myself intertwined with the slow food movement and working for the budding slow fashion and slow textiles movements."

Sasha's early work and thesis were "focused on direct parallels between slow food and slow fashion." She

Natural colors— healthy and happy.

developed partnerships and collaborations with women in the plant world from multiple angles—working with female slow food chefs, farmers, gardeners, herbalists, florists, perfumists, and ethnobotanists. She "learned so much and realized how plants tell deep stories and connect us more fully to both people and places," improving the environment—figuratively and literally—for both. "Working with plant-based colors that lend themselves to more environmental understanding and connectedness, I find that there is a poetic nature I love about being on nature's color schedule and not just on our own."

Currently, Sasha lives on an urban farm in Oakland, California, with her husband and children. She designs curriculum and teaches courses in the "intersection of natural color, slow food, slow fashion, and social practice." In 2007, she founded the Permacouture Institute "to encourage the exploration of regenerative design practice for fashion and textiles." She is the author of *The Handbook of Natural Plant Dyes* (2011) and *Natural Color* (2016). Her third book on plant-based color palettes and inspiration will be out in 2020.

OTHER INSPIRING WOMEN

◆ Marjorie Spock (1904–2008) and Rachel Carson (1907–1964), American environmental scientists. "Marjorie was a founder of the modern environmental movement. She was a strong influence on Rachel Carson as Carson was writing *Silent Spring*, regarding the dangers of industrial pesticides on the environment. Marjorie was a dear family friend and a teacher to me as a young child."

◆ Deepa Natarajan, program director, UC Botanical Garden at Berkeley. "A plant-dyeing colleague, supporting integrated and holistic approaches to working, designing with, and appreciating plants. Her work in natural dyes and fiber education has opened pathways that reveal how plants and people are inextricably connected."

◆ Amanda Rieux, former agricultural activist with the Edible Schoolyard movement. "She is teaching the next generation profound ecoliteracy skills. In Hawaii, she works with native food systems centered on the importance of reconnecting to native plants and nutrition. Nurturing communities and youth in knowing and loving plants at early ages is a profound, revolutionary act."

The color palette of summer flowers.

Fionnuala Fallon

HER WORK Gardening columnist, the *Irish Times*; flower farmer and florist, author, West Wicklow, Ireland

HER PLANT "Agrimony. Based on a dream in early adulthood in which I was healing an elder with some plant I could not identify. I was stunned to discover shortly afterward that not only is it an Irish wildflower, but it was traditionally used as an herb to halt bleeding and to help heal wounds. Needless to say, I now grow agrimony on our little flower farm."

HER PLANT JOURNEY The voices of long-marginalized plantspeople from diverse racial, cultural, and socioeconomic backgrounds have long cried for gardeners to "decolonize" gardens. Mainstream garden-and-plant print media have had generations of their readers gardening in the derivative shadow of privileged English and European tastes and conditions. However, in the past twenty-five years or so, plantspeople and gardeners from around the world have been making their voices known. Buttressed by the unprecedented access and connections made possible by digital platforms, they highlight historic plants and heritage gardens to the great benefit of us and our planet.

In the loveliest and most erudite way, Irish gardener, writer, flower farmer, and florist Fionnuala (pronounced fin-oo-la) Fallon stands out among international plantswomen. She explains, "I've always been deeply appreciative of the huge contribution the English gardening tradition has made to my own evolution as a gardener and a grower. But I suppose what I love about Irish gardening is it's this wonderful hybrid of that centuries-old tradition and what you might describe as a wilder, freer, less rule-bound sensibility."

Fionnuala has been the gardening correspondent for the *Irish Times* since 2011. Working in partnership with her photographer husband, Richard Johnston, she contributes regularly to a variety of garden publications including the *Irish*

> "The pure joy of magicking such beauty and sustenance out of the ground"

Garden and *Garden Heaven*. In 2015, Fionnuala and Richard began work to establish a "small, sustainably managed flower farm in a Victorian walled garden at a friend's manor house" close to where they live. She explains, "While I find both writing and gardening fulfilling, it's my work as a flower farmer/florist that gives me the greatest joy. It feeds into my lifelong interest in art, craft, and design."

Fionnuala and Richard's first book, *From the Ground Up: How Ireland Is Growing Its Own* (2012) profiles sixteen unique and often personal gardens located throughout Ireland. Many of the gardens integrate native plants, ancient cultivating tools, and traditional methods preserved over thousands of years.

Growing up in rural West Wicklow, "less than twenty miles outside Dublin, but it might as well be a different universe in terms of its climate, landscape, and way of life," Fionnuala has gardening in her blood. She comes from a "long and mongrel line of gardeners," and is happy knowing she is "following in the muddy footprints of others." She says, "My maternal grandfather was a fanatical tomato-grower and cultivator of sweet peas. His great-grandmother (my great-great-great-grandmother) was, I recently discovered through a diary of hers, equally devoted. Some of my earliest, happiest memories are of tiny, almost abstract moments in time—apple-green light flooding through the leaves of old beech trees, the sweet, clean smell of wild cowslips, the tang of ripe elderberries, the downy softness of the wispy bog cotton that grows in the damp, peaty soil of the Wicklow Mountains, where we used to cut turf with our father as children."

Fionnuala's father, Brian Fallon, was the chief art critic and literary editor for the *Irish Times* and her mother, Marion FitzGerald, was a well-known journalist. Among her aunts, uncles, and grandparents were a sculptor, painters, and a respected poet and playwright—so her thoughtful and creative tendencies come naturally. Following in family footsteps, she studied philosophy and classical civilization at Trinity College Dublin. After spending her early twenties working at the newly founded Irish Museum of Modern Art, often "staring longingly out the windows at the gardeners at work in its formal gardens," she decided to retrain. In 1994,

Buckets of Irish-grown ranunculus from Fionnuala and Richard's organic flower farm in Wicklow.

she embarked on a diploma in amenity horticulture at the National Botanic Gardens in Dublin.

"So often gardening is an underrated profession, seen as lowly, manual work, yet I believe the job of a good gardener is one that asks so much of an individual in terms of the different strands of knowledge that feed into it—you've got to be part scientist, part artist. My father introduced me to a wealth of great garden literature, bringing home countless free review copy books. I remember in my late teens picking out a copy of Russell Page's *The Education of a Gardener* (1962) from a bookshelf—a magic moment—and reading it with the wonderful realization that gardening is an art form in its own right."

Simply growing plants has never been enough for Fionnuala: "I've always been fascinated by plant combinations in terms of how they play off each other as regards the contrasting forms, textures, and colors." She is very aware of the symbolic impact and importance of flower farming and the local flower movement in Ireland, and in 2018 she helped to found the Flower Farmers of Ireland. "It's wonderful to be part of a worldwide movement that has radically redefined the floristry world by putting the focus firmly on the joys of seasonality and local, sustainable production. I think the flower-farming movement is part of a wider environmental movement where women are increasingly playing a significant role."

A spring bouquet design with Fionnuala's farm-grown blooms, buds, and greens.

OTHER INSPIRING WOMEN

◆ "Women who've lived their lives by their own rules—creatively, intelligently, productively, and with integrity—whilst having lots of fun along the way. The rich legacy they've left for future generations to enjoy is something I'll always hugely appreciate and admire."

◆ Helen Dillon, Scottish and Irish gardener and writer

◆ June Blake, Irish gardener

◆ Madeline McKeever, Irish botanist and founder of Cork-based Brown Envelope Seeds

◆ Joy Larkcom, English-born writer, organic gardener, and adventurer

◆ Rachel Ruysch (1664–1750), floral still-life artist

Severine von Tscharner Fleming

HER WORK Founder, Greenhorns; young farmers advocate, Pembroke, Maine

HER LANDSCAPE "Downeast Maine, with its intertidal zones and their ancient governance, are the landscape of my imagination."

HER PLANT JOURNEY Severine von Tscharner Fleming is a leading voice in the young farmers movement—an advocate and organizer focused on supporting the growing number of young people interested in farming and land repair.

According to the 2007 USDA agricultural census, the number of farmers under forty-five years of age doubled from the prior census, moving from 3 percent to 6 percent, a cultural shift that Severine finds worthy of celebration and support. From 2008 to 2011, she and a band of fellow young agrarians researched, filmed, and produced a documentary film entitled *The Greenhorns,* which was a direct counterpoint to the constant "doom and gloom" news about agriculture in the United States. The film, shown more than 3000 times around the United States, documented the energetic and hopeful young farming movement taking place "on campus farms, urban farms, historic farms, farms of retiring farmers, and farms on leased land." It suggested that, in the face of the "global economics crisis, climate crisis, and jobs crisis, starting a farm is a very practical approach to economic reform. Sustainable, family-scale ag is a sensible foundation for a new economy."

Accolades for *The Greenhorns,* and the gatherings around each screening, helped it grow into a grassroots organization of the same name, with a mission "to

> "How we dance in the commons: sexy young farmers outside engaged in land repair, land worship, land use, land health. How do we involve more people in caring for the land?"

recruit, promote, and support the rising generation of new farmers in America" and help them navigate shifting cultural perceptions and public policy.

Severine jokes that she's "basically a party planner," but it is this very approach to her work that energizes people and connects them to what she describes as "the agrarian cultural commons"—the joyous and often ritualized ways in which common resources such as land, water, and food, are shared and cared for on a family and regional scale—so different from the dominant industrial-scale, corporate-production model displacing family farms.

Born and raised in Cambridge, Massachusetts, Severine credits her grandmother—an avid gardener—with her first love of plants. Her first word was "flower," and she loved alyssum. However, her real awakening to the power of growing plants—especially as food and within food justice and land repair systems—happened while creating a "spontaneous and anarchic" community food garden with likeminded classmates and friends at Pomona College in Southern California. Severine ultimately took a few years off from school and traveled around the globe, volunteering on farms and at the National Botanical Gardens of South Africa. She completed her degree at UC Berkeley in conservation and agroecology, thinking she'd go into policy work.

In late 2009, Severine was instrumental in crafting the vision and forming the board for the National Young Farmers Coalition (NYFC)—the work this time including a "policy angle." The NYFC "works with farmers, consumers, organizations, and government to tackle the many challenges that young, independent farmers face in their first years operating a farm business." The challenges identified include "difficulties securing loans, land succession, access to affordable farmland, and student loan debt."

Between networking, workshop organizing, and "matchmaking," Severine found many ways to build the movement and expand its reach through the shared voices of those involved. She supported young farmers and helped them "to find their mates, find and intimately know their land, and learn the skills they need to navigate this complicated world." Under Severine's leadership, the Greenhorns have produced a weekly Greenhorns radio series, thirteen episodes of a web series entitled *Our Land*, a community film festival called *Up Up! Farm*, along with "guidebooks, posters, symposia,

Severine and friend on healthy, working farmland. Supporting young farmers in keeping farming viable and valued is at the heart of her work.

FarmHacks (an open-source farm tool development and exchange network), touring exhibits, mixtapes, and art stunts." They published an anthology, *Greenhorns: The Next Generation of American Farmers—50 Dispatches from the New Farmers Movement* (2012), which Severine coauthored, and four volumes to date (2013, 2015, 2017, 2018) of *The New Farmer's Almanac*.

After years of traveling and moving the group's center, Severine purchased the historic (circa 1896) Odd Fellows Hall in Pembroke, Maine, to house the Greenhorns' headquarters, their 8000-book agricultural research library, and their "agrarian celebratory equipment, like kitchen supplies, props department, silk screen supplies, printing equipment, and more." The hall is symbolically named Reversing Hall, both for the work done there and for a natural phenomenon unique to this part of the Maine coastline, the "reversing" tidal waterfalls between the rivers and bays of the Atlantic Ocean, which "gave the Passamaquoddy their name for the area." Here, Severine continues to work on the Greenhorns' workshops, publications, scholarship, and creative practice—all while tending a garden and orchard and harvesting wild seaweed and medicinal herbs.

Of her career, she reflects, "plant love, stewardship, land care—these impulses direct your life and can improve the world. From my earliest days of garden organizing in college, I've been in service, working at making, holding, shaping, and supporting individuals and groups who are interested in caring for land, plant life, animals, wildlife, watersheds, and the people in them."

OTHER INSPIRING WOMEN

- Darina Allen, founder, Ballymaloe Cookery School, Ireland. "She modeled matriarchal and activist methods of working, project management, and made a repertoire of action-supporting, horizontal, enduring collaboration—non-competitive and kinship based."
- Ruthie King, director, School of Adaptive Agriculture, a new agrarian farming collective
- Wendy Johnson, cofounder of the organic farm and garden program at Green Gulch Farm Zen Center, author of *Gardening at the Dragon's Gate: At Work in the Wild and Cultivated World* (2008)
- Barbara Deutsch, lepidopterist
- "Sustainable and regenerative agriculture is a ladies' mafia—a happy cradle rocked by the hands of women."

Lorene Edwards Forkner

HER WORK Editor, *Pacific Horticulture*, Seattle, Washington

HER LANDSCAPE "Ironically, I would say my soul landscape is the beach. Not the most diverse plant palette, but the rhythmic tide represents continuity to me. That great big sky. The sun is where all gardens begin."

HER PLANT JOURNEY Since people began interacting with plants, they have shared stories of these interactions—how, what, where, when, and how cool. Today, these kinds of stories are aggregated in something known as "garden communication" or "the garden media."

Today, garden media are diverse and fascinating: print, digital, audio, visual. From very local to international, nonprofit to successful consumer brands, plantspeople like to share their stories and their knowledge, and gardeners love to hear it, see it, and read it. Garden communication plays a vital role in the exchange of information that supports and grows the plant world.

Lorene Edwards Forkner edits the quarterly magazine published by the Pacific Horticulture Society, a not-for-profit organization founded in 1976. Its mission is to explore gardens, gardeners, and connections between beautiful, lively, nature-friendly landscapes and a healthy environment along the west coast of the United States—"from Baja to British Columbia."

Born in Southern California but raised in the Seattle area, Lorene had a "natural curiosity about the domesticated landscape" from the start. She remembers being "a four-year-old and planting an apple seed, certain the fruiting tree would appear the next day." In adulthood, the "garden became a backdrop to the rest of my life." She first became a backyard vegetable gardener as a way to retain part of her "paltry income" as an aspiring artist (her undergraduate

degree was in the fine arts, with a focus on "color, composition, contrast"). Once she had children, the garden became her escape. As relief from the occasional "boredom and loneliness of being a full-time mom to two young children, I nearly begged for a job at my neighborhood nursery, West Seattle Nursery."

It was here Lorene first glimpsed the shape of the horticultural world, while being, she quips, "the lowest of the low of nursery people, the girl at the end of the hose—but it's where my plant community education began." Here, she met her people, "others like me for whom every flower, bulb, grass, and twig was a constant source of wonder and possibility." It became clear to her that plants, and tending to them, were more than just an "internal" occupation, but rather "an ever-widening circle."

Within three years, Lorene was ready to try her hand at being an independent nurserywoman. She and a coworker from West Seattle Nursery opened Fremont Gardens on May Day in 1995, on a tiny triangular lot in Seattle. For thirteen years, she ran the beloved neighborhood nursery. Its warm community of people was as important as the exchanging of ideas and collecting of plants. It was "a time when independent and specialty nurseries were abundant"—before the economic recession of 2008, before the days of widespread plant patents, and before big box stores had taken on a large home and garden role.

The nursery's monthly newsletter was her entrée to the intimate and meaningful world of garden and plant writing, which she continued after it closed. She is now the author or coauthor of five books, including *The Timber Press Guide to Vegetable Gardening in the Pacific Northwest* (2013) and *Handmade Garden Projects* (2011).

It was also during the nursery years that Lorene's garden design gained ever-more acclaim in the larger gardening community, including her award-winning show gardens at the Northwest Flower & Garden Show. In the early 2000s, she was invited to be on the board of the Northwest Horticultural Society and act as their representative on the board of the more broadly based Pacific Horticultural Society (PHS). For nearly fifty years, PHS has developed programming and produced a publication that gathers and shares plant, garden, horticultural, and environmental news within its region, all with an eye

> "Gardeners are everyday superheroes—addressing challenges posed by climate change, urbanization, exploited natural resources, and a growing remove from the natural world"

to synthesizing, illuminating, and connecting the dots of patterns and trends.

Lorene became the first woman editor of *Pacific Horticulture* in 2012. According to her editorial philosophy, "the world is bigger than any one plant or any one plantperson. It's in the mixture and tending that you get a garden. What we find among plantspeople in their shared stories, knowledge, and experiences is the golden lining. It's more than pretty plants and a consumer. It's going down the rabbit hole of genera, species, and cultivars, or soil microbes and geologic and climate relationships. That's how you grow gardeners," and that, in Lorene's experience, is the "everlasting importance of garden clubs and horticultural societies."

Under her direction, PHS has continued sharing the stories of plantspeople along the West Coast—a region rich in biodiversity and under great climate change and human development pressures—with the personal details that bring such stories to life, and with an artist's eye to the larger regional connections and concerns. She has devoted individual issues to "The Urban Canopy," "Restoring the Landscape," "Pollinators," and "Changing Times, Changing Gardens," which focused on how our gardens can be proactive responses to climate change.

"I'd love to see a world where the best parts of tending a garden and working in horticulture—nurturing and connection—become a part of the fabric of society. Beauty is a seductive invitation to tend to the larger world. Delicious flavors keep us tethered to real food. Nuanced colors keep us learning to see. And hopefully our personal digging in the garden promotes respect and support for all."

OTHER INSPIRING WOMEN

- Sally Sykes-Wylie, British-born landscape designer/plantswoman based in the Pacific Northwest
- Eleanor Perenyi (1918–2009), gardener, writer, author of *Green Thoughts: A Writer in the Garden* (1981)
- Stefani Bittner, edible garden designer; owner, Homestead Design Collective
- Alice Doyle, owner, Log House Plants

Rose hip

Lorene's art and horticultural backgrounds come together in her explorations of the complex color narratives within even the most everyday plants.

Alys Fowler

HER WORK Horticulturist, educator, author, journalist, Birmingham, England

HER PLANT/LANDSCAPE "That little bit of wild that's hanging on in the most surprising of places, the weed growing out of the crack, the moss that's clinging to concrete. It's the bit of nature that's slowly dismantling our man-made world whilst we get distracted with shiny things. Those moss and lichen will undo our concrete jungle, turn roads back into paths, will car parks to return to forests. Whenever I see nature winning behind our backs, my heart skips a beat with joy."

HER PLANT JOURNEY At a time when most newspapers and general media sources are eliminating their horticultural coverage, Alys Fowler reaches a wide international audience and shares the joys and how-tos of gardening with a whole new generation and demographic of readers and plantspeople in the making. A contributor to the *Guardian*, a print and digital news source based in the United Kingdom, since 2010, she is the resident expert on gardening (her Ask Alys question-and-answer column on gardening ran through 2018), and she creates videos about garden life for the publication's online edition.

Of her work, she writes, "I am a horticulturist—not because of some special training or a certificate (which I have) but because I truly love both the art and science behind growing. I love every corner of my subject, and I'm lucky enough that my work takes me to every corner."

> I love sowing seeds more than anything in the world—I could sow seeds all day long for the rest of my life and be as happy as Larry. Sowing seeds is a true act of sustainability, running hand in hand with joy

Born and raised in rural Hampshire, in the south of England, Alys has long been a voice for eco-friendly and accessible gardening—especially small-space, small-budget, culturally diverse urban gardening in the United Kingdom. She carved her very first garden out of a semicircle of ground beneath an old fig tree at her childhood home and knew by fifteen that she wanted to make her life about working with plants and gardens.

Accepted into the Royal Horticultural Society's degree program at the Royal Botanic Gardens, Kew, and with several work-experience apprenticeships under her belt, she followed it all up with a year-long practical internship at New York Botanical Garden. It was in New York that space and budget constraints took on new meaning in her gardening. Returning to England, she completed her master's degree in society, science, and the environment from University College London in 2002, but "after five years of practical apprenticeship working as a gardener, I had so many ideas and nowhere to put them, no way to sort them. I realized I loved to write, and that perhaps all along, I was as interested in why *other* people are so interested in plants as I was in plants themselves."

Her new career as a garden journalist began at *Horticulture Week*. This

Enjoying every detail of the plants in her small urban garden.

led her, in 2006, to a head gardener position at the BBC's *Gardeners' World* demonstration garden at Berryfields, and finally resulted in a regular presenter position for *Gardeners' World* through 2011. In that time, she had the first of her many books published, *The Thrifty Gardener* (2007), based in part on her experiences with small-space gardening in New York. In it, she declared, "Gardening is something you do, not something you buy," a foundational belief that carries through her writing and gardening advocacy today.

Alys's work is also marked by a love for food and agroecology, as well as a deep interest in the structure, health, and societal implications of food systems. She explains, "I fell into writing about food because I wake up thinking about food, and because, after sowing seeds and gardening, my next happiest place is in front of a stove. Everybody has to eat—and so everybody, even if by proxy—cares about how food grows."

"Growing up, when cheap eggs were still more interesting to most people than free-range eggs, my mother, a small-scale organic chicken farmer, believed passionately that chickens have a right to run free and should be allowed to do so." If a chicken has a right to run free, Alys reflects, "then how is it possible that we have *people* in our society without access to healthful food and green space? Even more enraging to me is that we are producing food that won't ensure our long-term health on this planet. How is it possible that we don't care more about future generations than we do about producing too much cheap food poorly now?"

She sees entry-level gardening as one of the very best "tools for opening up conversations about food systems and larger cultural systems, and for dismantling gardening as a perceived leisure activity for wealthy, white people." She also sees limited access to affordable land and the risk of being unsuccessful as among the biggest barriers for young and culturally diverse people interested in household-supporting edible gardening or farming.

Since 2012, she has been developing an urban farm in the center of Birmingham, which she now calls home, "as an innovative way to look at public land and how it's used." Her interests are in everything from the way it's maintained, "without breaking the workers," to how it is valued. Opening such a farm is, she says, "the thing I want most to accomplish in my work. Anyone who grows anything in their back garden, or in a pot, or on their windowsill, or in their bathroom, is making a strong political gesture as to our food system and where our food comes from, because they're doing the obvious. They're taking themselves out of the multinational system and teaching themselves about food, creating a relationship with their food. When you have knowledge, you have power."

OTHER INSPIRING WOMEN

- Joy Larkcom, English-born writer, organic gardener, and adventurer
- Margaret Falk, associate vice president for landscape, gardens, and living collections, New York Botanical Garden
- Kristen Wickert, plant pathologist, social media educator on Instagram and YouTube—aka Kaydubs the Hiking Scientist
- Gayla Trail, founder of You Grow Girl, Canadian organic gardener, garden writer, seed grower

Tiffany Freeman

HER WORK Clinical herbalist and acupuncturist, Calgary, Alberta, Canada

HER PLANT "I feel a deep connection to the introduced dandelion. It's one of the first plants to come up in the spring in the city, along with the violets. I love its rebellious nature and how it will thrive just about anywhere—it's delicate, yet can surface from the cracks of the sidewalk. It's so common and abundant and often not considered as a powerful medicine. It has a quiet, humble power."

HER PLANT JOURNEY Tiffany Freeman is a registered acupuncturist, a traditional Chinese medicine doctor, and a registered clinical herbalist (certified by the American Herbalist Guild). An instructor, author, and educator, Tiffany is also the cofounder and codirector of the Lodgepole School of Wholistic Studies.

The greater integration and valuing of traditional plant-based knowledge, medicine, and healing practice within our broader culture is a powerful and hopeful movement in today's plant world. According to a 2017 article in UC Berkeley's *Public Health Advocate*, the integration of traditional medicines into mainstream Western medicine "is a crucial focus within the healthcare field as well as in public health."

Born in Winnipeg, Manitoba, and raised for the most part in Edmonton, Alberta, with her first five years in the wildness of the Northwest Territories along the Mackenzie River, Tiffany is of Cree descent on her father's side.

A plantperson from a very young age, Tiffany remembers she "loved to sit with plants and talk." As a teenager, she understood plants as medicine, a concept that ran in her family on both sides. Her maternal uncle, "who earned

> In Cree what we call *askiy*, meaning 'earth or land,' or 'of the land,' became part of my sacred name, Earth Medicine Woman, *Askiy maskihkiwiskwew*

his PhD in history but was called to a career as a Western herbalist, would drop by teas and green blends to help support my family's health. I remember one of the blends with lemon balm and red raspberry leaves he brought when I received my first moon." By nineteen, Tiffany realized working to help others transform their lives and perspectives through their health and with plants was "an honor," and that she wanted to be an herbalist, too.

Tiffany graduated from the Canadian Wild Rose College of Natural Healing in 2004, with a diploma in clinical herbology. She cites the approach of the college's founder, Terry Willard, PhD, as influential. "He gave a truly holistic perspective on plants and healing that honored indigenous voices. He spoke about plants' chemical constituents, therapeutic actions, and properties, but also about them as spirits with their own unique temperaments and energies.

He taught me about keeping an openness of mind and to consider the whole herb, not just its constituent parts." She served as an instructor at the college from 2004 to 2011, and during that time, obtained both her doctor of traditional Chinese medicine diploma from the Calgary College of Traditional Chinese Medicine (TCM) and Acupuncture and her Alberta acupuncture license.

At her clinic, Tiffany incorporates TCM, western medicine, and indigenous plant-based knowlege in her clinical and educational work. Her focus is on women and children, and reproductive and digestive health on physical and emotional levels. While she carefully sources some of her herbs from elsewhere, she also grows and forages many of her own, including calendula, echinacea, goldenrod, mint, Oregon grape, lemon balm, Solomon's seal, false Solomon's seal, tulsi (sacred basil), cottonwood buds, yarrow, and plantain.

She incorporates her traditional values as a person of Cree First Nations descent with her medical and healing work because she believes together they result in a deeper healing and vividly remembers a moment as a young adult when she gained clarity about her path. "During one of my vision quests—sacred ceremonies in which you fast for four days and nights while meditating in nature—sitting in ceremony, under the guidance of my Cree elder who mentored me through the medicine ways of my culture and dreamed my sacred name, I realized deeply in my core the interconnectedness of all things." She had always valued plants as unique spirits and as medicine—her Cree heritage holds plants as the "first people and first teachers, connecting all beings to one another and to the planet"—but at that moment it all clicked. "I sat outside my tent quietly observing the world. It felt very divinely feminine or motherly. I felt very comfortable and loved. A seven-legged grandmother spider (it had lost a leg on its travels) climbed on my blanket and she reminded me of the web we weave

Tiffany lovingly incorporates her traditional values as a person of Cree First Nations descent with her medical and healing work.

and the webs that are woven all around us, connecting everything together, above, below, within, and the four sacred directions, east, south, west, and north." This interconnectedness and deep respect are at the core of what Tiffany shares with her plant-based medicine.

"My goal is to include an indigenous perspective to the world of healthcare and herbalism, to share with people some of the teachings that have been passed down to me that can help or assist us in looking at the world from a different (indigenous) perspective. I want to show people the benefits of walking lightly upon the planet, and of working with respect and gratitude for plant-based medicines and all people."

Observing and knowing her plants in all their stages throughout the seasons allows Tiffany to harvest medicinal plants or their parts at just the right time.

OTHER INSPIRING WOMEN

- Rosemary Gladstar, cofounder, Sage Mountain Herbs. "A strong female voice in herbal literature and education—when I heard her sing songs of gratitude and honoring of the medicines, it rocked me to my core."
- Susan Johnson, teacher and practitioner of Master Tung acupuncture. "Passionate about helping people with HIV/AIDS, hepatitis, and other communicable diseases in San Francisco, California, she was instrumental in the legalization of TCM in the state."
- Blanca Estela Diaz, aka Mamá Maíz, herbalist and birth doula. "They are also the founder of Flora y Tierra, a space in Long Beach, California, that offers a variety of workshops and gatherings that honor the ancestral ways and prioritize BIPOC and LGBTQ2 folks."
- Leslie Lekos, director and educator, Wildroot Botanicals. "She is an herb teacher tucked away in the northwest corner of the United States, a humble plant enthusiast who works respectfully from the land and takes several students at a time through a bioregional herbal immersion program."

Kate Frey

HER WORK Garden designer, gardener, and author, recently of Hopland, California, now of Walla Walla, Washington

HER PLANT "Oak trees—they are beings who develop such great character over time and support so many different organisms, from gall wasps to screech owls to feral bee colonies and everything in between."

HER PLANT JOURNEY In horticultural circles, we have long discussed the direct correlation of our plant choices, gardening techniques, and garden designs to the health of wildlife. Certainly, this topical thread dates back to at least 1962, when marine biologist Rachel Carson raised the alarm that decimated songbird populations were the result of the widespread agricultural use of the pesticide DDT. A new urgency around pesticides arose in 2006, with the first reported cases of Colony Collapse Disorder (CCD) in commercial honeybee populations.

As investigators delved into the causes of CCD, the public became more aware of how important pollinators of all kinds are to our lives. People also learned more about the impacts of habitat loss and degradation and the detrimental impacts of toxic chemicals used in gardens and agriculture. These chemicals affect soil, water, food, worker health and safety, and wildlife of all kinds.

Kate Frey is a gardener, designer, educator, and consultant based in California and Washington State. Her work has always assumed the importance of cultivated landscapes to the health and well-being of the environment and all its moving parts—from microbes in the soil to insects and birds. In 2016, Kate's first book, *The Bee-Friendly Garden* (coauthored with Gretchen LeBuhn), brought together lessons learned in creating healthy and life-supporting gardens, but her career as a sustainable horticulturalist began decades ago.

> "I don't draw a design. I get to know the place, and every garden becomes a spontaneous community of plants that look like they decided to grow together"

Raised in Berkeley, California, she spent weekends on hours-long family walks in nature, during which she and her brother would pass the time listening to their father (a librarian at UC Berkeley) talk about "social, political, religious, and economic aspects of literature, while observing and enjoying the natural world." Her mother, she recalls, "had this way of treating animals as part of the family—as equal species—a free-range pet rat and guinea pigs were as much a part of the family as the rest of us."

The family had a vegetable garden for a short time, and "harvesting something you had sown—cucumber, corn, or carrot" impressed Kate. She came to believe "gardens should be more than pretty pictures to please us; they should intersect with nature. Gardens should have a beneficial purpose and a mission—they should contribute to the earth, not take away from it."

From 1978 to 1982 she worked for the California Department of Forestry and Fire Protection and California State Parks, as well as for the US Forest Service in California and Idaho doing fire prevention and working on trails. She bought her first house at age eighteen and started learning about gardens in earnest, "thinking about plants and gardens and how to work them in around a house to enhance its spaces." In her early twenties, Kate and her then-husband moved to Mendocino County and started a family. There was little opportunity for state work, so she stayed home with her children, gardened, grew just about all of the family's food, and read voraciously about gardening (Robin Lane Fox, William Robinson, Eleanor Perenyi, Katherine S. White).

Her first professional garden job was with Boonville Hotel—famous for its food and its garden, which was grown in part to supply the kitchen. "It was life changing seeing the people who came to eat there and walk the gardens—the intersection between the garden, their lives, and the food and the emotional power of gardens." The experience reinforced how deeply gardens touch people.

While Kate was working at the hotel gardens, Jim Fetzer (of the Fetzer wine family) visited along with Michael Maltas, the organic gardener he'd hired to help develop a food and wine center in Hopland, California. They were looking to study the model of organic gardens integrated into a restaurant setting—one that focused as much on lifestyle and a total experience as on a meal. They hired Kate for the Fetzer Valley Oaks garden project, where she worked for the next twenty years, helping establish the organic flower, vegetable, and beneficial insect gardens and eventually serving as garden director.

Michael Maltas's Rudolf Steiner–based biodynamic education emphasized soil health as the basis of plant health. Cover crops, compost, and flowers for beneficial insects were new concepts to mainstream American horticulture in the early 1980s. The Fetzer viticulturists and consulting University of California Cooperative Extension plant science advisor, Glenn McGourty, recognized that the organic methods used by Michael and Kate for the "healthy and abundant transformation of the garden project" would be beneficial to the vineyards. Kate reflects, "It was an incredible time to be there. Looking at the environment as a whole became

Tending California native clarkias, an early-blooming spring ephemeral wildflower.

a norm rather than an exception. They changed their 2000 acres of conventionally farmed vines to become organically certified in about three years," effecting change across the industry.

Over the years, Kate would develop this concept of organic and sustainable agriculture and business practices into designs and gardens for the Royal Horticultural Society's Chelsea Flower Show in London. Her first garden, in 2003, won a silver-gilt medal, and her second two won gold, marking the first time an American designer had medaled at Chelsea. "Each of the gardens were concepts of the organic vineyards in spring," she describes, "with wildflowers, weeds, agricultural plants, hedgerows, and vegetables." In 2003, a willow arbor and willow pathways were incorporated into the theme "Healthy Soil Means Healthy Plants." Her 2005 "Joy of Observation in a Healthy System" featured a vineyard tower built by her husband, Ben, and in 2007, the theme was "Sustainable Business Practices in Winery and Vineyards." The Chelsea Flower Show successes and connections moved Kate firmly into design, education, and land consultation. She has also continued to write, authoring *Ground Rules* (2018), which breaks her approach to sustainable gardening into easily accessible rules anyone, veteran and new gardener alike, will find useful.

Watching people walk into one of her gardens, seeing their faces light up and hearing them say something like, "Happy! This garden makes me *happy*," remains among Kate's greatest joys. "Of course, bee-friendly gardens also support all manner of life, and being in a garden filled with life changes us forever."

Kate designed and planted the Melissa Garden for a family in Healdsburg, California. The goal was to include a wide enough range of flowers year-round that the family's honeybees, as well as native bees and other flower-visiting insects, would have all the pollen and nectar they needed without human-provided supplement.

OTHER INSPIRING WOMEN

◆ Rachael Long, writer, educator, University of California Cooperative Extension farm advisor, Yolo County, California

◆ Gretchen LeBuhn, professor, San Francisco State University; director of the Great Sunflower Project, a citizen science program focused on pollinators

◆ "All the garden club and Master Gardener women who keep the garden world going."

Christin Geall

> As a gardener, writer, teacher, designer, and photographer, I can vouch that creative cross-pollination happens daily

HER WORK Gardener, writer, floral designer, photographer, educator, Victoria, British Columbia, Canada

HER PLANT "Poppies, particularly the Icelandic varietals of *Papaver nudicaule* and the Shirley poppies, *Papaver rhoeas*. I find them elegant and joyous, tough yet sophisticated, and love them from the delicate bud stage to the cracking reveal of pure color. The luminosity of the petals is entirely compelling."

HER PLANT JOURNEY In 1981, the writer Eleanor Perenyi's essay collection *Green Thoughts: A Writer in the Garden* culminated with a provocative essay entitled "Woman's Place." In it, she posits a theory for the centuries-long association between women and flower gardening: that it was a male-engineered "incarceration" based on the "superstitious fear that women were in league with nature in some ways that men were not." This male-dominated, societal "gifting" of the contained flower garden to the realm of women "thus simultaneously catered to and kept [women and their power] in check."

Perenyi's historical line of inquiry opens wide the issue of sexism in horticulture—including floriculture. It's refreshing. Rereading the piece spurs reflection about the self-actualized, successful women operating from positions of power through their use of flowers and floral design in this first part of the twenty-first century.

Christin Geall's career is a vivid demonstration that women are no longer incarcerated in the flower garden. In her work, flowers are a horticultural medium for leading and educating others about plants, acting not as pretty cages, but as colorful, Socratic-style critical thinking. Her photographs of her

carefully executed floral designs—often using organic, homegrown blooms, greens, branches, and fruits—are paired with prose that reflects on issues of time and place as much as on environmental and cultural literacy. Subjects range from changing tastes in and views on color theory, plant selection, ecology, and literary criticism, to personal and sociopolitical commentary.

Christin grew up in urban Toronto. She didn't have a strong connection to gardening until age seventeen, when her mother, then the owner of a bed-and-breakfast outside the city, left her in charge for a few weeks. "The house had a lovely perennial garden of peonies and delphiniums, and while I don't recall gardening, I know I delighted in making bouquets for the house."

At eighteen, she left home and apprenticed with herbalist Heidi Schmidt on Martha's Vineyard, who "grew medicinal and culinary herbs and flowers, made teas and tinctures, and educated others about the power of plants." Christin preferred to "work directly with the plants and tend house—cook up herbal meals, make preserves, and arrange flowers."

She attended an ecofeminism course taught by Indian soil scientist and ecologist Vandana Shiva at Schumacher College in England in her early twenties. "The ten days I spent with her and the other participants opened my eyes like nothing had before. We all knew the planet was in grave danger and that women, particularly in the developing world, were being hit hardest by environmental issues/ collapse. Ecofeminism helped me feel like I could make change."

After earning a degree in environmental studies and anthropology from the University of Victoria at age twenty-four, Christin took the opportunity of an inheritance from her mother to homestead on a remote island in British Columbia for five years, "clearing land for a garden, splitting cedar for fencing, and hauling drinking water in my wheelbarrow." During this time she also interned at the Royal Botanic Gardens, Kew, in England, where she worked with alpines, but also "begged her way" into the order beds, a floriferous area organized by genera. She was on her way to a career in ecological, hands-on, public horticulture.

A late-summer Geall garden arrangement of compelling color and form combinations—dahlias paired with airy sprays of saponaria.

Two life-changing events altered Christin's intended path—enrolling in her first creative nonfiction workshop and having a baby boy. She earned her master of fine arts degree in creative nonfiction as a single mother, and continued to learn, garden, write, and travel. By her early forties, she was settled back in Victoria, working as an editor and adjunct creative writing professor. In 2015, she started her business, Cultivated—an online home for her multidisciplinary work. "I was married for the first time, to my long-time American beau, in 2014. At the end of my wedding night on the Vineyard, I knew I wanted the next chapter of my life to bring together my loves: environmentalism, writing, flowers, and plants."

As a garden columnist, floral designer, writing teacher, and floral workshop leader, Christin appeals to keen, thoughtful people hungry for her intellectual consideration, rich aesthetic, and ecological commitment. "Ecologists and writers are interdisciplinary thinkers, so thinking about floral design holistically, as a form of ethnobotany, comes easily to me. I also love the workshop model of teaching—whether using flowers or words. It's interactive, conversational, and its creativity always catches you by surprise."

Floristry is a natural progression of her creative and intellectual expressions. "I love it when there's a confluence between the garden and the vase, or a moment of pure seeing through color, or when I know an arrangement or image is composed just the way I hoped. There's a feeling of accomplishment, and this opening of joy. Growing and designing with flowers is such beautiful work."

Christin is currently working on a book due out in 2020, *Cultivated: The Elements of Floral Style*, a literary marriage of her floral photography and essays on culture and design.

A cascading hand-held bouquet capturing the lush profusion of spring—clematis, ranunculus, geum, narcissus, fritillaries, foliage, and a nod to the past with a spray of dried hop bracts.

OTHER INSPIRING WOMEN

- Dr. Vandana Shiva, Indian scientist, ecofeminist, and activist
- Heidi Schmidt, American herbalist
- Molly Peacock, American poet and writer, biographer of eighteenth-century botanical collage artist Mary Delany

Flora Grubb

HER WORK Nurserywoman; co-owner, Flora Grubb Gardens, San Francisco, California

HER LANDSCAPE "The oak savannas of California. Live oaks speak straight to my heart. There's a gravity to a live oak that moves me."

HER PLANT JOURNEY In the world of independent urban plant nurseries, Flora Grubb Gardens stands out. "The history of the business is that we defied the reality of our industry at the time (2002/2003), opening a plant nursery in an industrial neighborhood of San Francisco at a time when small independent nurseries were closing everywhere." The nursery and its signature lush yet low-water, sophisticated yet natural, modern design aesthetic has had resounding success. Led by Flora, and co-owned with her business partner, Saul Nadler, the nursery sets a bar and tone for the entire industry of urban-based plant nurseries.

Flora (named for her Welsh maternal great-grandmother), was born and spent her early years in Bryn Athyn, Pennsylvania, a religious community formed in the early 1900s outside Philadelphia. "Gardens were important to the community, and the church had magnificent gardens."

When she was five, her family moved to Austin, Texas. She took to gardening naturally and would "cultivate little gardens in the backyard, and then I would paint the gardens—gerber daisies, celosias, petunias." She began gardening more seriously as an older teen. When she traveled to California to attend a friend's college graduation in the late '90s, she fell in love with the climate and landscape and "basically never went home. Texas was physically inhospitable to my constitution." In the Bay Area, she got part-time work doing landscape

> "The experience we craft is designed to wake people up—to delight them and to engage them in relationship with other living things"

105

maintenance and part-time work at a tech company. On the side, she did small, residential garden design and installation with her brother; Saul and Susie Nadler were among her clients.

Those close to her around this time remember her speaking constantly about her desire to start a nursery, and when she had completed the Nadlers' garden, Saul offered her the opportunity to do just that. The two found "an old business called The Palm Broker in a residential neighborhood. It was operating on a very low level, but the name and the concept were great, so we bought it." They quickly realized "that palm trees fetched a price that nothing else does," and palm trees bankrolled the early development of the nursery. In 2007, Flora Grubb Gardens moved to its current location in the Bayview district of San Francisco.

"We are many people's treat to themselves, and that's a very sweet space to hold in other people's lives. The experience we craft for our customers is designed to wake them up—to delight them and to engage them in relationship with other living things." Flora knows she is "very driven by an inability to be indoors," so while the experience is paramount, plants are integral. "My love of cultivating plants is the most important gift I have. It connects me to a larger sense of meaning and well-being. Being able to bring that to other people adds to how I create meaning in my life."

The plant palette at Flora Grubb Gardens is a signature combination of "really diverse plants like Proteaceae, cactus, and other plants from American deserts and Mediterranean climates of the world." There are also waterwise plants that, especially in artful blends, include a vibrant range of greens and evoke a sense of being lush and fresh—think ferns, palms, grevilleas, proteas, succulents, air plants. "Those bright greens tell you that there's enough—enough water, enough food, enough everything," Flora has said.

Though she herself is very taken with sculptural plants like palms and ferns in her own garden, in her view there are "plant people and there are garden people. Plant people focus on individual plants and collecting, garden people focus on the whole experience and space creation—we tend to carry plants that are good building

Flora Grubb Gardens—an iconic San Francisco modern-urban nursery.

blocks of gardens. I get obsessed with plants, but I don't abide a plant that isn't doing its job well in the garden."

She is also a team person, and says of those who work with her, "watching employees evolve and grow is a pleasure." The business, which currently focuses on the retail nursery and the 35,000 square feet of wholesale that supplies about half of what they sell at the nursery as well as supplying other independent nurseries, includes twenty-five employees. Four of them have been with her for twelve years or more, and another group have been there between five and ten years.

A self-described perfectionist, Flora has worked hard to direct this tendency in healthy ways for her team, her young son, and herself. "I garden to stay sane; it's time consuming, so that's hard, but gardening is very different than working/owning/running a garden business. My home gardening is how I retain the balance."

That home garden, surrounding her Berkeley bungalow, has gotten its own share of press. She describes it as a "normal-size lot with a very small house. The front garden was created when my father died and I was in the middle of a divorce. The garden is and was a very real structure that I needed internally as central to my existence. On a good week, I will spend one entire day in the garden. I work, I sit, I drink, I eat, I look."

The front garden portion of Flora's own home sanctuary.

OTHER INSPIRING WOMEN

- Annie Hayes, nursery woman, owner of Annie's Annuals and Perennials. "She defined something really different in nursery work with innovation and service. I admire her deeply for her long-term success and impact."

- Alta Tingle, owner of The Gardener, Berkeley, California. "She opened her first store in Berkeley in 1984—at the time the idea of outdoors-in was very new and her shop felt like the garden equivalent of Chez Panisse. She was a pioneer in lifestyle."

- Caitlin Atkinson, garden photographer. "So much of what we understand about gardens today comes from the photos we see of them. She captures gardens with sensitivity and understanding—their wholeness and the experience of them—inspiring us to live with and in our gardens more fully."

Annie Hayes

HER WORK Nurserywoman, owner, Annie's Annuals and Perennials, Richmond, California

HER LANDSCAPE "The romantic cottage garden flowers of nursery rhymes and fairytales—hollyhocks, Shirley poppies, silver bells, cockleshells—I'd lose myself in them as a girl, and they inspired the flowers I first grew from seed."

HER PLANT JOURNEY Finding your people and meeting them where they are is one key to success. Annie Hayes and her nursery, Annie's Annuals and Perennials, an eighteen-year-old retail, wholesale, and mail-order plant company does just this. "When I started, the retail nursery industry was going one way, and I went the opposite way."

Annie's, operating on close to 3.25 acres, is known for its almost completely seed-grown, 4-inch pots of unusual annual and perennial plants. The nursery and the woman are also known for the over-the-top, colorful, contagiously enthusiastic, descriptive information on each plant tag, which captures why Annie's loves this plant "soooooo" much and why you will, too.

Annie was born and raised in the Washington, DC, area. When her first-grade teacher, Mrs. Johnston, recognized her as a child who needed nature, "she created a terrarium in the classroom just for me and put my desk right beside it. It was an amazing gift. I am still grateful."

Annie ran away from home at twelve and by fourteen lived in a "hippy commune known as the Yurt Community in Franklin, New Hampshire." She credits the commune with "saving my life. I don't know what would have become of me without them." She vividly recalls walking through woods filled with lady slipper orchids in spring, very cold winters without electricity or hot water, and a two-acre garden where the food was grown. In her late teens, inspired by an

> Plants make my heart leap

ad in *Mother Earth News*, Annie became the catalyst for the Yurt Community moving to land near Ukiah in Northern California.

By the 1980s, in her thirties and a single mom, Annie got a job at Berkeley Horticultural Nursery. Her colleague there, Julie Snyder, "grew and sold plants to Berkeley Hort. When I walked into her studio apartment and saw her bed completely surrounded by fluorescent lights over seed trays, I thought 'she sleeps among germinating plants, how cool is that?' When I saw her potted plants growing three fire-escape staircases up on the roof, I thought, 'I could do this.'"

That day, Annie collected and sowed *Linaria purpurea* seeds. "They didn't come up, they didn't come up, and then my cat Jupiter walked across the tray and left little cat footprints." When the seedlings all came up where the cat had walked, she realized he had tamped the seeds down in a way she hadn't.

Annie insists that getting fired from Berkeley Hort for "having an attitude" was "the best thing that ever happened to me." She took on growing in her backyard in earnest. She knew these things from her experience at Berkeley Hort: selling plants in pre-bloom size (without hormones or neonicotinoid pesticides) led to the best result in the garden; selling them in small 4-inch pots was affordable; and the signs her friend Julie had made for her plants, "with the seed packet and a description of why she liked it," made a difference.

So she wrote labels in her own bright, fun-loving way, with photos of the bloom, habit of the plant, and how to care for it. The plants "flew off the shelves" of the nurseries she supplied—including Smith & Hawken and Berkeley Hort. "I grew flowers I loved, and I grew annuals and perennials that were easy to germinate but difficult to transport or hold in a nursery. I grew old-fashioned cottage flowers and plants for gardeners who showed me species in magazine pages and said they couldn't find the species anywhere else."

Annie outgrew her own backyard and after various rented spaces, she landed on the 3.25 acres she's still on today. The staff is comprised of sixty to sixty-five people. "We are mostly women—one man in management, many men in production—and we all like each other. We work collaboratively. We trial everything we sell, and once a month we walk the trial beds and decide as a team which plants are good, which will grow well here, are not invasive, will be successful for buyers."

Education is at the heart of what Annie's strives to do. "We try to teach people how to grow the plants—that's what's up in the catalogue, the demo gardens, regular free talks, simple basic helpful videos, anything we can do to teach staff and customers how to grow plants well where they live, and to grow the soil first. I am the queen of compost."

Besides plants, Annie has raised a total of eight children, including stepchildren and others she's informally adopted. Juni Samos is eldest of her two biological children—she

The nursery yard at Annie's Annuals and Perennials—known for its profusion of seed-grown annuals and unusual perennials in resource-thrifty and easy-to-transplant 4-inch pots.

One of the many informative and inspirational display beds at Annie's Annuals and Perennials, which provide ideas for plant combinations and eventual plant height, form, and color. Here, lupines blend with roses, mallows, dianthus, verbascums, and much more.

bought a computer for him when he was a teenager and asked him to "build Mommy a website and make it look like me—the kinds of things I like." The business still uses his original design.

"My business plan was always to be happy, to have a nice place to work, and nice people to work with. I have an endless fascination for plants—and if you're fascinated by plants, you can never learn it all. You will never be bored—*never*," Annie says with throaty emphasis. "I can go to the yard any morning of the week, and there's some new, weird plant trial we're growing, and it's blooming after two years (of sourcing, receiving, germinating, and growing on), and we are all so excited when a bud forms: 'It's gonna bloom, it's gonna bloom, it's gonna bloom!' I get that feeling at work all the time, and that's what I try to share."

OTHER INSPIRING WOMEN

- Julie Snyder, Berkeley Horticulture Nursery, Berkeley, California
- Marion Brenner, photographer of landscape architecture
- Erin Benzakein, founder, Floret Flower Farm, Skagit Valley, Washington
- Amanda Thomsen, aka Kiss My Aster, gardener and writer

Elizabeth Hoover

HER WORK Manning Assistant Professor of American Studies, Brown University, Providence, Rhode Island

HER LANDSCAPE "My first home landscape—the mountains and forest and fields of upstate New York—this is home. In the desert, I feel the beauty, but I also feel like a mouse about to get snatched up by a hawk."

HER PLANT JOURNEY Elizabeth Hoover is a voice for and gatherer of plant history, plant stories, and plant perspectives—for the value inherent in them, and for the way these stories shed light on so many other aspects of life and well-being. She studies how learning more about the plant and food ways of indigenous communities can add valuable insights to healthcare and environmental justice issues in these same communities. Elizabeth's research and community activism often rely on plants, as food, as medicine, as cultural signifiers—all keys to understanding human experiences more broadly.

Born in Albany, New York, she grew up in the "tiny" town of Knox, in the Helderberg Mountains. "I've been with the seeds and the plants in the dirt since I could move around. Both my parents did a lot of gardening, and my dad was very serious about it. We had all the Audubon nature field guides, and we'd go on all kinds of walks. Anything my parents didn't know, we would stop to look up—we looked everything up." Elizabeth is the first in a family of three daughters. Her father is of Mi'kmaq First Nations, English, and German descent, and her mother is of Mohawk First Nations, French, and Irish descent. "My parents' big gardens are where I learned how plants work—how to take care of them, how to tend, harvest,

> My deepest interests lie in food and medicine plants, ensuring there is unpolluted land for growing and foraging them, and getting them back into healthy relationships with the people who have a heritage and history with them

cook, and eat them—it started there, at home. Green beans, tomatoes, corn, zucchini, peas, potatoes, broccoli, winter squashes, berries in the good years, carrots, and onions—and cucumbers and dill and garlic because pickles were integral to my family life."

Elizabeth wanted to be a farmer after high school, but her school guidance counselor encouraged her to apply to Williams College, "a school I never would have looked at for its cost alone. She helped us figure out financial aid; she helped choose my classes for my first year at Williams and helped me decide on anthropology/sociology as my major." From Williams, Elizabeth went on to Brown University for a master's in anthropology/museum studies and her doctorate in anthropology, with a focus on environmental and medical anthropology as it applies to Native American communities responding to environmental contamination.

In her college and early graduate work, Elizabeth had the choice of "academia over plants," but when, in the course of the research for her dissertation, she moved to Akwesasne—the Mohawk Nation's homeland, which straddles upstate New York and Canada—she found herself naturally gravitating "to hang out and volunteer with" the plantspeople. In this pull "toward plants, foods, and working in the gardens" she connected the dots on "how gardens and food production as part of the way of life at Akwesasne had been impacted by environmental contamination." She was able to incorporate her research on gardens and gardening heritage, and the ways they are integral to the health and well-being of the Akwesasne community, into her work.

Her dissertation formed the basis of her first book, *The River Is in Us: Fighting Toxics in a Mohawk Community* (2017), a cultural look into the devastating industrial contamination of rivers in Akwesasne. The contamination badly impacted fish populations, a staple food of the Native peoples there, as well as soils adjacent to the rivers, which impacted food crops. Elizabeth's research explored the Akwesasne Mohawks' response, initiated by a concerned midwife, to the Superfund site's contamination. It also analyzed how environmental health research might be conducted better, with greater cultural awareness and understanding, thereby increasing effectiveness both for human and non-human communities of the affected environment.

While at Akwesasne, Elizabeth earned an environmental leadership program fellowship to help with the Akwesasne garden restoration. Working with a botanist from Massachusetts who shared heritage seeds from other northeastern Native peoples, Elizabeth realized these seeds tied into work that Dave and Mary Arquette and the Akwesasne Task Force on the Environment were already doing. Incorporating (or rematriating) more heritage seeds—those with long-standing association to Native peoples, lands, and foodways—into the Akwesasne garden became another important research thread.

Her work at Akwesasne took her to First Nations' food summits, powwows, and gatherings all around the country. Between 2014 and 2017, she visited more than forty garden project sites in Native American communities around the country. The more people she met and the more stories she heard, the more interested she became in documenting and sharing them. In her second book, *From Garden Warriors to Good Seeds: Indigenizing the Local Food Movement* (2020), she recounts her visits and what she learned there. She hopes that by documenting and preserving these stories, future communities will have help understanding "how they get started, who they accept funding from or not, how they get more of the community involved, how they get more youth involved."

In 2017, the Field Museum in Chicago asked Elizabeth to join their Native American Advisory Committee, which reactivated her museum studies background. The committee is working on a three-year project to revamp and update the museum's Native American displays and dioramas, continually asking themselves, "How do we tell a better, more complete story?" When she became aware of the Field Museum's heritage Native American seed collection, Elizabeth knew, "These seeds needed to be revitalized and re-energized by being sent back out into the communities from which they originated." A rematriation plan is now underway.

With fellow indigenous delegates at the 2018 Slow Food Terra Madre meeting in Turin, Italy.

OTHER INSPIRING WOMEN

- ◆ Angela Ferguson, Onondaga Nation Farm Crew, New York
- ◆ Diane Wilson, (retired) executive director, Dream of Wild Health farm, Hugo, Minnesota. "She worked on the rematriation of yellow flower corn stock."
- ◆ Rowen White, founder of Sierra Seeds, leadership member of Indigenous Seed Keepers Network, chair of the Seed Savers Exchange
- ◆ Lilian Hill, founder/director of the Hopi Tutskwa Permaculture project, Hopi Nation
- ◆ Linda Black Elk, instructor of ethnobotany, Sitting Bull College, Fort Yates, North Dakota

Elaine Ingham

HER WORK Soil scientist, microbiologist, ecologist, founder of Soil Foodweb, Inc., Corvallis, Oregon

HER LANDSCAPE "When I meditate, I retreat to a landscape that sits on the edge of a cliff overlooking the ocean. Starting in a well-cultivated garden, smelling all the flavors of the plants I love—lavender, heather, indigo, jasmine—I always get up and walk through the garden gate and into a forest—in the Pacific Northwest, in Hawaii, Costa Rica, Australia, or Minnesota. I return refreshed, and ready to keep on my voyage of discovery, fitting the pieces together, knowing it's critical that we understand how nature does things."

HER PLANT JOURNEY The soil world is integral—foundational—to the plant world. Since the 1980s, mainstream academic soil science has been transformed into a search for biological discovery. It is a fundamental shift from a science that seemed blindered by theories of the Green Revolution, which dominated from the 1920s through the 1970s. The term Green Revolution refers to innovations intended to increase food supply around the world, specifically through introductions of new, often dwarfed, sometimes genetically modified, varieties of cereal and grain crops developed for high yield. This coincided with introductions of synthetic fertilizers, herbicides, and pesticides, often derived from the chemical byproducts of World War II. The Revolution championed increased production and reduced pest and disease damage to crops managed with these methods over traditional agriculture. However, beginning in the late 1970s, many voices questioned the Revolution's long-term results and benefits versus its serious disadvantages. Many of the voices raised in opposition belonged to women, among them Doctor Elaine Ingham.

Elaine's work in microbiology at Colorado State University, Fort Collins, in the late 1970s through the 1980s illuminated the incredibly complex living systems

> "Explain old-growth forests to me"

116

at work in healthy soil. Her work is strongly associated with the concept of a soil food web—her lab group "was the first to publish the soil food web model."

Born and raised in Minnesota, Elaine seemed destined for a science career—thanks to her father, a large-animal vet, she could use a microscope to count *E. coli* in sample material by age six. Her career in microbiology started at St. Olaf College in Minnesota, and continued with a master's degree in marine microbiology from Texas A&M, where she also met and married her husband, Russ Ingham, who was studying nematology.

From Texas, the two accepted research assistantships toward their doctorates in 1977 at Colorado State University, Fort Collins (CSUFC). Elaine moved to soil microbiology. Russ joined CSUFC's Natural Resource Ecology Lab (NERL), which was working on research into "the roles of microorganisms found globally in soils: bacteria, fungi, protozoa, nematodes, microorthopods, and earthworms." While Elaine worked on methods to determine fungal activity in soil for her dissertation, she contributed to Russ's as well, researching the roles of bacteria and fungi in soil in relation to the nematodes he was studying. "His critters eat my critters," she laughs. When Elaine approached the CSUFC's soil science department, to develop a methodology for assessing fungal biomass in the soil, their response was, "those microorganisms aren't important, they're just there; they don't do anything."

This didn't make sense to Elaine. If "these organisms were present in the soils of every ecosystem on the planet, they had to be doing something. Nature doesn't keep useless things." Through their joint research, Elaine, Russ, and others in the lab "showed that these microorganisms are all-important in systematically providing the soluble nutrients plants require to grow." Soil scientists and agronomists, however, contended that plants need inorganic, synthetic inputs of nitrogen, phosphorous, and potassium to grow most effectively.

Elaine would counter: "Then explain old-growth forests to me? Every year for 2000 years or so in some cases, old-growth trees put away in their trunks, branches, and roots more nutrients than are removed by any crop in any agricultural field in a year. How can these trees stay alive without chemical fertilizers then? Where are they getting their nutrients from, year after year? Why don't they die from lack of nutrients? It's called soil life. Nature's been cycling nutrients very efficiently, without destruction of the soil, since long before humans were even a twinkle in nature's eye." But this flew in the face of everything the academic soil scientists had ever been taught. "Conventional chemical agriculture tills fields and adds inorganic fertilizers to the soil, destroying the organisms that would normally cycle nutrients into plant-available forms without the expense or damage involved when unneeded salts are applied."

In the 1990s, Elaine moved to Oregon State University (OSU) and joined the faculty in both the Forest Science and Botany & Plant Pathology departments. Her work included reevaluating testing the Environmental Protection Agency had done regarding "possible ecological effects of a genetically modified soil bacteria," *Klebsiella planticola*. Elaine's graduate student, Michael

THE SOIL FOOD WEB

Our soil teems with a multitude of organisms which provide the necessary work for healthy plants to grow free from disease, pests and infertility. These interconnected interactions and feeding relationships (quite literally "who eats who") help determine the types of nutrients present in soil, its depth and pH, and even the types of plants which can grow

Holmes, demonstrated that this genetically modified bacterium "had the potential for a devastating effect on soil health, namely the death of all terrestrial plants." Elaine presented these results in 1996 at a United Nations meeting in Madrid, in a session on biosafety protocol. "It changed everybody's view on the safety of genetically engineered bacteria."

This presentation was not well received by biotech companies, or by OSU. "Monsanto is a major funder of most land grant universities, including OSU." This struck her as a concerning conflict of interest, which resulted in her subsequent sense of being "persona non grata" at OSU after the Madrid presentation. However, no one could fault the methodology used in the research, and her graduate student earned his PhD based on the research he performed showing the potential highly negative effect of this genetically modified organism. While this particular genetically modified bacterium was never brought to market, the USDA has not changed the regulatory language regarding GMOs.

In 2001, Elaine moved full-time into the educational and consulting work she'd begun with Soil Foodweb, Inc. in 1996. The company "works with land managers around the world, evaluating their soil health with an eye to increasing microbiology to increase yields and decrease water and other inputs." Currently, she is working to expand her research and training programs by offering online courses and practical training programs to bring biological agriculture to food production all over the world—India, Brazil, Australia, New Zealand, Sri Lanka, the Philippines, Mexico, and elsewhere.

Elaine knows "we've barely scratched the surface in understanding soil life." Research demonstrates there are "fewer nutrients in chemically produced food. Plants grown in chemically treated soil provide fewer important trace minerals and fewer microorganisms to inoculate our digestive systems, helping us to process these foods. When we kill the soil, we diminish the medicinal qualities of our plants, and we diminish the complexity of our own gut biomes."

OTHER INSPIRING WOMEN

- Lady Evelyn Balfour (1898–1990), British farmer, educator, and organic farming advocate; cofounded the Soil Association in England, 1946
- Dr. Diana Wall, Colorado State University, Fort Collins, professor, Department of Biology; senior research scientist, Natural Resource Ecology Lab; founding director, School of Global Environmental Sustainability
- Dr. Vandana Shiva, environmental scientist and activist
- Alane Weber, owner, Botanical Arts, horticulture-based landscape design, and Soil Food-Weber, a sustainable garden consulting website

Robin Wall Kimmerer

HER WORK Professor and director, Center for Native Peoples and the Environment, College of Environmental Science and Forestry, State University of New York, Syracuse, New York

HER PLANT "I frequently refer to myself as a citizen of Maple Nation, so maples are highly valued by me. But right now goldthread, *Coptis trifolia* ssp. *groenlandica*, is also speaking to me. It's a powerful medicinal plant of the Adirondacks, well known in indigenous medicine and becoming so in Western medicine. A little evergreen forest floor plant you could easily overlook, but it holds great power and healing. It's very beautiful, but it's not big—reminding us we don't have to be."

HER PLANT JOURNEY Robin Wall Kimmerer states her mission simply: "The most important work I'm doing today is at the intersection of scientific botany and indigenous botany." Indigenous botany, in her experience, comprises "indigenous science and traditional ecological knowledge, combined with an understanding of plants and our relationship to them." What excites her most is "the symbiosis of these ways of knowing. Indigenous ways are often thought of as simple 'folklore,' but they are this entire body of knowledge about plant science and human relationships to and kinship with plants. In the graduate program I lead, in my research and teaching, it's an interweaving of these on behalf of Mother Earth."

From a child learning plant names to a student learning botanical knowledge to a woman passionately advocating for knowledge, Robin's journey included realizing she had to amplify and make heard the long-marginalized, colonized, and appropriated indigenous-knowledge voice. Her first non-academic writing, *Gathering Moss: A Natural and Cultural History of Mosses* (2005), was "tremendously unexpected, a pivotal personal transformation," because in this format she "could interweave the different ways of knowing" through storytelling. Her writing has continued to evolve, building to her book *Braiding Sweetgrass: Indigenous Wisdom, Scientific Knowledge, and the Teachings of*

"The teachings of plants: gratitude, reciprocity, democracy of species"

Plants (2013), a transformative collection of essays in which she brings all these concepts together.

Born of Citizen Potawatomi Nation and European descent, in rural upstate New York, to parents who were both "trained as engineers, avid amateur naturalists, and great readers," Robin grew up "in a science-y and nature household where our recreation was being out in the woods and swamps," often of New York's Adirondack Park, the "extraordinary ecological integrity" of which stands out as one of Robin's earliest and best teachers.

She always wanted to "know more" and remembers going to the library and searching through Peterson field guides for names and information about wildflowers and birds. As a fourth or fifth grader, she was given a book on wetlands written by a botanist, and for the first time she had "a name for this thing that I loved doing—botany."

While attending State University of New York, Syracuse, in the College of Environmental Science and Forestry (SUNY ESF) for her bachelor's degree in botany, Robin first understood how "unwelcome and dismissed indigenous ways of knowing were" in Western educational frameworks. "I didn't grow up in a Potawatomi community, but I did grow up in a family of Potawatomi values, in which plants as teachers and beings and companions was natural." At college, "I was asked to set aside my deep interest in our relationships to plants in order to learn about the mechanics of plants. Objectifying plants as opposed to understanding them as teachers and relatives was really different for me."

In her boat among the aquatic grasses.

In her undergraduate work, Robin studied under Doctor Edwin Ketchledge, one of her earliest professional mentors. "He took me under his wing, he turned me on to mosses, and he really gifted me the notion of being a botanist in service to conservation. He had a tremendous drive to use his knowledge to heal plant communities."

After completing her master's and doctoral work at the University of Wisconsin, Robin attended a gathering of "indigenous plant knowledge holders and elders," and "soaked up all this plant knowledge—completely in the indigenous idiom. It reminded me of all the plant ways I'd been asked to set aside." She came away energized. "It was this sense of homecoming, this sense of wow, there are these two really, really rich, amazing, and productive ways of understanding the world, and I have the great gift of being exposed to both of them." For Robin, "neither was wholly satisfying on their own," but together "the power of using those ways, coupled with a sense of responsibility to the plants for everything they have given us," showed her the path forward.

"The active marginalization of indigenous ways of knowing was and is a real truth," she says. While she held her indigenous knowledge "under the radar in college, it seems now the ethos has shifted, and there's a rising celebration of these different ways of knowing—to the enrichment of the whole. There are still many holdouts, but the door is now open to this consideration, which is gratifying."

Now an active member of the Citizen Potawatomi Nation and its communal culture, experience tells her that students crave this holistic way of thinking about plant science and ecology. "I have a Potawatomi graduate student who is studying the restoration of plant knowledge in our tribe. It's a dream come true. We have a whole cohort of indigenous students researching at ESF today in the realm of reciprocal restoration—work that restores ecological plant communities and cultural human relationships to those communities." And while funding in an academic and research institution is always a challenge, for Robin it is even more layered. "Every time we write a grant proposal, I remember that it's an educational endeavor to work to explain to people the value and role of incorporating indigenous ways of knowing into our Western ways of knowing."

OTHER INSPIRING WOMEN

- Keewaydinoquay Peschel (1919–1999), ethnobotanist, herbalist; lecturer of ethnobotany and philosophy of the Great Lakes American Indians, University of Wisconsin, Milwaukee
- Buffalo Bird Woman, nineteenth-century Hidatsa woman gardener/educator
- Jeanne Shenandoah (1927–2012), Eel Clan from the Onondaga Nation, midwife and herbalist, longtime mentor and influence
- Chun-Juan Wang, professor emerita of botany and mycology. "The single woman on faculty at SUNY during my undergraduate work."
- Dr. Wendy Makoons Geniusz, associate professor in languages, University of Wisconsin; author of *Our Knowledge Is Not Primitive: Decolonizing Botanical Anishinaabe Teachings* (2009)
- Linda Black Elk, ethnobotanist, restoration ecologist and instructor of science at Sitting Bull College, North Dakota
- Dr. Rosalyn LaPier, ethnobotanist, author, associate professor of environmental studies, University of Montana
- "Ancestors whose knowledge has been transmitted orally and whose names we don't even know anymore."

Jamaica Kincaid

HER WORK Antiguan-heritage American writer; professor of African and African American Studies, Department of English, Harvard University, Cambridge, Massachusetts

HER LANDSCAPE "The desert, though I could never really live in it for long periods of time. I grew up surrounded by two bodies of water: the Caribbean Sea and the Atlantic Ocean. When I was a child, I would grow so afraid and tired of the overwhelming force that was the water, I often would wish there was a plug, which I could pull, and all the water would run out. And then what would that be like? The desert I suppose. And then again, as a child, I read the Bible, the entire book over and over again, mostly because I had nothing else to read and I liked to read. It must not have been lost on me that a great many good things came out of the desert, not least of all some very good writing."

HER PLANT JOURNEY Between 1993 and 1996, writer Jamaica Kincaid, an avid home gardener, wrote a series of garden columns for the *New Yorker* magazine, where she'd been a staff writer since 1976. When initially approached about such a series, she had made it clear to editor Tina Brown, "I don't want to write about rich people and their fabulous gardens, I just want to write about the garden. I wrote the first piece about the conquest of places and the naming of the things found growing in them because, of course, to name something is to possess it. And I think it was quite unusual to look at the garden in that way, with history and power at the center of it—and the joy of it too because for me one led to the other."

> "Plants contain the world. The garden, better than any college education, gave the world to me"

Ms. Kincaid was born Elaine Cynthia Potter Richardson in St. John's, Antigua. At the age of seventeen, her mother sent her to the United States to work as an *au pair* to help support her family. Over the course of her first ten years in the United States, she cut ties for a time with her family in Antigua, took night classes at a community college, quit her job as an *au pair*, got a full scholarship to college, then dropped out to live in New York City and become a writer. She changed her name to reflect her new sense of self and possibility. In the early 1970s, she made her debut at the *New Yorker*, where the longtime editor, William Shawn, championed her voice—the signature style that would become well known through her many novels.

It wasn't until her second Mother's Day, when her husband and young daughter Annie gave her a gift of some garden tools and seeds, that Ms. Kincaid "became a gardener." She immediately dug up a patch of their Vermont lawn and planted the seeds. "I seemed to have been overtaken by my own childhood in Antigua and the spirit of my mother, who was not so much a gardener in the way I would become, because she did not have the luxury of growing things just for their beauty. She grew mostly things she had eaten and liked the taste of them. I went back to her, I suppose, and from there, because of the way I am, I became interested in the origins of the flowers I was growing. I had Latin as a child, and my favorite subjects have always been botany, history, and geography, and plants contained those three things—overwhelmingly really—plants contain the world."

Once she started gardening, she also started asking questions. "Where did this peony come from? Who brought it from there to here? How did it come by its name? Once you're on this path, looking at where something comes from, you can really find all those topics right there." Ms. Kincaid's garden columns and their 1999 collection, *My Garden (Book)*, were revolutionary in their exploration of the tangled history of European conquest and expansion. She questioned her relationship to this history as a woman of color from a colonized nation. Her questions about gardens, gardening, gardeners, and our often-unseen biases inherent in cultural perceptions of them, mark a significant starting point for a larger cultural conversation we might refer to now as "decolonize your garden." This conversation helps reframe our cultural understanding of horticulture and its limitations and exclusions. "My greatest challenges in the plant world are the same as they are anywhere: racism," she wrote. When she would research plant names and end up reading about a white, European male colonizer, she would rightly ask herself, "where am I, and people who look like me, in this narrative?"

In her essay, "In History," Ms. Kincaid questions "what to call the thing that happened to me and all who look like me? Should I call it history? If so, what should history mean to someone like me? Should it be an idea; should it be an open wound, each breath I take in and expel healing and opening the wound again, over and over, or is it one long moment that begins anew each day since 1492?"

In her exploration, she describes how the European history of disregarding other cultures was definitively codified as the earliest binomial nomenclature by Swedish Botanist Carl Linnaeus in his 1735 *Systema Naturae*. For example, Europeans first encountered the plants we now call dahlias when

Spain colonized the land we now know as Mexico. The Spanish sent samples back to their homeland, and in a Spanish botanic garden, the Aztec name *cocoxochitl* was replaced with *Dahlia* after the Swedish botanist Andreas Dahl—effectively erasing the plant's existing history. "The naming of things is so crucial to possession—a spiritual padlock with the key thrown irretrievably away."

"How Europeans would get rid of the people, but keep their things—the absence inherent there is fascinating. And I love the dahlia, but can also see its tarnished history, but then, you know, we *all* have a tarnished history. All humans left to themselves will do something that will tarnish their name."

As an American woman living and gardening in Vermont, who has traveled the world to see plants in their homelands and to collect seeds in China and Nepal, Ms. Kincaid sees her feet now being in two worlds—that of colonized and that of colonizer. And she feels passionately that "the thing we have liked the most about gardens is the love of a flower from somewhere else. Most people don't know that the marigold and the dahlia were part of Montezuma's gardens. If we could just honor one another, it wouldn't feel so bad to have taken them. Honoring one another is one way perhaps we redeem ourselves; I am very interested in redemption."

This portrait from Ms. Kincaid's plant-collecting travels to Nepal was the cover image for her book *Among Flowers: A Walk in the Himalaya* (2005).

OTHER INSPIRING WOMEN

- Sacajawea, "Guide to Meriwether Lewis and William Clark, who would have given them information about the many new plants they were encountering. She is not given any recognition at all in the history of plant collecting for the part she would have undoubtedly played in their westward journey of conquest."
- Gertrude Jekyll (1843–1932), English garden designer, plantswoman, and writer
- Mac Griswold, cultural landscape historian, author of *Washington's Gardens at Mount Vernon: Landscape of the Inner Man* (1999) and *The Manor: Three Centuries at a Slave Plantation on Long Island* (2013)
- Sue Wynn-Jones, Welsh plantswoman, plantseeker, and co-owner of Crûg Farm Nursery

Lauri Kranz

HER WORK Founder and owner, Edible Gardens LA, Los Angeles, California

HER LANDSCAPE "It is the place where the land meets the sea. It is wild, mysterious, and full of possibility."

HER PLANT JOURNEY According to a 2014 United Nations report, "54 percent of the world's population lives in urban areas, a proportion that is expected to increase to 66 percent by 2050." Nature-deficit disorder, and the correlation between our contact with natural green spaces and our quality of life is well researched and established. Many plantspeople and researchers are addressing how to keep city dwellers in touch with a sense of nature and their food supply. Lauri Kranz is one of these plantswomen, working to add green, edible, gardened spaces to urban home and educational environments, undaunted by location or circumstance.

"My children led me to the garden—that's what started my journey. When my now-eighteen-year-old son was four and just starting school, the parents of his class were asked to volunteer in some capacity—on the list of choices I saw 'garden' and though I wasn't even sure what that would consist of, I signed up. And I fell in love with it—everything about it."

After her volunteer experience at her son's urban school garden, she subsequently read every book she could, started her own home garden, befriended farmers at urban farmers markets, and let her "imagination run wild." When her younger son started preschool and his school did not have a garden, she volunteered to get one started. The school said, "Great!" That extraordinary experience with a very supportive community gave her a start with school and residential garden design, school garden curriculum development, and a life in the soil. Reading Kristin Kimball's farming memoir, *The Dirty Life* (2010), "opened up a larger world—women were farmers! I was inspired by her strength,

> "A garden can be anywhere"

wisdom, and honesty. How extraordinary that there is room for everyone to bring their own unique view of the world to the farm, to the garden."

Lauri was born and raised in a small town outside of Hartford, Connecticut. "Growing up, we had a dense patch of woods behind the house where my sister and I would roam and create stories around the skunk cabbage, fireflies, and berry plants. Our neighbors had a large sunflower patch in their backyard, and in the height of summer, I would wander into the center of it and just stand amid the towering, mammoth sunflowers, awestruck."

These days, she is referred to by the *Los Angeles Times* as the "vegetable whisperer." "I work in the soil, in the gardens, six days a week. I can't be away from the gardens for too long—they are like children and need attention. I ache for the scent of the soil, herbs, and flowers all around me. I spend my days in a wide variety of home and restaurant gardens as well as developing school curricula. I help clients harvest and care for their vegetable gardens organically, keeping in balance with nature."

Garden education in urban schools both public and private plays a large role in her current work. She actively gardens at several schools, and she developed the garden curriculum for many more. "The private schools are, sadly, generally better funded for supporting an edible garden," but she's been honored to help with underserved school programs and hopes to continue to expand on these. She also hosts adult-education classes and workshops each year and loves to witness the "excitement of the many different kinds of people upon seeing what

happens when you put a seed in the soil." A big part of the curricula she designs "is having the students eat the harvest."

"I don't want to eat the same things every day—I'm deeply interested in the foods that come from other cultures. Walking through the Hollywood Farmers Market on a Sunday morning is to see the vegetables and foods of the world." For her, this captures one of the great gifts of living in a big city: access to the farmers and growers of the world, their plants, food, and knowledge. "Farmers (and my own failures) have been my best teachers."

By way of example, Lauri grows all kinds of mustard greens, tatsoi, and bok choy in her gardens (crops she learned about from local farmers). Sharing this knowledge with her school gardens and "watching students grow plants from seed and develop relationships with these foods that they might not have had on their plates before" is exciting to her. "The mustard greens might be spicy, but when students try them with a little lemon juice, or sautéed in olive oil and a touch of salt to cut the spice, they eat them by the bowl."

For Lauri, seeing "people connect to where their food comes from—it's very powerful to bear witness to this journey and see how this experience leaves an indelible mark on the person moving through it. Each garden I work in teaches me something new. As the gardens have grown, I have grown."

Her philosophy is simple: "A garden is for everyone," and, as indicated in her first book, *A Garden Can Be*

An edible garden in Los Angeles full of successional flowers, fruit, and edible and medicinal foliage.

Anywhere (2019). Ideally, it's a place far away "from the everyday noise" all around us. Being in a garden is a "privilege that belongs to everyone. In the middle of the city, I want to be with the trees, and the green beauty, and this magic that exists. Everyone should experience this. I hope the work I'm doing—writing, gardening, curriculum—finds its way to and is a lasting presence in the lives of the children who might be looking for this same sense of peace, shelter, respite."

OTHER INSPIRING WOMEN

- Georgia O'Keeffe (1887–1986), American artist, known internationally for her distinct flower and landscape paintings, often of the American Southwest
- Beatrice Wood (1893–1998), San Francisco, California–based ceramicist and painter, noted for her unique use of colorful and unusual glazes
- Claire Zarouhie Nereim, Los Angeles, California–based botanical illustrator
- Victoria Morris, California ceramicist. "Her use of color in her glazes is glorious and unexpected, like nature itself."

Barbara Kreski

HER WORK Director, Horticultural Therapy Services, Chicago Botanic Garden, Chicago, Illinois

HER LANDSCAPE "I find the shore of Lake Michigan to be the most receptive, restorative, inspirational, and soothing place I know. Not a year of my life has passed that I haven't made the six-hour trip around the southern tip to the sandy eastern shore for the sole purpose of walking on the beach. It's never wasted time."

HER PLANT JOURNEY In 1973, the American Horticultural Therapy Association (AHTA) was founded with a vision to "expand and advance the practice of horticultural therapy." Horticultural therapy (HT) is defined by the AHTA as a "practice of strategically incorporating horticultural engagement and garden environments into a broad range of healthcare and other therapeutic modalities."

In 1999, the Chicago Botanic Garden (CBG) dedicated the Buehler Enabling Garden, an 11,000-square-foot display garden "that was the first public garden in the world to be interpreted around accessibility." Barb Kreski explains proudly, "Combined, the CBG's Community Gardening and Horticultural Therapy departments serve more than 100,000 adults, students, youth, teachers, community residents, and human service agency clients each year."

"This garden demonstrates methods and tools to make gardening accessible to people with a wide range of health-related challenges and/or disabilities. It incorporates universal design principles," and the demonstration of these principles in relation to accessibility are updated regularly to incorporate new evidence-based research results. This diligence is crucial to Barb's department, which serves clients who range from preschool-aged children with extreme

> "The power of a plant-rich environment"

Petunia x hybrida
'ColorBlitz Sky Blue'
ColorBlitz Sky Blue
Petunia

disabilities such as "being on a gurney or with a feeding tube," to trauma and disease survivors—those with persistent mental illness, war veterans, hospice patients—and an aging population, who might be "losing their memories, their vision, their hearing, or their mobility."

Elements of the garden include "raised beds and other containers, which provide a user-friendly way to bring plant and soil life up to a manageable height. Six of these are table beds with space under them so they can be approached straight on from a wheelchair or seated position without contorting the upper body. Another bed is forty-one inches tall so that it's standing height, and we have vertical wall gardens and hanging baskets that crank down on a pulley system."

The spatial layout of the garden itself is key. "The enabling garden is fully paved and basically walled for safety, monitoring, and a sense of shelter.

Two entry and exit points are directly across from each other—the walls are trellised above shoulder height to allow a sense of openness." She elaborates, "We do a lot of work with veterans who cope with hypervigilance. Here they can monitor the entry and exit points and feel protected by the walls without a sense of mystery. The boundaries also allow young and old to have the freedom to wander without getting lost or without someone on top of them all the time."

For the plantings, "we research and incorporate interesting plants (grown on site) each season that are safe (non-toxic, without thorns, hypoallergenic) and easily propagated for hands-on activities. We go for a high sensory impact: scent, taste, textural, or plants that might provide sounds, and finally, bold, high-contrast colors—think purple against gold, red against white." Annually, the garden goes through three full planting rotations and provides programs designed to engage visiting groups with plants and nature.

Horticultural therapists "need an understanding of horticulture and an expansive and sympathetic knowledge of human beings and the multiple ways that human beings can be." What is compelling to Barb in this work is "the power of the medium of plants in all their forms and stages of life."

At work planting in the CBG therapeutic gardens.

Prior to her work at the CBG, Barb had a thirty-year career as an occupational therapist, which "emphasized purposeful, meaningful physical tasks" to foster improved function in patients. At CBG, she observes "the reactions and interactions of people with plants, and something always resonates deeply. As therapists, we gauge our client's reactions and adjust our offerings and methods so they are responding with their strongest, most functional, and most heartfelt self."

She was "generously mentored" by the previous department director, Eugene Rothert, Jr. "Gene drew on his own experience as a gardener in a wheelchair and his keen powers of observation and problem solving to improve access and include people with all sorts of challenges in gardening."

Early in her work at CBG, Barb had an interaction with a veteran in treatment for PTSD. He rarely left home and had a lot of trouble sleeping. "His therapist encouraged him to think about where he felt less anxious and to write in a journal." Barb invited him to CBG, and during a tour of the gardens, "he kept remarking on all the locations where he would enjoy writing in his journal." The following week, he wrote Barb an email about visiting CBG "on his own, to do some journaling. He found a quiet bench, wrote for a while, and dozed off. He was astonished to realize the level of relaxation he had experienced." This left her in awe of the power of a plant-rich environment.

Based on "connecting engagement with nature to various measures of well-being," Barb steers CBG's programs toward "what that research can tell us, directly or indirectly, about best practices for HT." An essential element of her work is "partnering with researchers to collect data from our programs and to work with the researchers to produce publications" about and in support of the professional field. She strongly believes HT addresses an urgent need for "healthcare that incorporates holistic and preventative—non-drug-based—interventions. While HT is not a complete care solution, it's a controllable variable that gives us all a better baseline. We'd be crazy to not provide this for ourselves."

The Buehler Enabling Garden's design creates open, safe, and welcoming accessibility.

OTHER INSPIRING WOMEN

- Patsy Benveniste, retired vice president of education and community programs, Chicago Botanic Garden
- Clare Cooper Marcus, professor emerita in the Departments of Architecture and Landscape Architecture at the University of California, Berkeley. "She is a foundational researcher in the world of evidence-based therapeutic landscapes."
- Teresia Hazen, MEd, HTR, QMPH, coordinator of therapeutic gardens and horticultural therapy for Legacy Health Systems, Oregon

Mia Lehrer

HER WORK Founder and president, Studio-MLA, Los Angeles, California

HER LANDSCAPE "The rolling California oak savannas. The dotted oaks grew on me, having come from the tropics of El Salvador. I love going to Catalina Island and taking long walks; it's a unique environment, and I can get lost in those hills. It grounds me in different ways than the familiar lushness of the tropics, with the long vistas across the terrain and the exoticism of cactus."

HER PLANT JOURNEY Since landscape architecture and public planning began to develop as fields, designers, builders, thinkers, and dreamers have worked to interweave nature—its sense of green, of refuge, of peace—into otherwise very inorganic areas, to benefit both the ecological and built worlds. Think of Frederick Law Olmsted's work in New York's Central Park and every other urban park across the country at the turn of the nineteenth century. To varying degrees of success, generations of landscape architects since Olmsted have carried this torch.

One of our generation's leading lights in bringing nature to urban areas is Mia Lehrer. Mia is the founder of Los Angeles–based Studio-MLA, whose large-scale public and residential garden design work in urban environments embodies her belief in the power of landscape to enhance the livability of a city and encourage nature as part of a city's environments. Her award-winning work includes rewilding and community integration projects along the Los Angeles River and the Nature Gardens at the Natural History Museum of Los Angeles County.

Born and raised in El Salvador, Mia is the daughter of European-immigrant parents who cultivated an awe and respect for the natural world. She describes her early life as a paradise of rainforest, volcanoes, parakeets, and weekend outings to engage with the world. Her father founded an organization similar

> Urban nature— making cities more livable

to a land trust, which continues in El Salvador today. Her mother was involved in projects to provide economic stimulation to women.

While at Tufts University for her undergraduate work, Mia encountered a retrospective of Frederick Law Olmsted's drawings for the design of Central Park. The magic of those drawings introduced her to the existence of landscape architecture as a career. Due to civil war in El Salvador in the mid-1970s, she was unable to return to her home country after graduating, so she completed a master's of landscape architecture from the Graduate School of Design at Harvard University. There, she met and married Michael Lehrer, who was completing his architecture training at Harvard, and they moved to his hometown of Los Angeles, California, after graduation.

Mia spent years designing and building residential gardens, learning her new climate and new city. In the early 1990s, working in a volunteer capacity with her young children on behalf of their schools, Mia was involved in the annual *La Gran Limpieza*, The Great LA River Cleanup, hosted by Friends of the Los Angeles River (FoLAR). The most important thing to know about the Los Angeles River is its history—over the course of several decades, from the late 1930s to 1960, it was almost completely channelized with concrete in an effort to control flooding, forming a fifty-one-mile engineered waterway through the city. This channelization destroyed plant and animal habitat, the seasonal rhythms of the river, and human interaction with the river's greenspace and life.

Mia's initial pro bono and community-minded involvement in the river cleanup marked a turning point in her professional journey. In the process of the cleanup, she met Lewis MacAdams, cofounder of FoLAR, with whom she subsequently collaborated, employing her design lens "to give vision to his dream of making the river accessible to all." Her work with FoLAR, TreePeople, and other environmental organizations produced an epiphany—an opportunity for a firm that could work with like-minded environmentalists to deploy the skills that landscape architecture and planning require. The goal would be balancing environmental and social justice. Her career path shifted away from private gardens to what she is known for now: bringing diverse communities together through ecologically significant, large, public spaces of beauty, utility, and integrity.

Her diverse, forty-member team at Studio-MLA includes landscape architects, urban designers,

The living walls, pathways, and native plants of the Los Angeles Basin invite human engagement in the Nature Gardens at the Natural History Museum of Los Angeles County.

community advocates, botanists, ecologists, and technical experts, with a purposeful 50:50 men-to-women ratio from different ethnic and cultural backgrounds. The office includes native Spanish, Cantonese, Mandarin, French, Portuguese, Hindi, Gujarati, and Marathi speakers. This diversity of perspectives adds depth and meaning to their collaborative process, something Mia values for its resulting "culturally sensitive and environmentally responsive design."

In addition to several parks and plazas, which have been instrumental in the revitalization of the Los Angeles River, one of Studio-MLA's showcase projects is the Nature Gardens at the Natural History Museum of Los Angeles County. With more than four hundred species of trees, shrubs, perennials, and annuals—70 percent of which are native to the LA Basin watershed—this 3.5-acre garden and living laboratory in the heart of downtown transformed what was once a parking lot into a lush landscape. The plants provide refuge for both humans and wildlife, air and water filtration services to the environment, and a natural setting for the venerable cultural institution. More than one million people a year visit the Gardens.

Mia's work has always investigated how different cultures and demographics use space. "I think it was my empathy for other immigrants from El Salvador that led me wonder, How do you manage public space for people who use space differently? How do we invite everyone to make use of public space for gathering, for quiet reflection, for rest, for recreation?" She lives by her belief that "landscape architecture can transform the quality of life for people and, through design and beauty, we are uniquely positioned to leave the world better off than we found it. The complexity of the natural and built systems have to be negotiated carefully. We know more every day about the negative impact that we have had on the world, but through opportunities with technologies and science, we are better positioned to effect change."

OTHER INSPIRING WOMEN

- Rosa Kliass, Brazilian landscape architect, contemporary and friend of Roberto Burle Marx; created beautiful and significant gardens in South America
- Cornelia Oberlander, Canadian landscape architect known for her ecologically functional landscapes
- Celeste Cantú, from the Santa Ana Watershed Project Authority. "She developed a regional watershed management plan to achieve sustainability in the Santa Ana River watershed."
- Arancha Muñoz-Criado, a landscape architect, planner, and writer working in green infrastructure and using innovative geodesign technologies

Lady Arabella Lennox-Boyd

HER WORK Founder and principal, Arabella Lennox-Boyd Landscape and Architectural Design, London, England

HER LANDSCAPE The hillsides and wildflowers of her childhood home and garden, Palazzo Parisi, Oliveto, Italy

HER PLANT JOURNEY "One has to look at what's around when designing— it's a visual and gut feeling to start with," says Arabella Lennox-Boyd, who for more than four decades has been a leading landscape designer and plantswoman in the United Kingdom and beyond.

Arabella is known for her luxurious and expertly composed plantings, born of horticultural knowledge and instincts, and for her career-long service and voice in horticultural institutions of note, including serving as a trustee for the Royal Botanic Gardens, Kew, for nearly a decade. Since the 1990s, in both her design and public service roles, she has helped to define the nature and direction of horticulture in the United Kingdom.

Born in Rome and raised there and at Palazzo Parisi, Arabella moved to London in her early twenties and attended a course in landscape architecture at Thames Polytechnic, later the University of Greenwich. In the late '60s, she began designing gardens noted for their combination of Italianate structure and symmetry with English plantsmanship, and in 1989, she officially formed Arabella Lennox-Boyd Landscape and Architectural Design. Her work illustrates an appreciation for "grand effects of earth and plants—big gestures." She's been known to declare, "I must have something strong and powerful in my designs."

Her commissions, numbering more than five hundred and ranging from small-town gardens to large landscapes for historic homes, can be found around

> "There is an essential relationship between a design and its surrounding environment—the light, the topography—it's absolutely essential"

Lady Arabella at Palazzo Parisi, Oliveto, Italy—her home garden since childhood. The scale, feel, and history of this garden have informed her design sensibilities throughout her career.

the world, notably in England, Italy, France, Germany, Ireland, Scotland, Spain, Barbados, Canada, the United States, Russia, and Ukraine. Her own home gardens at Gresgarth Hall in Lancashire, England (to which her family moved in 1978), and Palazzo Parisi, Oliveto, Italy, remain among her most important and most public. They are ongoing training grounds for her own learning and experimentation. In *Designing Gardens* (2002), Arabella wrote, "For me the most important garden of all is my own in Lancashire. It has been a source of inspiration and something of an experimental station for other commissions. I can try out different gardening techniques, planting ideas, plant combinations, and designs. Living and working there in all seasons, it's impossible to lose sight of the fact that a garden is a living, changing thing and not a static object."

On Gresgarth Hall's 150 acres, Arabella laid out the 12 acres of gardens with terraces coming down from the house to the lake. These are richly planted with "roses, clematis, and more tender plants in season, and the predominating pinks, purples, and silver-whites compliment the rugged gray stone of the Gothic house." The gardens include renowned pebble mosaics, a potager, greenhouses for potting up and growing from seed, and a now nearly thirty-year-old arboretum.

A special passion since her time as a trustee for Kew Gardens, the arboretum "is now looking really good. It's not mature, but it's looking like an arboretum. I planted about 7000 trees and shrubs, but of course, lost some along the way." The collection includes "*Quercus, Sorbus,* euonymus, and birch, a collection of *Styracaceae, Stewartia,* magnolia, *Daphne bholua,* and rhododendron."

Arabella's display garden designs at RHS Chelsea Flower Shows have earned her six gold medals. Designers' Flower Show names only began to be included with their designs and sponsors' names in 1976—since 2000, only 70 of the 225 garden designers have been women. In 1998, Arabella was among the first women awarded Best in Show, an honor first bestowed in 1984.

Other professionals still talk about the beauty and effect of this Best in Show garden. The design, sponsored by the *Evening Standard,* could be seen as her hitting her full confidence in experimental design and expression. It "was based on a garden I had done in Normandy, France, some years before, but simplified and pared down to convey a contemporary simplicity. I particularly wanted to have a lot of water and to use Portland stone to edge the steps for contrast with the green of the grass, trees, and shrubs. The entire site seemed to be filled with water, the pools and grass giving an air of calm, and the woods and sculpture adding a sense of mystery or hidden meaning." The herbaceous borders were lush with her signature "impressionistic" muted color palette in phlox, foxgloves, verbascum, heuchera, iris, yarrow, and airy, dynamic seed heads of ornamental grasses. "Over the years, I think my designs for Chelsea have become simpler and more contemporary. In each of my gardens I have tried to show a concept or a design idea, which is not always possible when working for a client where there are always constrictions."

Lady Arabella's home garden at Gresgarth Hall, in Lancashire.

Throughout her career, Arabella has served as a member of the Historic Parks and Gardens Panel of English Heritage and served on the heritage panel of judges for six contemporary heritage gardens. She has been a patron of the Painshill Park Trust and served on The Yorkshire Arboretum Trust (once known as the Castle Howard Arboretum Trust) and on the council and the scientific panel of the International Dendrology Society. She also served on the Woody Plant Committee of the RHS. Currently, she serves on the board of directors for the historic Chelsea Physic Garden, London's oldest botanical garden, founded in 1673. After almost fifty years designing gardens, Arabella is "more at ease, more determined in my ideas" and "knows quite quickly" what she should do in a space. Many of her clients have turned out to be friends for life, and she has three or four gardens that she maintains. Of this annual work, she says, "it's a wonderful link with something interesting that carries you through the years."

OTHER INSPIRING WOMEN

+ Sarah Price, British landscape designer

Cara Loriz

HER WORK Executive director, Organic Seed Alliance, Port Townsend, Washington

HER LANDSCAPE "The high desert. I love the tenacity of the plants that grow there, and I am fascinated by the Native American history of farming in this landscape."

HER PLANT JOURNEY Cara Loriz has long believed that "human ingenuity pressed into service for the common good is the antidote to the enormous footprint our species is imposing on our natural environment." When she "learned about the organic seed movement, how it's growing the biodiversity of our food supply by training farmers to breed the heirlooms of tomorrow," she saw all the pieces of her own education, training, and experience come together for her current life's work—executive director of the Organic Seed Alliance. "Incredibly constructive work is underway to build an alternative system with farmer-scientists at its heart. By connecting farmers with university plant breeders, seed companies, food distributors, chefs—the entire supply chain starting with seed—we can change the way we grow food on this planet."

Having grown up in Omaha, Nebraska, Cara was marked early on by a culture of farming set against the "farm crisis" of the 1980s. She clearly remembers the powerful cultural force of Farm Aid, the movement that started as a benefit concert, held September 22, 1985, in Champaign, Illinois, to raise money for family farmers in the United States. This national conversation was poignant and personal for her as a young adult. "Many of the farmers in my family and town circle had bought into the whole Green Revolution mindset of Big Ag—monoculture, big equipment—and they were all defaulting." There were several famer suicides in her region at the time.

> The plants we live with today are largely those whose seeds we saved

But her path to becoming a seed and farming advocate was not a straight line. After studying geology and technical writing at the New Mexico Institute of Mining and Technology, she completed a master's degree with a geotechnical focus at California State University, Fresno. In all her subsequent work, "this foundation in the mechanics of soil and soil formation would prove invaluable."

Her subsequent work would run the gamut—she moved around the country a lot and worked as an educator in almost every place she lived, teaching "geology at College of the Sequoias in California and physical science for educators at both Utah Valley State College and Miami University in Oxford, Ohio." She and her husband started a family in Salt Lake City, Utah (she credits him with giving her the gardening bug). When their children had graduated high school, they moved to Shelter Island in New York, where she worked as reporter and then editor of the local community paper before becoming the executive director of the newly formed not-for-profit, Sylvester Manor Educational Farm—an organic educational farm. Formed out of what was once a northern slaveholding plantation, the farm had been home to more than eleven generations of the original European settler founders. She served at the farm for five years, putting to work all that she had learned about "developing lines of communication and building community," only this time around, "reviving a heritage around local food, farmers, soils, and history."

Since her first garden in Utah, Cara has grown food everywhere she's lived and "been a native plant gardener in each region as well—the mountain West, the heartland of Ohio, coastal New England, and now the Pacific Northwest."

When her husband was diagnosed with aggressive cancer, they decided to return to the West and relocated to Port Townsend, Washington. Soon after arriving, all the puzzle pieces of her research, community building, and advocacy would come together in her work with OSA.

The Organic Seed Alliance (OSA) uses "research, education, and advocacy to advance ethical seed solutions to meet food and farming needs in a changing world." OSA educates "farmers and other agricultural community members, conducts professional organic plant breeding and seed production research, and advocates for national policies that strengthen organic seed systems." State of Organic Seed reports from OSA "provide ongoing monitoring of organic seed nationally and a roadmap for increasing the diversity, quality, and integrity of organic seed available to American

Fieldwork and carrot seed project evaluations.

farmers." Cara's personal philosophy and OSA's mission match up perfectly. "For me, the plants we steward are an intrinsic part of food, family, and place. One of the biggest revelations coming from a deeper understanding of my work is that people and plants have evolved together. There is no bright line between mankind and nature, with one surrounded by artifice and the other a pure ecological creation. The plants we live with today are largely those whose seeds we saved, helping the process of natural selection along its way."

Among the research that OSA conducts, Cara notes its work as a fiscal sponsor of an organic seed symposium for graduate students working in organic plant breeding. OSA also teamed up on a carrot project with Doctor Phil Simon of the University of Wisconsin, Madison, and the USDA, "trying to harness the genetic strength of a wide diversity of carrots to develop new varieties that meet the needs of today's farmers by being resilient, adaptable, nutritious and great tasting."

When she considers the question of how to "develop a food system that is good for people and good for the planet," she comes back to "what we have now is a food system that puts profits before people and the planet; if there has ever been a testament to the fact that capitalism can go too far and has run amok and become rapacious, it is in the idea that we can patent life. OSA works hard for all their work to remain in the commons and be available to all. To use our research to improve food, make it more resilient, nutritious, and delicious and connect that food to our communities—I can't think of a better way to a brighter future."

Evaluating the carrot seed-saving and breeding project with the team.

OTHER INSPIRING WOMEN

- Edith Lammerts van Bueren, a vital force for organic plant breeding in Europe; author, *Organic Crop Breeding* (2012)
- Amy Goldman, seed saving and heirloom advocate; author, *The Compleat Squash: A Passionate Grower's Guide to Pumpkins, Squashes, and Gourds* (2004), *The Heirloom Tomato: From Garden to Table: Recipes, Portraits and History of the World's Most Beautiful Fruit* (2008), and others
- Micaela Colley, seed educator and advocate, program director, Organic Seed Alliance
- Kristina "Kiki" Hubbard, seed and farmers' rights advocate, Organic Seed Alliance

Clare Cooper Marcus

HER WORK Professor emerita, Departments of Architecture and Landscape Architecture, University of California, Berkeley; leader in the field of evidence-based research, education, and design of therapeutic landscapes in healthcare settings

HER LANDSCAPE "Perhaps the most significant single moment in discovering I was a plantsperson was at age six or seven, when we had been evacuated to the countryside from London during World War II. I experienced a deep sense of awe when, one spring, I came upon a field where thousands of daffodils were blooming."

HER PLANT JOURNEY Most plantspeople would affirm the importance of plants to the overall quality of their lives. At a very basic level, our physical health (from the air we breathe to the food we eat) depends on plant life, but beyond that, the presence of plants and outdoor landscapes contributes to our mental, emotional, and spiritual well-being in myriad ways. Measuring exactly how and why plants and green spaces are valuable is particularly important with respect to design in our ever-more-urbanized world. This became apparent to urban planners in the early twentieth century, when an increasingly industrialized landscape in United States cities led to widespread advocacy for parks to improve the health of residents.

Clare Cooper Marcus is a leader in the field of evidence-based research, education, and design of what are alternately known as healing gardens and therapeutic landscapes. A longtime researcher into the relationship between people and their environs, Clare focused early in her career on assessing and measuring how and why people make use of designed landscapes in cities, "trying to link the social sciences with the design professions."

She first bonded with a landscape as a child, when she and her mother and brother were evacuated from London to live in the safety of the British countryside during World War II. A maternal aunt "took me for walks through the fields and woods, teaching me the names of wildflowers and pointing out which mushrooms were edible. One day, she brought me a six-pack of pansies, helped me plant them, taught me how to water them and pinch off the dead blooms. These were the first plants I took care of—I was hooked!"

The work for which she is best known today began toward the end of her tenure as a professor at the University of California, Berkeley, when her graduate student at the time, Marni Barnes, suggested they apply for a grant researching the effects on visitors of different hospital gardens. This was an area not yet covered in research, and they were intrigued. They got the grant and conducted the research, which launched Clare's subsequent twenty-plus-year career on the benefits of, and best practices in, healthcare garden design.

Clare and Marni were encouraged in their early hospital garden work by the evidence-based healthcare design research of Doctor Roger Ulrich from Texas A&M University. His work showed improved outcomes for hospital patients with views outside into green spaces. After that first grant, their award-winning report on their findings, and Clare's retirement from formal academia in the mid-1990s, the two women continued their research. Ultimately, they coauthored/edited the book *Healing Gardens* (1999), which reflected a deep interest in the links between nature and healing, and the importance of incorporating gardens into healthcare facilities.

> "Passionate about sharing the researched beneficial effects of plants and gardens for those who are sick or under stress"

Shortly after her retirement, Clare was diagnosed with breast cancer. While conducting research on the therapeutic benefits of hospital gardens, she was going through cancer treatment at one of those same hospitals. "The fact that these two things coincided seemed almost like a cosmic joke. But the importance of that hospital garden immeasurably deepened my understanding and commitment to promoting the healing power of nature. My garden at home, in particular, brought me great solace and joy." Her healing process and its relation to place and landscape is recounted in her memoir, *Iona Dreaming* (2010).

As a retired professor, Clare realizes the importance of educating people in many fields related to incorporating therapeutic green spaces in healthcare settings. She teaches each summer at the Chicago Botanic Garden in an annual, eight-day intensive Healthcare Garden Design Certificate program, which is attended by professionals from diverse fields including landscape architects, educators, horticulturalists, scientists, and healthcare professionals and administrators. This course is registered with the American Society of Landscape Architects as a Landscape Architecture Continuing Education System–approved provider.

She also works as a "consultant with design teams creating therapeutic gardens. The needs of each patient group—from cancer care to those recovering from burns to those experiencing memory loss—are subtly different. And patients are just one of the user groups; there are also visitors and the healthcare providers to keep in mind. It's incredibly rewarding work."

In order to update the research and design recommendations presented in her first book, Clare collaborated with colleague Naomi A. Sachs (founder and director of the Therapeutic Landscape Network) in writing *Therapeutic Landscapes: An Evidence-based Approach to Designing Healing Gardens and Restorative Outdoor Spaces* (2014). In addition to her books, Clare has written many articles in *Landscape Architecture Magazine*, in her mission to "publish what is known about the beneficial effects of plants and gardens for those who are sick or under stress, to provide case examples of exemplary gardens in hospitals, senior living, Alzheimer's facilities, hospice, etc., and to offer clear design guidelines for landscape architects who will be creating gardens in the future."

Healing garden with clear pathways, places to rest out of the flow of traffic, sun protection, and a welcome sense of both visibility and enclosure.

OTHER INSPIRING WOMEN

- Teresia Hazen, coordinator of therapeutic gardens and horticultural therapy, Legacy Health Systems, Oregon
- Marni Barnes, Deva Designs, Palo Alto, California
- "My Aunt Jean, who taught me to garden."

Mary Pat Matheson

HER WORK President and CEO, Atlanta Botanical Garden, Atlanta, Georgia

HER LANDSCAPE "My husband and I have a farm in Athens, and we named it 'Triple Poplar' after a triple-trunked tulip poplar that graces our yard. This farm, with its beautiful oak and hickory woodlands where we ride horses, hike, botanize, and enjoy friends, is our Camelot; the Triple Poplar stands as the tallest in the forest and welcomes me home."

HER PLANT JOURNEY "For people in public gardens, this is our century," declares Mary Pat Matheson, president and CEO of the Atlanta Botanical Garden (ABG) since 2002. "Never before in human history have more people lived in urban areas," she goes on. "I recently heard from Sarah Milligan Toffler, director of the Atlanta Children & Nature Network, that children in the United States spend less time outdoors than prisoners. That took my breath away and puts fear into my heart. Public gardens are one antidote to that. They are a safe place to get kids into nature. Once there, being there, learning there, loving and caring about nature there—they are inoculated for life!"

Mary Pat thinks everyone should be able to answer the question, "How did you acquire a love of nature?" She believes for most people it happens early in life, from in-person, hands-on experiences. "Botanical gardens can help provide this kind of experience—especially to kids—and we need to do more!"

As leader of the ABG since 2002, and an active member of the American Public Gardens Association, the Directors of Large Gardens, and the Botanic Gardens Conservation International's Leadership Advisory Council, Mary Pat sits in a unique position to help form and inform the ways in which public gardens are resonant and welcoming places of refuge, education, and meaningful, relatable experiences for the widest possible range of visitors. She also helps

> "Gardens are where people go to feel human again"

model how public gardens are centers for plant research and conservation efforts worldwide.

    She has served her entire professional career, more than thirty-five years, at botanical gardens. She grew up in the Washington, DC, area but headed to Utah for college. Graduating from the University of Utah with her degree in natural resource management, she began her career as the director of horticulture for the university's campus arboretum. In that position, she was an integral part of the team that researched, planned, and created the university's Red Butte Garden, which opened in 1985. While working there, she went back to school for her executive master of public administration degree, and then went on to serve as executive director at Red Butte Botanical Garden for twelve years.

    Mary Pat's true skills and passion lie in "thinking forward and into the future" within the unique resources botanical gardens have to offer. "I often compare my work to that of a symphony conductor—I lead the music but the team makes

A view over the pond (planted with aquatic edibles such as rice) in the center of the Edible Garden's colorful vegetable amphitheater at the Atlanta Botanical Garden.

the magic happen. The ABG has always been committed to plant collections, but we're not only here to save plants, we're here to connect people to them as well." The mission of the ABG is to "develop and maintain plant collections for display, education, research, conservation, and enjoyment."

Mary Pat sees the work of public botanical gardens as having changed "a great deal in the last four decades, but all in good ways. More people visit public gardens than ever before, so we are far more successful at mission fulfillment. In large part, we have shed the prevailing notion that only garden lovers come to the gardens, and that we're only here to serve one segment of the population."

When she was hired, both she and the garden's board of directors dreamed of really "cracking the doors open for everybody." Mary Pat realized that vision "through programming and fundraising." When she arrived, garden membership was at 10,000 and annual visitation was around 130,000. In 2018, membership was 46,000 and visitation was 600,000 per year, on average.

"Part of how you open your doors to people of all backgrounds is in looking closely at how different populations feel welcome and reflected, where you market, what kind of programming you do. We looked long and hard at how to get people of different economic levels to come to the garden in a long-term, meaningful way—and we looked directly to the people supporting the community: city employees, staff and faculty within the public school system, the public transit system, and the regional Level 1 trauma hospital." She and her staff then wrote a successful three-year grant to provide free and reduced memberships to all employees of these institutions over an initial period, and to underwrite development and implementation of programming to ensure these populations felt "welcome and included, wanted and connected." The ABG now has 11,000 household members with average annual incomes of $36,000. "This is phenomenal new reach, and it's relevant programming that's key."

Mary Pat is well aware that her city's full population needs to be modeled in garden staff, research departments, and administration. She sees the garden's recruitment and training for these arenas starting with the garden's partnerships with the Atlanta Public School System, wherein "every single kindergartener comes to the gardens every year, and then up through sixth grade. We've just launched a high school program, and we have an ongoing internship placement program with Spelman College. This is the pipeline for professionals entering the field."

She has also encouraged botanical gardens' roles "as leaders in plant conservation, leaders in science research, and leaders in training the next generation of biologists, botanists, taxonomists, and conservationists." She recently participated in a conservation project "at Torreya State Park in Florida with one hundred botanists working to save the beautiful *Torreya taxifolia*. I was both uplifted and depressed. The tree is all but gone in the wild, and the challenges of bringing it back are immense. We need to strengthen funding to support the conservation of native plants and restoration of wildlands—maybe even save half of the planet for biodiversity as E. O. Wilson wants."

The Fuqua Orchid Center at the Atlanta Botanical Garden is the largest orchid center in the United States and comprises two display houses, a conservation greenhouse, and labs for conservation and research.

OTHER INSPIRING WOMEN

- Ann Crammond, Mary Pat's predecessor, the second executive director of the Atlanta Botanical Garden, who served from 1979–1992
- Judy Zuk, (1951–2007) American horticulturist and conservationist; served as president of the Brooklyn Botanic Garden from 1990–2005
- Dr. Emily Coffey, vice president of conservation and research, Atlanta Botanical Garden
- Dr. Kayri Havens, director, plant science and conservation, senior scientist, Chicago Botanic Garden

Marta McDowell

The sweet spots are where gardening and literature dovetail

HER WORK Writer, author, and historian; landscape history and horticulture teacher, School of Professional Horticulture at New York Botanical Garden, New York City

HER LANDSCAPE "My great Aunt Mary (Ryan Brandt) grew flowers in sunny beds behind her bungalow in Atlanta, Illinois. The garden was magical, especially for a small person. She seemed to like tall plants, or so it seemed to me at the time. Was it because the surrounding prairie was so flat? Perhaps she wanted the height. The tiger lilies, hardy amaryllis she called 'magic lilies,' and colorful annuals were bigger than I was at the time. There was a hand pump and watering can for any child interested. It is still a garden I can conjure up in my mind's eye, like some sort of *Doctor Who* time machine. In my garden, you'll also find tiger lilies and 'magic lilies' (*Lycoris squamigera*), those hardy amaryllis from Aunt Mary's flower beds."

HER PLANT JOURNEY There are myriad ways people engage and interact with the plant world—expanding what and who we as a broader culture might consider to be horticultural.

Marta McDowell has spent the last twenty years researching and writing books that explore the horticultural and garden pursuits of people, often women, primarily known for other things—poets, painters, writers, and presidents—but for whom the garden, horticulture, and the natural world were sources of inspiration. In her first book, *Emily Dickinson's Gardens* (2004), she introduces readers to the classic American poet this way: "Emily Dickinson was a gardener."

Marta's other books include *Beatrix Potter's Gardening Life* (2013); *All the Presidents' Gardens* (2016), and *The World of Laura Ingalls Wilder* (2017).

A revised color edition of *Emily Dickinson's Gardens* came out in 2019. In each book, she explores and expands on what we already know of the lives and pursuits of her subjects through the lens of their interest in horticulture.

Raised in Chatham, New Jersey, where she still lives, Marta was "a suburban kid in the '60s, lucky enough to spend most waking hours outdoors." She liked "solo wanderings, and there were still scraps of woods and streams in our north Jersey town, not to mention a river (the Passaic) and the vast and aptly named 'Great Swamp,' now a national wildlife refuge." She liked "to explore and collect—acorns, rocks, and the like."

An appreciation of gardening came in her twenties, when she got her own "bit of earth," to quote Frances Hodgson Burnett's *The Secret Garden*. Over the course of her twenty-year corporate career, gardening was a beloved hobby and respite. When she was almost forty, she started taking classes and doing some garden writing and teaching in her spare time. She earned her certificate in landscape design from the New York Botanical Garden (NYBG) and has been an instructor and lecturer in landscape design, history, and horticulture ever since. Then, as she puts it, "a miracle happened. Prudential funded my midlife crisis by offering a buyout package as part of a downsizing, and I went, as a friend put it, 'from leading to weeding.'"

Marta teaches and lectures regularly on garden history and the subjects of her many books.

Marta recounts that she's "smitten with the world of plants, especially its intersections with place, people, and the past." She "gravitated toward the study of landscape history," and throughout her own life has wondered what drives the human compulsion to "grow plants—and not just for sustenance. We arrange plants in functional and symbolic ways. Our species has the urge to select, shape, and control their growth."

Marta has been a "book person" from childhood and "the spots where gardening and books dovetail, well, those are sweet spots for me. Maybe writers are drawn to gardening because it is outdoors and tactile. Exchanging pen (or keyboard) for trowel moves the brain into a nonverbal, multisensory world."

In the mid-1990s, while still engaged in corporate life, Marta chanced to visit Dumbarton Oaks, while in Washington, DC. "I was enchanted by the gardens—an orchestrated series of outdoor rooms that flowed down a wide hillside, from house down to Rock Creek Park. Dazzling. A landscape architect I'd never heard of designed it, a woman—Beatrix Jones Farrand. [She] was my first landscape history obsession. The first class I taught at NYBG was about her life and work."

Around the same time, Marta was on a business trip in Massachusetts and she "took a detour to Emily Dickinson's house museum in Amherst. It was quiet—as the only visitor, I had a private tour from the curator—and I discovered that this poet had also been a gardener. A door opened that day, and I stepped through it."

She took her readers through this door with her. She also helped others rethink the role of horticulture in people's lives. In 2010, by way of example, the NYBG opened a major exhibit—*Emily Dickinson's Garden: The Poetry of Flowers*. In 2018, Marta served as Gardener-in-Residence at the Emily Dickinson Museum.

Delicate sprays of martagon, or Turk's cap, lilies bloom in Marta's garden. She has a fondness for historic plants and flowers, and these garden cultivars date back centuries.

OTHER INSPIRING WOMEN

- Elizabeth Lawrence (1904–1985), American gardener and garden writer. "She touched my heart, or maybe my soul. One of the first gardening books that made a deep impression on me is her *Gardening for Love*."
- Ruth Bancroft (1908–2017), California gardener. "Her Walnut Creek succulent garden inspired the founding of The Garden Conservancy."
- Susan Fraser, the head of the LuEsther T. Mertz Library at the New York Botanical Garden. "To me, librarians are the great unsung heroes. I could not do my work without the resources and expertise of the guardians of the archives and collections of the great botanical institutions."
- Jenny Rose Carey, director of the Pennsylvania Horticultural Society's Meadowbrook Farm

Jekka McVicar

HER WORK Founder and co-owner, Jekka's Herb Farm and Herbetum, Bristol, England

HER PLANT "Rosemary, *Rosmarinus officinalis*, because it is evergreen, is useful all year round, restores the memory, and flowers generously twice a year giving early nectar to the bees. The Lamiaceae family is wonderful—it has been proven to help heal bees."

HER PLANT JOURNEY "We've traveled around the world through herbs, and the more we've traveled, the more I've realized that in many parts of the world, herbs are still a primary source of medicine," says Jekka McVicar, co-owner and founder of an herb farm, educational display herb garden, and school near Bristol, England. The organic farm grows more than 600 varieties of herbs from around the world, from seed and cuttings, specifically to be used in the garden.

Jekka has been growing herbs professionally since 1975 and founded her herb farm in 1985. Sometimes referred to as the "Queen of Herbs," she has contributed to Royal Horticultural Society displays and gardens since 1993. Her hand-grown herbs form the main plantings in her award-winning garden designs, and she has won sixty-two RHS gold medals. In 2012, she became the first woman (and sadly still the only, as of 2018) to be chair of the judging of the great floral pavilion at the Chelsea Flower Show.

As a plantswoman, designer, author/educator, and RHS senior judge, Jekka has spent her career expanding the public's understanding and appreciation of organically grown herbs—not just as medicine but as a pathway to improved environmental and community health and well-being. She was born and raised near Bristol, and she grew up gardening. When she had children of her own, living in a semi-detached suburban home, with her husband, Mac, away for

> The herb garden is the modern apothecary

work, she came to understand "we are what we eat," and she determined to begin growing and selling her own herbs.

She started off supplying local health food stores, but soon enough, her fresh tarragon caught the attention of the celebrated London food purveyor Fortnum & Mason, and they placed an order. From there, her business grew. In the early 1980s, it outgrew their suburban home, propelling Jekka and Mac to put all their savings into the renovation and establishment of what is now Jekka's Herb Farm.

In 1992, a significant drought left her "moaning" to another nursery friend about all the excess plants retail nurseries weren't buying. He told her to "stop moaning and enter them for display at the RHS." At an October show, her herbs caught the attention of a well-known judge who suggested, "We don't see many herbs. Would you apply for Chelsea?"

Jekka remembers this as a turning point. "If I had not entered those shows, you would not know about me now. The British system of horticultural and floral shows provides a platform that is worldwide and unique for nurseries, for really good specimen plantspeople, designers, and others."

Her first book, *Jekka's Complete Herb Book* (1994), was followed by her first gold medal at Chelsea in 1995. She exhibited the organic herbs she grew herself in winning plant-stand displays annually through 2009, and every single year, the Queen and Duke of Edinburgh would stop in to see her herbs and greet her. In her intended final stand in 2009, "bees, ladybirds, and hoverflies" formed a central part of her display. She was "the only certified organic grower at the show," according to the *Telegraph*, and she used the platform to "make a call for more insect-friendly gardening," saying she would like "to show what is possible without any chemicals in a show garden."

In 2016, Jekka created her first main show garden for Chelsea, entitled "The Modern Apothecary," ultimately sponsored by St. John's Hospice, which received the garden after the show ended. It was an entirely organic, herbal enclosed garden, with a large central vessel fountain providing the sound of water and underplanted with flowering thyme. The space was based on interconnected pathways, two on the interior and one running organically around the perimeter "so people feeling low could actually walk somewhere." The two interior pathways were paved with cobbles stood on end, designed in the Asian tradition for the "reflexology benefits of walking on them." Even the edges were herbal grasses. Espaliered pears lined the walls, because pears are "the least allergenic food and recent research had shown that organically grown pears are rich in nutrients." Finally, the garden was hedged with yew, from which the cancer-treating drug Taxol is derived, and the entrance archway—inspired by Asian garden moon gates—was covered in scented climbing roses. "All good gardens include an entrance—just going through them puts you into a different frame of mind."

When the garden was relocated to its home at the hospice, Jekka added a third, outer ring made of smooth paving, so "wheelchairs had easy access. Florence Nightingale said fresh air was the best cure. Fresh air and the feeling of life going on—watching the butterflies and bees and birds taking a bath in the central basin—is therapeutic."

In 2017, she worked with St. Mungo's, a homelessness advocacy organization in London, and Jo Malone London LTD, who together sponsor a charity civic garden every year, to create The Quiet Garden, a community-based garden in Notting Hill. She oversaw the St. Mungo's client-crew who installed the herbal and edible garden; through their work on the garden, they had the opportunity to earn official certification to work as gardeners. The transformation of the crew, "who seemed to grow in confidence with the garden, and the ownership of and pride in the garden from the surrounding community" made the effort one of the "most moving" projects she's been involved in.

To be a nurserywoman in the public eye with such pursuits as designing, teaching, speaking, and judging, Jekka feels strongly that "you have to be prepared to listen, because in plants you can get it technically wrong so easily. And you have to love it, because you are never going to make a lot of money, but you are going to make a wonderful life. To walk into the glass house in morning and greet everything coming on—it's the same every year—every spring is a joy, seeing the seedlings, creating cuttings."

"The Modern Apothecary" won silver-gilt at the 2016 Chelsea Flower Show.

OTHER INSPIRING WOMEN

- Beth Chatto (1923–2018), British plantswoman, nurserywoman, writer and designer
- Penelope Hobhouse, British plantswoman, writer, and designer
- Derry Watkins, British nurserywoman, writer, author; owner of Special Plants Nursery
- Sarah Raven, British plantswoman, nurserywoman, writer, and cook
- Charlotte Harris, British garden designer; in 2017, first LBGTQ designer to create a Chelsea main avenue show garden with a fully female team

Amy Merrick

HER WORK Floral designer, writer; owner, Amy Merrick Flowers & Styling, Brooklyn, New York

HER LANDSCAPE "A native meadow. It's seemingly peaceful to the human eye, but behind that beauty is a thrilling, ever-evolving community striving to grow to its full potential."

HER PLANT JOURNEY Amy Merrick is a floral designer and writer. "I travel extensively to teach flower arranging and write about gardens, design, and flowers. I've learned to give my business a lot of freedom to chase whatever interests me next." Since her early floral design successes in New York City in the 1990s, she has embodied an ideal for a generation of thoughtful, global, and botanically minded people in search of meaningful beauty.

As comfortable in a field in rural New Hampshire as in a Chinese skyscraper, a temple garden in Kyoto, the flowery herbaceous borders of an English estate garden, or a back corner of a research library, she tries to work beyond profligate consumerism to connect more deeply to culture and place. Her creativity taps into global conversations around design, cultural literacy, economics, and how a botanical knowledge and sensibility are part of a well-lived life and a more hopeful future for our planet.

Amy grew up outside Annapolis, Maryland, and went to college in New York City for fashion design. Not long into her time in New York, she missed the wildness of her rural childhood and actively sought flowers to soften the city around her. Unable to afford traditional floral courses while juggling freelance writing jobs, she instead found an internship at the flower shop Saipua with Sarah Ryhanen, where she worked one day a week and was paid in flowers.

The internship lasted for a month before it turned into paid work and then into a full-time designing position. Within the year, Amy went from having no experience in the field to managing, sourcing, and arranging flowers for the

> To follow flowers where they lead me

high-end weddings Saipua had started to book. "The experience honed my skills in learning through observing and doing. It was an incredible education in how to navigate as a woman in the city, and in the commercial value of flowers." In addition to her work at Saipua, Amy was also establishing herself as a writer with her personal blog, contributions to websites such as *Design Sponge*, and to newspapers and magazines.

In 2011, she launched her own company out of her apartment bedroom and bathroom. She slept in her tiny office, her bedroom became her studio, and her bathtub was one large flower bucket. Her designs were known for their expansive and spacious extravagance—wild and natural with softness and romanticism.

Her reputation as a designer, writer, and stylist allowed her to move right into high-end weddings and floral workshops around the world, doing events for fashion designers such as Ralph Lauren and Oscar de la Renta and styling for publications like the *Wall Street Journal* and *Kinfolk*. "I basically worked every day for seven straight years without a day off to establish my business."

But, at the age of twenty-nine, she realized the effort had taken its toll. "I began to wonder where all this success was going? I didn't only want to arrange flowers for fancy New York parties. I knew there was something else out there, but I never had so much as a moment to look." In 2014, she closed her Brooklyn studio and set off to explore. "It is easy for people to follow on a very narrow path and never look up to check course. It was scary to close up shop, but it was scarier to imagine living a life I wasn't fulfilled by."

Her first stop was Japan, which held up a mirror for her to see the excess of much of traditional floristry. It inspired a more thoughtful, simple approach to arranging, and Amy realized how much she didn't know about the world, or about the world of flowers. So began her international journey to both teach and learn. She visited China, France, England, and more, and as she traveled, she returned to Japan over and over as source of inspiration and as a second home of sorts. She intensively studied *ikebana*, a traditional Japanese art of flower arranging, and ultimately taught her own style of arranging in a series of floral classes throughout the country. "Japan helped me

One of Amy's designs featuring seasonal wildflowers, seed heads, berries, and branches.

remember that picking flowers is the truest kind of joy in arranging—being outside, looking, and finding them is the art."

After a three-month apprenticeship in the United Kingdom at the famed Great Dixter House & Gardens, her eye turned toward horticulture and gardening history. While she learned to garden, she also learned how little she knew about plants themselves. "Arranging flowers is a world away from ornamental gardens, and I left Dixter hungry to know more."

Today, her work is a delicious cycle of trying to dig deeper and always learn more. "Nature is always changing, so I'd like to have the same freedom to grow. This is the gift of flowers—appreciating their moment and learning from that ephemerality—nothing lasts, so I might as well follow my curiosity wherever it leads. Flowers help me not grasp my creativity with such a tight fist."

Amy is an ongoing contributor to the *Wall Street Journal,* where she reflects on design, gardens, and flowers. Her first book, *On Flowers: Lessons from an Accidental Florist* (2019), comprises her evocative floral photographs and stories and is a reverie on her experiences working with flowers all over the world.

OTHER INSPIRING WOMEN

◆ Marianne North (1830–1890), British botanist and botanical artist. "She traveled to the farthest reaches of the natural world alone to paint flowers in their native habitats."

◆ Constance Spry (1886–1960), British floral designer and writer. "The original visionary English florist who bucked tradition by arranging weeds and lettuces and all sorts of bizarre things for royalty. She was also a whip-smart writer."

◆ Lady Tania Compton, British garden designer and plantswoman, Spilsbury Farm, Wiltshire

◆ Charlotte Molesworth, British gardener and plantswoman, Benenden, Kent. "Known for her whimsical topiary, which she travels worldwide to create for clients."

A selection of local and in-season flowers, grasses, and branches for a workshop in Japan.

Julie Moir Messervy

HER WORK Owner and founder, Julie Moir Messervy Design Studio and the Home Outside app suite, Saxtons River, Vermont

HER LANDSCAPE "I have been lucky to travel to landscapes around the world and to have experienced some of the most beautiful and sophisticated gardens one can ever see. They always touch something deep in my soul, transporting me back to my favorite childhood landscapes that in turn inspire the gardens I design for others."

HER PLANT JOURNEY Julie Moir Messervy believes that "most of us want, on some level, a garden that encourages us to daydream, allows us to reflect, and supports us in finding meaning and magic in our own backyards." For more than forty years, Julie, an award-winning landscape designer and garden design theorist, has worked to "compose landscapes of beauty and meaning, further the evolution of landscape design, and change the way people create and enjoy their outdoor environments." She has focused on helping people—individual homeowners, municipalities developing public parks, and institutions creating public gardens—to realize garden spaces that achieve these ends.

As second oldest of seven children growing up in Northbrook, Illinois, and later in Wilton, Connecticut, Julie often felt the need to get away into nature. "I created cherished hideaways in the fields, forests, orchard, and pond adjacent to our property. Nature was my earliest playground; plants created an ever-changing display of delight to inhabit, admire, pluck, smell, taste, touch, or harvest. The landscape was full of daydreaming spaces just for me." Her mother loved gardens, and Julie grew up surrounded by a wide assortment of plants and plant people. She attended Wellesley College for her undergraduate degree in art history, and went on to study and earn her master of architecture and master in city planning from Massachusetts Institute of Technology (MIT) before starting her design firm.

> "Deep within each of us lies a garden"

Two years into her graduate work at MIT, she "opened up a book full of pictures of Japanese gardens and fell madly in love." She felt an immediate "kinship with these mossy landscapes," so, as a Henry Luce Scholar, she took time off from MIT and went to Kyoto to study Japanese gardens for a year and a half with Professor Kinsaku Nakane, a "renowned garden designer and scholar." Professor Nakane had Julie spend her first three months in Kyoto visiting and observing eighty gardens. He instructed her to "go to these gardens and look at them with your heart, not your intellect, and take in their beauty and meaning." After those first three months, she joined the garden crew, building and maintaining gardens. She learned pruning techniques and stone placing, all under the "orchestration" of Professor Nakane.

In 1988, in what felt like a "wonderful finale" to her apprenticeship, Julie served as the United States associate for Professor Nakane's design of the

Museum of Fine Arts, Boston's *Tenshin-en*, The Garden of the Heart of Heaven. On his behalf, she liaised with the museum's director and staff, selected the stones and plant materials, trained the contractors, and helped interpret the garden in books and lectures. It remains a remarkable oasis and contemplative viewing garden in Boston's Fenway neighborhood.

The earliest of Julie's eight books, *Contemplative Gardens* (1990) and *The Inward Garden* (1995), showcase her signature design process, which elicits her client's "inward garden" and melds it with her own, "to create a landscape that is both completely unique and deeply personal." Her groundbreaking design theory of the seven spatial archetypes—Sea, Cave, Harbor, Promontory, Island, Mountain, and Sky—expresses both feeling and form as a landscape image. These seven fundamental forms apply to all spaces, whether natural or built. Each suggests a vantage point along a continuum that moves from most inward to most outward, deepest to outermost, lowest to highest. And they suggest the journey of human development, from womb (Sea) to death (Sky).

They also offer a "language of landscapes" to explain a client's particular longing for home, which all good design seeks to fulfill. For example, "at times we long for a place to feel immersed, other times to feel enclosed and safe, still others to take a long view of unfettered horizons, and, at special times, for transcendence."

While many of the projects Julie and her team undertake are for residential clients, their designs for public spaces are also well known. In her public work, she gathers stakeholders together to help determine what she calls "the big idea"—the organizing strategy for the project's design, which may be inspired by a particular image, vision, or idea.

For the Toronto Music Garden, which opened in 1999 in the Harborfront neighborhood, eminent cellist Yo-Yo Ma asked Julie to create a three-acre public park whose design was inspired by Johann Sebastian Bach's six *Suites for Unaccompanied Cello*. When she first listened closely to the music, she noted that "each suite feels

One movement in the Toronto Music Garden, a collaboration with Yo-Yo Ma, interpreting Bach's suites for cello through a garden.

like a landscape; each movement a garden. In Suite 1, the prelude sets the mood of the overall 'site,' a place designed as a study in continuity and change. The courante is like a wildflower meadow being pollinated by a swarm of bees." The resulting garden is a joyful landscape of clef forms, swoops, and swirls, with each of the different garden rooms corresponding to one of the six movements of the suite.

Nearly two decades later, at the Southern Connecticut State University Reflection Garden, the big idea began as a way to honor the four teachers who had matriculated there and were killed in the 2012 mass shooting at Sandy Hook Elementary School in Newtown, Connecticut. This small memorial garden is the first of several gathering areas, paths, and gateways that together will become a living expression of the university's core ideals of social justice—civility, respect, dignity, compassion, and kindness—for the entire campus and its neighboring communities.

Julie finds joy in the gardens and parks she designs for others around the world. "Nothing is more fun than being able to dream up, refine on paper, shepherd into place, and maintain into the future a space that you conceived and birthed. It's like being a mother."

At home in a Vermont garden's perennial border and orchard.

OTHER INSPIRING WOMEN

- Gertrude Jekyll (1943–1932), British plantswoman and garden designer
- Beatrix Farrand (1872–1959), American landscape architect
- Denise Scott Brown, architect, Venturi, Scott Brown and Associates, Philadelphia, Pennsylvania
- Kathryn Gustafson, landscape architect and principal of Gustafson Guthrie Nichol in Seattle. "Her work at the Lurie Garden at Millennium Park in Chicago inspires."
- Claudia West, landscape designer. "Her ideas, work, lectures, and book (*Planting in a Post-Wild World* with coauthor Thomas Rainer) are groundbreaking."

Julie Kierstead Nelson

HER WORK United States Forest Service botanist, Shasta-Trinity National Forest, California

HER PLANT "Curl-leaf mountain mahogany, *Cercocarpus ledifolius*. It's very tough, beautiful even in great age, grows in scrappy places, breathtaking when backlit in fruit with the feathery tails of the achenes all aglow; it is a plant of western North America, and it is found in my two favorite landscapes—the Great Basin and the eastern Klamath range."

HER PLANT JOURNEY Botany is the scientific study of plants, and field botanists are those plant scientists who have chosen to primarily work in the field in direct relationship with plants and their larger environments. Many field biologists studying plants and plant communities *in situ* are public servants who work to research, document, protect, and communicate about the life of plants and plant communities on public lands. They map changing environments and needs and interpret them for the rest of us, alerting us to the loss of plants or habitats, to the presence of new, rare, or endangered species, and providing us with a direct connection to the living science of our plant world.

Julie Nelson is a career field and conservation botanist for the United States Forest Service (USFS), an agency that manages 193 million acres. She has responsibility for the 2.2 million acres of the Shasta-Trinity National Forest. For her, this work "in botanically interesting places" provides a powerful "connection to something bigger than me, a sense of purpose and satisfaction with an expertise developed over time, a deep connection to a tribe of other plant people, and understanding that plant conservation

> There's great pleasure in finding a plant I've never seen before and figuring out what it is (or maybe that it's new to science!)

and gardening are as much about relationships with other people as with the plants themselves."

Her region includes all of California plus Hawaii, and she is responsible for ensuring the Shasta-Trinity National Forest complies with law, policy, and regulation regarding plant conservation and management. Through biological evaluations of plants, lichens, liverworts, and fungi in field surveys and impact analyses associated with Forest Service work, Julie helps ensure work in her part of the National Forest system does not increase any plant's risk of becoming listed as endangered. Evaluations take place before activities such as road or campground maintenance, timber or other sales, trail work, post-fire activity, or watershed restoration. She also helps with general ecological restoration, monitoring and restoring pollinator host plants, monitoring and controlling invasive species, and, her favorite, "finding and publishing new species and sorting out messes in older [plant identification] taxonomy."

Born and raised within a nature-loving family in Coos Bay, Oregon, Julie recalls fondly that her "mom had a flower garden, and we spent a fair amount

Julie with an aged mountain mahogany (*Cercocarpus ledifolius*).

A herbarium specimen prepared by Julie, of the Shasta snow wreath (*Neviusia cliftonii*), a rare and endemic shrub of interior Northern California, only identified and named in 1992 despite being linked through fossil evidence to shrubs from prehistoric times.

Plants of Shasta County, California

Neviusia cliftonii J. R. Shevock, B. Ertter, & D. Taylor
SHASTA SNOW WREATH

Pit Arm between Silverthorn and Jones Valley, south side of
Shasta Lake. T33N, R3W, NW ¼ Sec.8. Growing in full sun
with *Toxicodendron diversilobum, Vitis californica*. Elev. 1200
feet. Bella Vista 7.5 minute quadrangle, 1992.

Julie. Kierstead. Nelson 2010-004   May 1, 2010

of time outdoors catching crawdads, picking berries, swimming in creeks and lakes." She became "hooked" on botany and fieldwork at Lane Community College. The greatest lesson she learned was, "Not everything is nailed down in the botanical world."

After going on to finish her bachelor's degree in botany at Oregon State University (OSU), she held her first field position at Malheur Field Station in southeast Oregon, which exposed her to the very different environment of the northern Great Basin, "a place largely without trees." She spent her time "camping for months at the edge of the Alvord Desert, collecting and keying out plants using a dissecting scope with a light run off a car battery—it was glorious." She "polished her plant ID skills and developed a love of herbarium work" at OSU, and then, after earning her master's degree in biology from Northern Arizona University, went to work at the Berry Botanic Garden in Portland, Oregon. Hired to start a seed bank for rare and endangered plants of the Pacific Northwest, she would serve as conservation director from 1982 to 1988.

The Berry Garden was "chock-full of thousands of plant species from all over the world that weren't available in nurseries—and they were labeled. Most had been grown from seed by Rae Berry, [whose home and grounds were the basis for the garden]." Julie spent many hours "wandering around the rock garden, the rhododendron forest, the traditional borders, and the native conifer forest underplanted with all manner of things." Here, her interest in native plants of the American West "broadened to an interest in all plants."

When the Forest Service hired her in the late '80s, she was the inadvertent beneficiary of several circumstances: a class-action lawsuit against the USFS for discriminating against women, and several congressional acts, including the Clean Water Act and the Endangered Species Act. "All these forces converged at the exact time that I was looking for a job. The USFS needed women and minority employees, as well as employees who could help them comply with these new laws and regulations." Julie was the first permanent botanist ever hired for the Shasta-Trinity National Forest, the largest national forest in California, established in 1905 by proclamation of President Theodore Roosevelt.

In 2001, Julie worked with forester and University of California extension agent Gary Nakamura editing the *Illustrated Field Guide to Selected Rare Plants of Northern California*. She coauthored papers naming several new, rare northwest California endemic plants, including *Vaccinium shastense*, *Adiantum shastense*, and *Erythronium shastense*. *Sedum kiersteadiae* was named in her honor. She also served as an editor and scientific reviewer for *Wildflowers of the Trinity Alps* (2017). Through her field work, writing, photographs, drawings, and discoveries about the "particular slice of nature" she has spent her adult life getting to know, Julie contributes creatively as a leader and teacher for improving plant-human relationships.

Sedum kiersteadiae is a newly described species of sedum in California's Klamath region and named in Julie's honor.

Her work reinforces her own knowledge and appreciation that the "natural world is familiar, it's not foreign or frightening. For native plants and gardens to thrive, they need regular, careful tending."

OTHER INSPIRING WOMEN

- Jean Siddall (1930–1997), pioneering Oregon plant conservationist. "She was an early advocate of native plant conservation. One of her favorite quotes was 'You may not like living with us now, but conservationists make great ancestors.'"

- Happy Hieronimus (1930–2014), "Portland Garden Club member, who with others, saved Rae Selling Berry's estate and its plant collections as a nonprofit botanic garden."

- Sheila Logan, ecologist, US Forest Service, Shasta-Trinity National Forest. "Sheila was my first supervisor. She taught me that it's possible, even necessary, to both have serious passion for our work *and* find great humor in bureaucracy, and that, beyond competence in one's professional specialty, the most important key to success as a bureaucrat is in creating and tending relationships."

- Linnea Hanson, botanist (retired), Plumas National Forest, California; founder of the nonprofit Northern California Botanists, a cooperative association of federal, state, academic, consulting, and other botanists in the Northern California region

- Jessica Orozco (1987–2018), botany graduate student, Claremont Graduate University. "Her work at the intersection of science, conservation, social justice, and Native American wisdom was impressive."

Ngoc Minh Ngo

HER WORK Landscape, botanical, and interior photographer, New York City

HER PLANT JOURNEY "I have spent a lot of time photographing a garden in a remote village in Northern Morocco, atop a hill overlooking agricultural fields and the Atlantic. The hillsides there are dotted with olive and fig trees, and the roads are unpaved. People travel on foot or on donkeys. I have photographed this landscape through all the seasons—the combination of the wild and the tamed that makes the place at once earthy and majestic. Those hours I spend in the garden photographing, no matter the weather, are almost magical."

HER PLANT JOURNEY In the introduction to her second book, *In Bloom* (2016), the artist, photographer, flower lover, and writer Ngoc Minh Ngo says, "Like a Robert Frost poem that begins in delight and ends in wisdom, flowers seduce us with their piercing beauty, but they also have much to teach us about the impermanent nature of life."

The book, which profiles in text and rich photography the work of eleven artists inspired by the natural world, is part literary history, part art history, part impassioned elegy for the importance of nature nurtured in the day-to-day aspects of our lives. In pursuing her own curiosity at the juncture between human creativity and nature, Ngoc is as much a poet as she is a photographer. She illuminates how "the beauty of the botanical realm continues to be the perfect foil for the magic of the human imagination." At the same time, she recognizes how the best of our humanity can be witnessed through our expressed relationship to the natural world—how we design and live in our gardens, how we arrange and display flowers, how we create art from botanical inspiration.

> "I set up my camera and wait for the sky to rearrange itself and for the morning to unfold as if for me alone. It's always different but always full of wonder"

Ngoc grew up in a small seaside town in Vietnam, with seasonal flowering trees and plants. Her memories of this time are vivid: her father's love of flowers; her great aunt's night-blooming cereus and being allowed the privilege of staying up late to experience its once-a-year, white, spidery, and fragrant bloom as a girl; the flame trees' vibrant bloom lining the streets and marking for her the freedom of summer vacation; quince branches brought indoors to slowly open as a welcome to the Vietnamese New Year Tết celebrations.

At the age of twelve, Ngoc relocated to the United States with her family as refugees at the end of the Vietnam War in 1975. After undergraduate work at the University of California, Berkeley, she went on to study landscape design at Columbia University in New York. She fell in love with photography and began studying and learning it, shooting film and developing her photographs in the bathtub of her studio apartment. By the early 2000s, Ngoc was a sought-after food, interiors, and lifestyle photographer.

Her first book, created in collaboration with floral designer Nicolette Owen, *Bringing Nature Home: Floral Arrangements Inspired by Nature* (2012) documents Nicolette's use of seasonal, local, naturalistic garden and foraged florals throughout interiors that are rich with life. This book and collaboration were a direct response to Ngoc's frustration with being on photo shoots and seeing flowers and foliage used as merely decorative objects and meaningless placeholders for a splash of color in a shot. She wanted to model how the plant elements in these spaces could be carefully chosen and thoughtfully incorporated to vastly increase the overall effect and meaning.

"As a photographer, I see myself as a storyteller, and the story I aim to tell is that of the fascination and inspiration that plants and flowers have had on people in all cultures and times. Our love of plants is expressed in our art, literature, science, and culture throughout history. It's this intersection of nature and culture that interests me, and my work is to explore the beauty and tension within it." She sees this tension in the delicate balance between human imagination and creativity and nature's abundance without us.

Ngoc's work includes "photographic portraits of plants that serve both to identify their botanical features and emphasize their individual beauty, much in the way botanical illustrations have done for centuries." She also documents the works of "people

A study in light.

who are inspired by plants"—top-rated garden designers, horticulturists, floral and interior designers, and artists—"as part of the larger narrative of the way plants shape our work and vice versa." In her images of individual plants, of flowers artfully arranged in interiors, and of homes, gardens, and landscapes—classic and modern share a sense of depth, lightness, and romance.

Thanks to her deep "love of being around plants," her own small New York City garden is a "meeting point of all these different ways of looking at the world." She has "come to appreciate more and more the importance of keeping the wild places on Earth, even while our natural impulse is to dominate nature. Seeing flowers growing wild in their natural habitats has touched me deeply." In future work, she would like to devote "more time to documenting wildflowers and to be more involved in preservation efforts."

OTHER INSPIRING WOMEN

- Valerie Finnis (1924–2006), English photographer and plantswoman. "Acclaimed for her skills in collecting and growing alpine plants, she left a library of 50,000 images of plant portraits, and a book called *Garden People* (2007), which documents notable people in English horticulture. She established the Merlin Trust to help young horticulturists travel and gain experience."
- Mary Delany (1700–1788), English artist. "She invented a new botanical art form she called 'paper mosaicks' at the age of seventy-one. Using paper, which she painted and cut, she made intricately detailed collages of plants—scientifically precise and employing her vast botanical knowledge and lifelong interest in plants."
- Marianne North (1830–1890), English biologist and botanical artist. "She traveled alone to various continents to paint exotic flora in their natural environments."
- Carmen Almon, American-born artist. "Known for her botanical toles, flower and plant sculptures made of metal, her works are like beautiful eighteenth-century botanical illustrations brought into 3-D."
- Anna Atkins (1799–1871), English photographer and botanist. "Considered by many to be the first female photographer, she made beautiful cyanotype images of ferns and seaweeds."

Ngoc at work with light and flower fields.

Frances Palmer

HER WORK Ceramic artist/potter, Frances Palmer Pottery, Weston, Connecticut

HER PLANT "I cannot get enough of dahlias in my own home garden. In the winter when the dark is never-ending, I just keep ordering more."

HER PLANT JOURNEY Frances Palmer is an artist whose pottery helps us to see the flowers, fruits, vegetables, and foliage of a given season from our gardens in new ways. She asks us to consider how the vessels will show off the character of the plant life. Her work elucidates how plants and flowers grow and behave, drape and move in life and in display. For Frances, her pottery is the perfect bridge to bring her garden, her kitchen, and her art together.

Born in Morristown, New Jersey, she grew up surrounded by an abundance of local farming and farm stands. Her mother was a great gardener and cook. "She always set the table, and she was always the one to host dinner parties." Frances made art of her own from an early age, and while she considered going to art school, she ultimately knew she would always make art, so the academics of art history—learning to look and analyze and understand art in a cultural context—became her focus. She studied art history for her undergraduate degree at Barnard College and for her graduate degree from Columbia University.

The interrelationship between artistry and our daily lives in the home and garden has always interested her, and she is a longtime admirer of the famed English painter and interior designer Vanessa Bell. Sister of writer Virginia Woolf, Vanessa Bell and the extended Bloomsbury Group at Charleston Farmhouse in East Sussex are known for their handcrafted artistry,

> "My garden and my art are in symbiotic relationship—each feeding the other"

interwoven into all facets of living. Under their Omega Workshops, Ltd., this community of artists came together to create and sell their furniture, hand-painted wallpaper, fine arts, pottery, and more.

After studying the pottery of Omega Workshops, Frances thought, "Wouldn't it be nice if I could make all the pieces for the table?" She went on to teach herself how to do just this with a second-hand potter's wheel she uses to this day, her own natural and voracious curiosity, and the daily discipline required to be successfully self-employed.

Today, she creates plates, platters, and bowls, but she is best known for her vases, urns, and pots specifically designed for displaying flowers, vegetables, and fruit. From the beginning, she took particular care in photographing her work, to help "tell a story with it" and to illustrate its scale, color, and luster to best effect. From petite bud vases to footed platters and tall-footed or handled urns, her pottery is a perpetual exploration of the fruit, flowers, and foliage of the season, and of the changing weather and light. "What looks well in any given moment, season, or year presents a different set of issues. It's never the same garden or plant palette," and as a result, she's never throwing exactly the same pots. "From colors to forms to season, the garden, photography, and pots are all interwoven."

Everything in her garden has to work as a cut flower, and if it doesn't work, it comes out. In addition to cut flower borders and extensive raised beds, she also has an orchard of apples, medlars, peaches, pears, persimmons, paw-paws, plums, and quinces. Everything she grows earns its keep on display with her pots and then on the table. She has a particular affinity for dahlias and grows up to 500 different varieties as well as teaching classes on their history and cultivation at the New York Botanic Garden (NYBG) annually. Every time Frances throws a new piece, she thinks about what would best be displayed in it, on it, or with it, and while planting and harvesting,

In the studio.

she's thinking about the best pot or piece for showing off the harvest.

Her ceramics are often imbued with rich historical and cultural references from a wide range of cultures, both ancient and modern—those of Greece, Egypt, China, Japan, England, Mesoamerica, the Netherlands, and Spain. Humans have long been making vessels in which to display treasured plant companions and harvests—as beauty, as food, as status symbols, and as spiritual totems. Many of Frances's pots contain references to these histories, narratives, and lessons about the time-honored human relationship between growing and displaying flowers and plant life.

In her travels, she seeks out ceramic traditions, histories, and examples in museums, open houses, and gardens. Travel, as another form of study, further informs her work. She's "always looking for an elegant expression of classic forms in the simplest gesture possible." She loves using interesting, traditional glazes, such as historic Chinese celadon, blue and white oxide, oxblood, and tenmoku on her high-fired porcelain to help enhance and express the form.

A Frances Palmer vase showing off late-summer flowers to great advantage individually and as a group.

In 2018, Frances began taking botanical drawing classes at the NYBG, and she was pleased to stretch herself. It "helped so much to see plants in a different way." She wanted to be able to understand how to draw the flowers she grows, to know how, for instance, "to appropriately draw a tulip, how to dissect it, and look closely at its structure and anatomy."

"Every day that I sit down at the wheel or prepare and arrange flowers, fruit, or foliage for display in one of my pots, I learn something new," she says. "And that's the goal at the end of the day—to push all these ideas further."

OTHER INSPIRING WOMEN

- Eudora Welty (1909–2001), American writer and gardener
- Nicole de Vésian (1919–1996), French fashion designer and gardener, known for the Provençal formal garden she created in her seventies
- Rosie Sanders, British botanical artist; author and illustrator of *The Apple Book* (2010)
- Emily Thompson, floral designer and owner, Emily Thompson Flowers, New York

Anna Pavord

HER WORK Writer, gardener, Dorset, England

HER LANDSCAPE "Mountains—from the Highlands of the west coast of Scotland to the Himalayas in Sikkim."

HER PLANT JOURNEY Anna Pavord is among the most influential garden writers of the last twenty-five years, charting a course far beyond the boundaries of how-to and inviting us, through her own abiding curiosity, far back into plant and garden history. Her scholarly narrative nonfiction works, *The Tulip: The Story of a Flower That Has Made Men Mad* (1998) and *The Naming of Names: The Search for Order in the World of Plants* (2005), explore in wholly new ways the dramatic relationship between humans and plants over thousands of years of recorded history.

"It's good to have the opportunity to write stuff that occasionally goes beyond saying 'Now is the time to plant your potatoes.' That's important, but I've had the great good fortune to always be allowed to expand into why it's the right time to plant your potatoes and why digging them up later on is a treat you shouldn't deny yourself." She also enjoys explaining how and why planting potatoes (or anything else) in the first place sets a person in world history.

Anna's extensively researched writing reframes perspectives on the importance of plants to human endeavor, elevating them from secondary characters in history to primary agents of change. "I wouldn't call myself a person who first and foremost is interested in the content of a garden, rather than its wider impact."

She was born and brought up in Abergavenny, Monmouthshire, on the border between England and Wales, within miles of where her parents were born and raised. Her parents were both avid gardeners, her mother tending to the "aesthetics and a beautiful classic herbaceous border," and her father becoming an alpine rock gardener and heirloom fruit orchardist.

As an adult in her own first garden, Anna "realized that gardening was not necessarily about an end result. The doing was what mattered." She learned about gardening "as a sustaining activity," a lesson that has served her throughout her adult life—a respite from parenting small children and from illness. Along with walking, she found gardening one of the most useful palliatives during "life's inevitable periods of melancholy." It "allows you to be part of a world that moves to a different, more primal beat. Like walking, it brings a correcting perspective to your own place in that world."

In 1973, her family moved into what would become one of the great gardening projects of Anna's life, The Old Rectory at Puncknowle, where she lived and gardened for forty years. "The place was without a roof and had been long abandoned. It was magnificent, built in 1701, and ruled our lives for all the time we were there. It had a big walled kitchen garden and, eventually, I grew every fruit and vegetable that was possible to grow outside."

The Old Rectory, which was always "ravenous" for time and money, became a living character in the life of the family. It also provided source material for many of Anna's garden columns for the *Independent* from 1986 to 2016, a period during which she also served as associate editor for *Gardens Illustrated* magazine and chaired the Gardens Panel of the National Trust.

Her first book, *Growing Things* (1982), was followed by five more before *The Tulip*, which she worked on purely out of her own love of tulips and her curiosity about their centuries-old history. "It was incredibly exciting to watch *The Tulip* storm its way into the world and become, very surprisingly, a bestseller. I had not written it for publication, but for myself, to find the answers to questions I couldn't find anywhere else. I finished the whole manuscript and pasted in 126 of my favorite pictures. Every one of those 126 pictures made its way into the printed book." When she told her agent about the book, "he thought he might as well have a look at it."

> "Of course, I love plants—magnolias, arisaemas, and spurges especially. But they are always only part of a wider story that has to do with the way the space works, and above all the atmosphere, the spirit of a place"

Anna reflects, "*The Tulip*'s success was in large part due to timing." It was the first book launched by Bloomsbury in America, the physical book itself was an "object of great beauty," and the genre of narrative nonfiction was newly established and very popular. But perhaps most timely of all, "the dot-com boom had just happened, making the story of the wealthy excesses of 'tulipmania' relevant to the late 1990s. People could read it and consider the lessons from these historic booms and busts." It wasn't only a book about a flower, but about human nature, economics, fashion, and passion.

The success of *The Tulip* allowed Anna the time to spend close to eight years writing *The Naming of Names*—the book she says she is "gladdest to have been able to write. It was a story that had not been told before." Like *The Tulip*, *The Naming of Names* had "a strong narrative with which to engage, and some magnificent and charismatic characters." It starts with the ancient Greek philosophers Theophrastus and Aristotle and their efforts to sort and order the natural world. Aristotle was to describe all known animals, and Theophrastus to name and describe all known plants. Anna documents the story through the extraordinary work done by men engaged, as she saw it,

"in a kind of relay race. The thinkers of one time and place would get the story as far along as they could, and then pass the inquiry onto the next generation or civilization trying to find order in chaos, fighting to find logical ways of grouping things, interrogating the evidence as to why were things similar and why were they different."

In 2013, Anna and her husband left The Old Rectory and moved to a more remote twenty-acre piece of working land in Dorset with grazing sheep and an orchard. From the new garden, she wrote *Landskipping: Painters, Ploughmen, and Places* (2016), a history and celebration of the changing ways in which the English have responded to, valued, and viewed their landscape. It was a good excuse to walk even more of the country and was "a way of saying thank-you for the sustenance I have drawn throughout my life from looking out over the ever-changing beauties of the land around me."

Joy, she says "comes from standing in my own garden, in a remote part of west Dorset, looking out over the valley at the shadows lengthening on the hill, watching the rooks wheel and clatter around the tops of the alder trees. From that comes serenity."

Susan Pell

HER WORK Deputy executive director, science and public programs manager, United States Botanic Garden, Washington, DC

HER LANDSCAPE "Because I grew up in the Midwest, my chosen landscape will always be a good agricultural field surrounded by woods—it's just kind of where it's at for me. I love to look at paintings of this landscape, I love to drive through it, I love to be in that space."

HER PLANT JOURNEY "Effectively communicating cool science to people who thought they were just going to come see a pretty garden is just fantastic for me," enthuses Susan Pell, who is one part educator, one part administrator, and one part research scientist exploring the fascinating intricacies of Anacardiaceae, the cashew family of plants.

Established by Congress in 1820, the United States Botanic Garden (USBG) is among the oldest botanic gardens in the country. It is a "living plant museum that informs visitors about the importance, and often irreplaceable value, of plants to the well-being of humans and to Earth's fragile ecosystems." It comprises a conservatory of living plant collections that explore and celebrate plants from the world's iconic ecoregions—tropics, deserts, the Mediterranean for example—as well as exhibit space for plant-focused exhibitions curated annually. USBG also includes the National Garden, "a three-acre outdoor laboratory for gardening in harmony with natural ecosystems," and Bartholdi Park, "a two-acre garden demonstrating accessible water-conservation methods and native plant and habitat gardening on a home-landscape scale."

The USBG "maintains approximately 65,000 plants for exhibition, study, conservation, and exchange with other institutions. Noteworthy collections include economic plants, medicinal plants, orchids, carnivorous plants, cacti and succulents, and Mid-Atlantic native plants." With more than a million visitors a year, the USBG must prioritize ways to communicate plant knowledge.

Luckily, Susan's favorite activities include leading tours. "Tours are instant gratification—everyone's so excited to learn all these crazy things, and you can tell people all kinds of deep science stories about the plants, and they ask great questions. It's super invigorating. I love giving talks, I love teaching classes, I

> "The awesomeness of plants every day"

love working with our team to craft well-written interpretive materials. You can sneakily provide people with all this botanical knowledge in ways that are really enjoyable to them."

Susan was born in Indiana and raised in the Midwest. She "became a plant person really early on." As a girl, she spent a lot of time on the farm her mother had grown up on, visiting with her grandparents and her Japanese-Hawaiian great uncle, "who had beautiful flowers, an orchard, a vineyard, and a large vegetable garden." There, she would explore the woods, then enjoy the fruits of the farm.

At St. Andrews University in North Carolina, she gravitated toward biology, and her advisor, Frank Watson, was "the person who gave me an understanding of and love for the science of botany and taxonomy." She was also involved in Beta Beta Beta, the biological honors society, which "had a program teaching science after school to elementary school students. I loved it—I got super jazzed about teaching and super jazzed about plants."

On a break between undergraduate and graduate work, she lived in Baton Rouge, Louisiana, where she worked at Louisiana State University's molecular systematics lab and was soon accepted into the fellowship program that would start her molecular research into the cashew family. In 2000, she took advantage of a visiting scientist opportunity at the New York Botanical Garden (NYBG) to further her research with one of the world's experts on Anacardiaceae, John D. Mitchell, with whom she still collaborates and goes on plant-collecting expeditions around the world.

After defending her thesis in 2004, Susan accepted a position to head the Brooklyn Botanic Garden's molecular lab. Within five years, she became the director of science there, overseeing its herbarium, its longstanding history (since the 1930s) of fieldwork surveying flora within a fifty-mile radius, and its collaborations in restoration and survey work with other institutions and organizations. While in New York, Susan continued her love of teaching as the garden's part-time botany program coordinator in adult education.

Susan, her wife, and their daughter relocated to Washington, DC, for Susan to take a one-year science and technology policy fellowship with the American Association for the Advancement of Science. This gave

Susan answering visitor questions on a garden tour.

her the opportunity to work on everything from public and external affairs to exhibits at the USA Science and Engineering Festival to legislation and social media. The energy, range of projects, and people "were fabulous!" and springboarded her right into her jobs at the USBG.

As science and public programs manager, she's responsible for the garden's science education programs, communication, interpretation, visitor services, volunteer program, and special events. As deputy executive director, she assists the executive director in direct oversight of the daily operations of the garden including developing and guiding vision and strategy, managing the $12-million budget, congressional communications, and coordinating with Friends of the U.S. Botanic Garden. In addition to overseeing 70 employees, 200 volunteers, major construction projects, facilities, educational programs, and horticulture, Susan integrates her "expertise in botany, science communication, education, and mentoring to show people, through engaging and accurate science, the awesomeness of plants every day."

"Plants sustain us—everybody eats plants every day, we wear plants every day, we live inside buildings made out of lots of plants. We're surrounded by plants all the time, but are sometimes not aware of it. Bringing awareness to people about how vital plants are for our world, connecting this day-to-day importance to the importance of sustaining plants in the wild, for the health of the earth, gets people jazzed."

OTHER INSPIRING WOMEN
- Dr. Barbara McClintock (1902–1992), American scientist and cytogeneticist, awarded 1983 Nobel Prize in Physiology or Medicine for her groundbreaking work in genetic transposition, by which genetic characteristics are turned on or off
- Dr. Shirley Tucker, botanist, professor emerita, chair in plant systematics, Department of Biological Sciences, Louisiana State University. In 2015, the LSU Shirley C. Tucker Herbarium was renamed in her honor.
- Dr. Barbara Schaal, Mary-Dell Chilton Distinguished Professor in Arts & Sciences, dean of the faculty of Arts & Sciences/professor of biology, Washington University, St. Louis, Missouri. Her lab work focuses on the evolutionary genetics of plants—from the molecular evolution of genetics to systematics and quantitative genetics.
- Dr. Allison Miller, professor of biology, St. Louis University, research associate, Missouri Botanical Garden. Her lab work focuses on wild progenitors of crop plants and perennial plant diversity and evolution.

Leah Penniman

HER WORK Cofounder, codirector, and program manager of Soul Fire Farm, Grafton, New York

HER PLANT "Hard to pick just one, but this past season I felt very connected to horseradish, which was really speaking to me—it's so tenacious, and fierce and multiplicitous and just badass. I love its spice and spunk and use in Jewish ritual, because our family is also Jewish. And of course, I have strong connection to plants of cultural resonance for my Black community—the fish pepper, the 'Paul Robeson' tomato, collard greens, sweet potatoes."

HER PLANT JOURNEY Leah Penniman describes her land- and plant-based work in this way: "I'm helping turn sunshine into nourishment for our community. I feel really connected to the food sovereignty movement here at Soul Fire Farm. We are able to provide 250 individuals, who otherwise do not have access to that nourishment, with a bountiful, life-giving box of farm-grown fresh vegetables, herbs, and fresh eggs, delivered right to their doorsteps." She and her husband, Jonah Vitale-Wolff, founded Soul Fire Farm in 2011, a seventy-two–acre, mission-driven farm, centered on "the needs of the Black community," and working to "end racism and injustice in our food system."

Leah is dedicated to "reconnecting African-heritage people to the land after centuries of land-based oppression and alienation." Her book, *Farming While Black* (2018), documents her journey and vision for "African-heritage people ready to reclaim our rightful place of dignified agency in the food system. To farm while Black is an act of defiance against white supremacy and a means to honor the agricultural ingenuity of our ancestors."

Born in Ashburnham, Massachusetts, to a Black Haitian mother and a white father, Leah has felt "deeply connected to plants" since she was a little girl. "As one of the few brown-skinned children in my town, kids were super mean to me for the most part, and plants were kind and tender. I would go to the forest after school and

> "Black land matters"

wrap my arms around the sticky trunk of a tall white pine, and receive solace." After she learned about photosynthesis she "visualized exhaling carbon dioxide and the tree taking it in and breathing oxygen back to me. There I was, breathing with this tree as a young person. My relationship to plants has always been true."

Both her parents are ministers in the Unitarian Universalist tradition, and both were involved in the civil rights movement in the 1960s. She remembers her maternal grandparents living in Boston, having been disenfranchised from the land but hanging on to their relationship to it "in really beautiful ways." Her grandmother harvested crabapples for jam and grew strawberries for pie. "These plants were part of our experience."

"For a time, I thought that to be a plant lover I had to abandon my Blackness because I was shown mostly white environmentalists, and Black people were supposed to be concerned with housing and education and issues of gun control. My plant love came home again to me when I was sixteen and working at the Food Project, a nonprofit food organization in Boston that embraced the dual missions of environmental stewardship and social justice."

She learned that farming and growing food "could be leveraged to improve both environmental conditions and social conditions. They were caring for the soil, they were providing habitat for pollinators, and they were providing healthy food to the communities who needed it the most." However, subsequent work experiences were so "dominated by white people, it took me another decade to really grasp and understand all of the ways in which Black and brown people had been erased from the environmental, sustainable food, and farming movements in history and narrative."

After receiving her undergraduate and graduate education, Leah volunteered in Ghana, restoring her heritage connections to the West African religious tradition of Vodun, into which she was initiated and given her spiritual name of Manye Amidede. In 2003, she and her husband started their family and settled in the South End of Albany, New York. Leah worked as a high school biology and environmental science teacher with "some chemistry and physics thrown in." The South End is a neighborhood Leah describes as living under "food apartheid," where obstacles imposed by the dominant culture make access to fresh, affordable food almost impossible. "There were no community gardens, no farmers markets, no real grocery stores, and we didn't have a car, so it was very difficult to get fresh food for our family despite our education privilege. We knew we needed to buy land and start a farm that could help feed our neighbors."

Soul Fire Farm
produce and people.

In 2006, they found their land. "It had no electricity, no septic, no well, no buildings. It took us until 2010 to build up the soil and build a home." The farm opened the next spring. It now includes two acres cultivated in vegetables, another three acres of orchard and pasture for chickens, a half-acre pond with fish, and the rest they left as natural forest.

These days, the farm has three cooperatively determined top goals. "One: grow 80,000 pounds of food intensively on two acres of land using low-till methods, sequestering 2400 pounds of carbon, growing over a dozen African-indigenous heritage crops, and demonstrating several African-indigenous sustainable farming practices. Two: train eighty-plus new farmer-activists of color through our Black and Latinx Farmers Immersion and its apprenticeship program, and mentor eighty-plus BLFI alumni. Three: train and inspire 250-plus youth of color through our food-justice empowerment program and immersion."

"My joys are centered on seeing what this work means to people," says Leah. "For instance, the youth who come to the farm arrive pretty beaten down, pretty checked out. They've been fed the message that your only value is as a consumer, and your only future is hardship, prison, or untimely death. Being around mentors who deeply respect and see the humanity in them, and being with the land, which is just so ready to soak out that trauma and compost it into hope—creates transformation even in a day: eyes brighten, smiles engage, and they connect to the place's fullness of spirit. I see it every time. And the land is our partner and ally in all this; we have to make the introduction and just be careful to get out of the way so the relationship between the land and the people coming to it can come to being."

OTHER INSPIRING WOMEN

- Harriet Tubman (circa 1820–1913), Black abolitionist, activist, and nurse. Known for her work as an herbalist and healer both on the Underground Railroad and as a Union soldier.
- Fannie Lou Hamer (1917–1977), women's rights and voting activist, Mississippi Freedom Democratic Party, avid farmer and preserver of food. "She said, 'If you have your gumbo soup put up for the winter, no one can push you around and tell you what to do.' She helped infuse food sovereignty into the civil rights movement."
- Larisa Jacobson, codirector and farm manager/farmer, Soul Fire Farm. "She talks about herself as a plant, and she just has some magic with those beings, and so much reverence."
- Yonnette Fleming, urban farmer, social and food justice advocate with Hattie Carthan Community Garden in the Bedford-Stuyvesant community of Brooklyn, New York

Hemlata Pradhan

HER WORK Botanical artist, West Bengal, India

HER PLANT "Orchids! They have been my inspiration and motivation ever since I can recall. Orchids are highly evolved, the oldest group of flowering plants, with 25,000 species in some 850 genera, inhabiting and thriving in all the regions of the world except Antarctica, very dry deserts, and the sea. Orchids represent a biodiversity that is of immense value to human beings. For me, this represents both hope and strength. Likewise, I live my life as a botanical artist in the remote foothills of the Himalayas and am spreading my knowledge and experience in this field at the grassroots level, with a hope that it adds value not only to human lives but also to our rich biodiversity, helping them to thrive and grow."

HER PLANT JOURNEY While the original intent of what we now refer to as "botanical art" was to document known species and to amass information on how they could be useful, botanical artistry has more recently developed to capture details about species before they are lost altogether because of human-caused ecosystem degradation, destruction, and climate change.

In all corners of the globe, scientists, naturalists, and artists are at work documenting species and habitats. Born, raised, and working "in the lap of the Himalayas," Hemlata Pradhan is one such botanical artist, "by passion and profession." The intention of her work is to "highlight India's wild orchids and other plants in their natural habitats, to bring about an awareness of what we are unwittingly losing, so this work can complement and enhance the crusade to save this wonderful heritage of our planet." Her art highlights plants "as extremely important subjects for conservation—immortalized on paper." Each portrait is intended to "assist conservation biologists in their works, help bridge the gap between art and science, and raise public awareness of our flora and fauna." In particular, her work features "rare and unique species of orchids,

> "The artistry of biodiversity, the lessons of perseverance in an orchid"

lilies, and other plants I've seen and observed growing in and around Kalimpong, Darjeeling, and the Sikkim Himalayas. It's my hope these works will bring joy and kindle and foster interest in these irreplaceable plant treasures and make us all join hands to conserve them for all times."

Hemlata's work—begun in childhood while watching and working with her orchidologist father—has provided her with "rich opportunities to directly connect with the plants and the natural world," as well as "with the platform to connect with like-minded and beautiful souls from all around the world with whom sharing and exchanging knowledge, ideas, and experiences has been invaluable and enlightening. It's all helped me grow as an artist and a human being!"

Growing up surrounded by the rich biodiversity of the Himalayas and a family "deeply involved with plants for over four generations," Hemlata recalls her father, "a keen orchidologist, horticulturist, author, botanical illustrator, and a hard taskmaster, trying to teach us the names of plants, trees, insects, and birds that surrounded us and taking us out on field trips to nearby forests and jungles so we could observe nature at its purest."

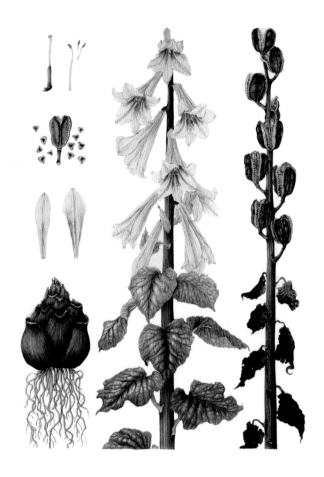

A botanical study of *Cardiocrinum giganteum* stages and plant parts.

She first painted flowers when she was eleven years old. When she was thirteen, she discovered her father's field drawings of orchids and rhododendrons and was inspired. "I understood then that this was exactly what my heart desired: to draw and paint plants. I began my journey by painting single flowers of *Cymbidium* orchids in all their gorgeous hues—apple greens, shades of pinks, yellows, whites, and maroons—and each one I painted made me crave more."

In 1993, Hemlata earned a BFA at Kala Bhavan, Visva-Bharati University, Santiniketan, in West Bengal. Although she was interested in painting, her advisors coaxed her toward graphics, which, though frustrating, taught her "new mediums like lithography, serigraphy, and etching," which she found "required meticulous handling, quite similar to botanical art techniques."

When she learned that the Royal Botanic Gardens, Kew, England, offered diploma courses in botanical illustration to Margaret Mee Scholars from Brazil, she applied, even though she was from India. They appreciated her "keenness" and accepted her, and in 1998, having won two rounds of scholarships, she completed her post-graduate diploma in botanical illustration. From there, she went on to England's Royal College of Art, and earned her master's degree in natural history illustration and ecological studies.

While she was studying in the UK, the Teesta hydro-electric dam project destroyed large areas of trees and huge portions of hills in the Himalayas, irreversibly damaging unique spots of natural beauty. "Thousands of orchids and other plants of great scientific and aesthetic interest, which formed a complex web of life, were eliminated without a second thought. It was heartrending to see the hills 'crying' on my return home!"

With a new awareness of the planet's "dwindling natural heritage" and "as someone passionate about nature and as a botanical artist, it became my urgent passion to observe plants and document them exactly as I found them in their natural habitats." She joined the Indian-Subcontinent Regional Orchid Specialist Group of the Species Survival Commission of the International Union for Conservation of Nature and Natural Resources, and her paintings have become far more complex and habitat filled, which requires what she affectionately refers to as "donkey patience." A final piece can take months to years to complete. "While I paint and exhibit my works to spread a message of conservation, I am also deeply involved with training young children in the field of botanical art, ecological studies, and conservation."

Hemlata's "great joy in sharing creativity, knowledge, and experience with children in a grass roots way" inspired her to found the Himalayan Trust for Natural History Art in 2003. The trust hosts "hands-on workshops and classes, with help from visiting tutors and volunteers from different corners of India in the field of natural history art." Students learn close observation in "sketches, paintings, doodles, words, and maps, using traditional techniques, methods, and materials." The program builds skills and confidence as well as "a deep respect for and understanding of the natural environment."

Hemlata with a botanical art student.

OTHER INSPIRING WOMEN

- Pandora Sellars, Indian botanical artist. "Her paintings have led me to believe that perfection can be attained using paint and a brush to a great degree."
- Margaret Mee (1909–1988), British botanical artist
- Abhisheka Krishnagopal, Indian artist
- Sangeetha Kadur, Indian artist

Sarah Price

HER WORK Garden designer, principal, Sarah Price Landscapes, Abergavenny, Wales

HER PLANT/LANDSCAPE "Sessile oaks (*Quercus petraea*) grow on the mountainsides where I live—they are full of character, shaped by the wind and often intertwined. The landscape of the Black Mountains of Wales is also magical."

HER PLANT JOURNEY *Painterly.* That's the word often used to describe the gardens and designs of Sarah Price. Her artistic public and private garden designs place her in a position to influence large numbers of people on how to see and think about plants, garden design, and the importance of both in the twenty-first century. Her eye and knowledge have been integral in post-games legacy design work for London's Olympic Park.

Sarah grew up in Surrey, in a large family, both sides of which were from Welsh border country. "Holidays were all about exploring remote areas. We would stay in my family's stone cottage, rebuilt from a ruin in the Black Mountains. It was accessible only by foot." She was always "walking and looking," observant by nature, with a strong visual memory, and attuned to landscapes.

Growing up, she found expression in the arts—painting, drawing, ballet, and later, art school. When she was twenty-one, her grandmother, an inspiring gardener, died, leaving a beautiful garden in Abergavenny, Wales, and Sarah spent subsequent holidays tending to the garden with her father. She came to realize that while she loved creating art, it was in the garden that she felt "really alive and attuned."

Upon visiting the Royal Horticultural Society (RHS) garden at Wisley in the early 2000s, to see the Glasshouse Borders designed by Dutch plantsman Piet Oudolf, she was "really struck by how different they were to most planting schemes." Inspired to learn more, she read, studied, and ultimately got a job at the Hampton Court Palace gardens. Here, she realized that, thanks to a

" Creating spaces with plants, light, and shadow "

childhood immersed in the outdoors and plants, her plant knowledge was pretty good. After being asked to help other designers with their planting plans, she decided to enter competitions to test her skills and see if she could get interesting work.

According to Sarah, "Show gardens are an opportunity to experiment. New designers can quickly find out what they're about." Soon enough, she had established exactly what she was about and had no trouble attracting admiring sponsors. After a gold medal at RHS Hampton Court Palace Flower Show, she had several sponsored appearances at RHS Chelsea Flower Show. From her "Bejeweled Garden," for QVC, which she describes as "subtle, with a simple palette of a few rich colors," where she "instinctively arranged plants in a naturalistic way, layering the species, threading sanguisorba and nectaroscordum, for example, through tufted grasses," to her 2008 garden, in she which took direct inspiration from hedgerows and verges, choosing plants that looked like they could easily be "cousins of their wild counterparts," her Chelsea gardens received a lot of press and public attention because of their unconventional and evocative nature, so "different to the accepted, blocky style of planting." It was through Chelsea that she met designers/plantsmen Nigel Dunnett and James Hitchmough, with whom she would work as one of the three plant consultants on the 2012 gardens at Queen Elizabeth Olympic Park in the lead-up to London's hosting of the Olympic Games.

The vision for the park was "really original, brave, and brilliant," she says, looking back. "We had a fantastic, knowledgeable, and energetic client in John Hopkins. His vision was that the landscape was to come first." There were to be forty hectares of meadows, "which had never been done on such a scale." Sarah worked quickly to communicate to a large team of landscape architects (LDA Design and Hargreaves Associates) a vision of plantings in a naturalistic style that would spark something like the thrill of seeing plants grow in great swathes in remote locations—incredibly beautiful spectacles usually reserved for globe-trotting plant hunters. She hoped "to stretch the aesthetics of perennial planting design, exaggerating the layers of a plant community, introducing greater variation in height as well as in transparency. I wanted strong visual repetition to increase the depth of field and colorways. It was like composing a three-dimensional, continually changing painting in space." Thankfully, she was passionate and could articulate the science and artistry well, translating between groups on the whole team.

After the Olympics, Sarah continued to create award-winning gardens for Chelsea. She won her first gold medal there with a Main Avenue garden that incorporated native English wildflowers, including rare orchids, interwoven with native birch trees and interspersed with pools of water in granite. In this garden, her skill at "creating visual links through a garden with swathes of flowers knitting the whole composition together," shone. She won gold a second time in 2018 with a Mediterranean-themed garden—"a completely fictional space, a romanticized haven in a

A small part of Queen Elizabeth Olympic Park's 40 hectares of meadows, with swaths of layered flowers and grasses.

warm, sunny climate, designed during a cold, Welsh winter. Using Mediterranean flora and raw materials dug directly out of the earth—clay, aggregate, pigment, and tile—the garden celebrated the expressive and sensual language of color and texture, light and shadow." She designed it to be "like stepping through a portal into a different world, with color and texture but also shadow as focal points, those kinds of subtleties we often overlook."

Sarah's gold-medal-winning, Mediterranean-themed design for the 2018 Chelsea Flower Show.

"Every time I do a show," Sarah observes, "I gain a greater depth of understanding," about gardens, about design, about where she wants and is able to expend her creative energy. Today, she has relocated from London to Abergavenny, where she lives with her young family. In moving to a focus on her own home garden, which is almost two acres—and a fragment of her grandmother's original garden—she continues to experiment with spatial relations and plants. She wants to "value this garden as much as I value client gardens," and put it to good use for clients, "as a forest school, or as a host site for storytelling or drawing in the garden with local primary schools." She reflects, "I could always make a beautiful space, but now I am increasingly aware of the complex needs of wildlife and people; caring for an elderly father and having young children can only heighten your awareness. I love to invite people to engage with plants, to get in close, to slow down and observe, and to even think like a plant." As her work has matured, she makes "carving these spaces in which to pause amongst plants, wildlife, and daylight" a priority.

OTHER INSPIRING WOMEN

- Sylvia Crowe (1901–1997), English landscape architect and garden designer
- Mien Ruys (1904–1999), Dutch landscape and garden architect
- Marina Christopher, English plantswoman; owner Phoenix Perennial Plants
- Chris Marchant, English plantswoman; partner, Orchard Dene Nurseries. "Supplying plants to most of the UK's best designers."

Milla Veera Tuulia Prince

HER WORK Educator, advocate, ancestral plant medicine, Lopez Island, Washington

HER PLANT "My main plant ally is nettle, an ancestral food medicine plant for me, one that also grows in the bioregion I live in, on unceded Coast Salish territory off the coast of Washington. Nettle is a deeply nutrient-dense plant, which actually helps us absorb other constituents and nutrients from the rest of our diets, and this quality made it vital to my people's resilience, survival, and ability to thrive in the harsh climate of the taiga."

HER PLANT JOURNEY Milla Prince writes of her childhood, "I grew up in the subarctic taiga, in the boreal forests, lakeshores, hills, and ecotones of my home city in eastern Finland, about 200 miles from the Arctic Circle and less than 100 miles from the Russian border." She is an educator and plantswoman advocating for and modeling an embrace of traditional, culturally based plant knowledge as part of broad cultural literacy.

Like many of us, she works as an immigrant, far from the homelands of her heritage, a fact she actively strives to consider with compassion and responsibility, despite the inherent dichotomies. Her work centers on exploring and sharing a plant- and land-loving way forward in an age rife with separation: forcible and chosen separation of people from their historic lands, separation of our greater lives from how we make our livings, separation of our food from our plants from our medicine from our spirituality, and finally, our proximal separations from one another due to diaspora and the digital age.

Milla is known online as The Woman Who Married a Bear. She writes a somewhat regular blog of the same name, and her tagline, *Old ways in a new age*, speaks to her belief in working to embrace and embody life's many dichotomies. One branch of her plant work is crafting "spirit-based, vibrational plant medicines, or 'potions.' These medicines contain such esoteric ingredients as plant spirits, elements, moons, weathers, animal essences, and old deities."

Some of her earliest memories are about plants—talking to them, eating them, making "soups" and "potions," playing games. "Once I acquired the words for my

> " Old ways in a new age: connecting folx with all kinds of ancestry to their own plant medicine traditions "

plant medicine practice, it came to me these practices were as old as my own body—they were ancestral, and intuitive." The wild and cultivated experiences of her childhood combined to teach her "a lot of my people's ancient practices, resilience, and plant relations," a form of knowledge she descriptively refers to as an "ambient endemic cultural knowledge model."

In her early twenties, Milla lived in England where she continued her herbal education through some formal and some experiential learning. She returned to Finland for college before meeting her husband and immigrating to the United States when she was thirty. As an outsider who sometimes sees cultural nuances in the United States with a different clarity than people who've always lived with them, Milla is "interested in fostering land connection for folx with settler ancestry, to facilitate allyship and reciprocity with the land and her people." Her great hope is that in "connecting folx with their own ancestral herbal practices and the medicines of their people, we can also be of service in preserving and restoring habitat on the lands we currently occupy. We can also follow indigenous leadership in learning to be of service in these places, in the hope of reducing appropriation and helping usher in a more land-based mindset as we shift away from an extractive, colonial culture."

The climate, weather, and topography of the Salish Sea around Lopez Island where she and her husband live resonated immediately with Milla's Finnish heritage. Here, she started her first real garden, growing "local native plants, healing plants from around the world, and traditional kitchen herbs, as well as food medicine for my family." Because many of the native and naturalized plants are similar to those in Finland—wild roses and rose hips, 100-year-old plum trees, plantain, nettle, pine, fir—she could continue with a lot of her practices around plant foods and medicine, although with a keen sense of the land not really being hers and trying to work with the grief of that, but also the empathy available in that understanding.

"For the longest time, my plant medicine practices were private and intimate," but for the last few years, she has shared her work "with others outside my immediate family and friends. That's been a huge growth edge to me, at times really uncomfortable, but also rewarding and magical."

One challenge for Milla has been to "fill in the gaps in my education, and stay true to my unique path in honoring my people's medicine, and cultivating and reviving those practices. *Braiding Sweetgrass* (2013) by Robin

Foraged medicinal flowers and leaves drying for later use in teas and preparations.

Wall Kimmerer taught me so much about plant-human relations in an ecosystem, and the reciprocal exchange that's part of our land-based ancestral knowledge. Learning about the practices of other land-based cultures helps me reconnect to those parts of my own heritage that can still be salvaged and rekindled, and also grieve for what is lost."

Milla sees so many people as "fragmented from their own spiritual and plant traditions and so hungry for this kind of meaning and belonging, that when they see something more intact, they feel entitled to take it—to adopt it as if it were their own without naming or crediting it." In her education and outreach work, online writing, and in-person workshops or gatherings, she is "really blunt. I say, 'Think about and check in about whatever you do with plants—if it's an asshole move, don't do it. And check in with someone other than yourself, check in with folx who might be affected differently as a result of these forces you benefit from.'"

Her plant practice, "focused on the ancestral food medicine of my people" and including learning more about her biological father's Palestinian ancestry, "is inseparable from my spiritual practice, the cosmology of my people, an animistic worldview. My spiritual practice is inseparable from my activism; the idea that as an offering for Earth in this age, we must do what we can to protect and nourish the diversity of life."

OTHER INSPIRING WOMEN

◆ Grandmothers, hedgewitches, womxn with folk remedies for any ailment, mighty kitchen gardens, and simple herbal healing knowledge. "My grandmother communicated directly with plants—her windowsill was covered in geraniums. She would chat with them daily as she watered them, pinching off old leaves, and making sure they were well nourished."

◆ Mary Siisip Geniusz, plantswoman, writer. "Her book, *Plants Have So Much to Give Us, All We Have to Do Is Ask: Anishinaabe Botanical Teachings* (2015), has been a foundational and comforting text to me. This book is the affirmation of reciprocal, animist, storied plant ways, and while I wouldn't use it as a guidebook since I'm not Anishinaabe, its teachings are healing and affirming of my own ancestral practices."

◆ Layla K. Feghali, founder, River Rose Apothecary. "Her South West Asia and North Africa project (SWANA) is 'dedicated to the remembrance, resurrection, and reclamation of ancestral medicine and the ancient traditions' of those areas."

◆ Rachel Budde, founder, Fat and the Moon. "Her work encompasses preserving, gathering, and cultivating her own ancestral Slovenian plant knowledge as an American-born descendant of immigrants."

Debra Prinzing

HER WORK Writer; founder and owner, Slow Flowers, LLC, Seattle, Washington

HER LANDSCAPE "My landscape is an ocean beach. I always feel at peace when I can sit quietly and watch the rhythmic and irregular patterns of waves advancing and receding. Beachcombing is one of my favorite ways to experience the amazing diversity of our natural world, and I confess to filling my pockets or the hem of an upturned shirt to carry my special finds home with me."

HER PLANT JOURNEY Garden journalist Debra Prinzing, founder of the Slow Flowers movement, has been a leader in shifting our national consciousness and conversation around where and how the flowers in our life are grown. She focuses on how floral consumers (gardeners, growers, floral designers) can help resolve concerns about a flower industry that is not sustainably grown nor locally sourced. Much of her advocacy is communicated through her books, *The 50 Mile Bouquet* (2012) and *Slow Flowers* (2013), and her website slowflowerssociety.com, which she founded in 2014. She also has a weekly Slow Flowers podcast and an online directory connecting American flower farmers with one another and a larger market.

Debra seems to have inherited a gardening gene that skipped from her grandfathers on both sides of her family directly to her. One grew great banks of peonies in Illinois, the other prize-winning dahlias in Indiana. Her parents didn't garden, but they loved nature, and regular family road trips taught her this love, too—of national parks, seashores, and seasonal colors.

Since her first home and garden of her own, with her husband Bruce Brooks, Debra has been "intentionally involved in plants. There's an urge to tend to the earth when you feel responsible for it." Her favorite quote, by the twentieth-century English writer Beverley Nichols, speaks to that sentiment: "Surely, if

> "Slow flowers: seasonal, local, and sustainable"

you are privileged to own a plot of earth, it is your duty, both to God and man, to make it beautiful."

After a career in business and lifestyle journalism, Debra says "the universe kept putting flower farmers in my way, and when I looked back at all the flower people I'd ever interviewed for books or magazines, I knew there was something in that realm that really appealed." She just kept meeting them, and "it felt like a clear sign. I knew—this is what I want to write about, this is what I want to document, these are the people who don't have voices—I could give them voice."

"Frustrated and disturbed" that she could grow the same flowers in her back garden, and "yet the marketplace was not offering anything but foreign-grown imported flowers with this huge transportation footprint, to say nothing of the unknown environmental and human rights impact in the country of origin," Debra felt keenly "the injustice of what was happening in the floral industry domestically."

As her Slow Flowers manifesto summarizes, "For various reasons, be it economic, trade, or government policy, the floral industry since the early 1990s has undergone a major shift in the way flowers are grown and marketed. Slow Flowers began in the United States, where 80 percent of cut flowers sold are imported from other countries and continents. The movement recognizes that this is not sustainable for people or for the planet. . . Slow Flowers believes it is irresponsible to support the continued production and consumption of a perishable product that devours so many valuable resources (jet fuel, packaging material, water, to name a few), especially when there is a domestic alternative to imported flowers."

Since 2012, Debra's work has "100 percent focused on helping flower lovers—gardeners and consumers, as well as professionals (florists and designers)—embrace a new floral ethos and make conscious and informed flower-buying decisions to source domestically and locally." She explains, "I am a documentary storyteller who gives voice to doers and makers, artists and farmers, the people behind the flowers." Through the many branches of Slow Flowers, reintroduced in 2019 as the Slow Flowers Society, she "strives to shine

The Slow Flowers cutting garden.

light on positive successes in flower farming, floral design, and every point along the floral continuum. In many ways, it's a form of social persuasion. I like to showcase positive examples of success that (I hope) will disrupt industry apathy about the origin of flowers." The Slow Flowers movement "has become part of the floral industry's vernacular to describe seasonal, local, and sustainable practices."

At work on the weekly Slow Flowers podcast.

Despite success and headway, Debra acknowledges "there've been many weeks and years where I've had to repeat myself like a broken record, saying the same things about seasonal, local, and sustainable flowers. The needle is moving slower than I wish. But then I see changes in the floral industry, and I feel optimistic again. When I'm interviewed for the *New York Times*, when leading NYC-based and DC-based wedding and event designers—people whose work and careers have been heavily reliant upon imported flowers—go out and buy farms where they can grow some of their own flowers, well, that is pretty gratifying." Being asked by *Florists' Review*, the top floral industry trade magazine, to launch a print version of her online *Slow Flowers Journal* "similarly validated" Debra's work and subjects, "sending a message that my mission is relevant to the broader floral community."

"The inspiration for Slow Flowers begins in gardens, meadows, orchards, and fields, where the timeless act of cutting or harvesting botanicals season by season is part of the natural cycle of a year. Having a relationship with the grower who planted and nurtured each flower is nothing short of magical. They are the unsung heroes—the faces behind the flowers we love."

OTHER INSPIRING WOMEN

- Karen Page, landscape designer, Chimacum, Washington
- Jean Zaputil, garden designer, writer, and artist, Davenport, Iowa
- Diane Szukovathy, co-owner, Jello Mold Farm, Mt. Vernon, Washington. Cofounder of the Seattle Wholesale Growers Market (2011), a Pacific Northwest flower farmers' cooperative in Seattle, Washington
- Christina Stembel, founder and CEO, Farmgirl Flowers, San Francisco, California

Sarah Raven

HER WORK Gardener, writer, founder of SarahRaven.com and Perch Hill Farm, East Sussex, England

HER PLANT "*Dahlia* 'Babylon Bronze', this is a large decorative dahlia, really curvy, and literally two or three years ago, I would have hated it, but now I love its soft color and its soft shape and the way it develops and sort of opens out. I'm a restless sort of mind, and to be honest, I like new things. I don't want to get stuck, and so maybe part of what I like about this flower is that I didn't like it a few years ago."

HER PLANT JOURNEY "To just be, for me, is to be able to go out and walk among wildflowers and then to come home and harvest some fruit or veg from the garden and cook it up in a gentle sort of way. We live in an incredibly impatient world, and I'm one of the most impatient people, and you just can't be that when you're gardening. It's very calming and I know it's good for my state of mind and spirit—it's a cure-all in many ways," says Sarah Raven of the importance of her work as a gardener, educator, and garden designer.

Sarah is something of a superstar in the garden world, in England and farther afield, in large part because of her prolific production of gardening and cookbooks, garden courses, and seeds and plants from her working home and garden, Perch Hill Farm, in East Sussex. Rounding out her impressive gardening credentials are Sarah's love for botany and her studies in history and medicine. Sarah's current work combines all of these skills and passions into her roles as successful businesswoman, eminent floral designer, and gardening and ecology advocate and educator.

Her many gardening and cookbooks combine her love of gardening, cut flowers, good health, and good food—including her first book, *The Cutting Garden: Growing and Arranging Garden Flowers* (1996) and her most recent, *Good Good Food: Recipes to Help You Look, Feel, and Live Well* (2016). She has written

> "We're all better for a bit of gardening"

influential books on garden history, including *Sissinghurst: Vita Sackville-West and the Creation of a Garden* (2014), in which she charts the course of the famous garden and gardener through the lens of her own years spent living and working at Sissinghurst with her husband, Adam Nicolson, Vita's grandson. She has also written natural history books, including *Wild Flowers* (2012), in which she celebrates, documents, and advocates for the preservation of Britain's remaining wildflower diversity. Between 2008 and 2011, she turned her ecological concerns about pollinator declines and wildflower and habitat loss to advocacy in the television documentary series, *River of Flowers* and *Bees, Butterflies and Blooms*.

Born and raised in Cambridge as one of five children, Sarah grew up in unconventional gardens. Her parents were both gardeners, and "their garden was full of things they'd collected in Greece and the Mediterranean, which is quite fashionable now but wasn't fifty years ago." She remembers, "They encouraged self-seeding camassia and allium, biennial foxgloves and smyrnium, and their garden was full of bearded iris, peonies, and eremurus. It was absolutely beautiful from late May to late June." Her father was a classics don, but a noted amateur botanist as well. Sarah spent a good deal of time botanizing with her father, who retired early with emphysema. In a 2017 interview with the *Telegraph*, she shared that her father's poor health "meant he couldn't walk very far, so he'd sit in the car while I'd go into a field to see if I could spot the plant he was looking for. If we found it, we'd take great delight in adding its whereabouts to the official *Atlas of the British and Irish Flora*." She recalls a time visiting Ireland's vast limestone Burren, known for its wildflowers, and finding "wild orchids, including a very fragrant species (*Gymnadenia conopsea*). I was maybe eight or nine, and while it wasn't hugely rare, it was very exciting to find this fragrant, pink, columnar orchid growing in a crevice."

She studied history for her first degree, and then studied, trained, and worked as a medical doctor, a period of time in which she'd retreat to her tiny flat's garden "and grow as many things as I could—the antithesis to the ward and the white coat." Eventually, she retired from medicine while on maternity leave with her second child, realizing it wasn't conducive to the family life she wanted.

Her professional life has been concerned with gardening ever since. Not long after publishing her first book, she started her official business at Perch Hill

Sarah's colorful cutting garden at Perch Hill, with poppies, penstemon, and pinks.

Farm. The ninety-acre farm was relatively derelict when she and her husband bought it, but today it supports 2.5 acres of production gardens—inclusive of a cutting garden, trial beds, perennial gardens, and vegetable gardens, which are managed with the help of long-time head gardener Josie Lewis. The rest of the farm is "an organic beef cattle and sheep farm, with between 10 and 15 acres of oak and hazel woodland, tended with light coppicing to encourage the wildflowers, such as bluebells and early purple orchids."

In 2017, Sarah collaborated with well-known color artist Tricia Guild to design her first display garden for the Chelsea Flower Show, entitled "The Anneka Rice Colour Cutting Garden." It interwove softly colored cut-and-come-again blooms with Tricia's trademark bold, saturated colors. Although Sarah states, she "*absolutely* hates the combining of white with any dark color or bright color," thereby "ruining a dark, lush palette," she also reflects, laughing, "the thing about age is, it makes you slightly less dogmatic." She now really thinks that "every color has a place—it just has to be carefully used and combined more than anything." These days, she'll admit she "likes white on its own, or with green and gray or with soft colors." Similarly, "the peachy, milky, coffee colors used to feel too girly" to her, but not anymore —"combined in the right way, any color can be quite beautiful."

Sarah sees her wildflower and biodiversity passions interfacing strongly with current research, which shows the importance of gardens to help address the plight of pollinators. "It's so easy to think we can't make a difference, but the happy thing about gardening is you absolutely can—and the more of us who garden in a pollinator-sympathetic way really can make these pockets of nectar- and pollen-rich habitats. So for me, the fact that I love a richly embroidered, absolutely jam-packed flower garden and the birds and bees do, too, is quite perfect."

OTHER INSPIRING WOMEN

- "Faith Raven, my mother, and Vita Sackville-West. Vita's garden writing and her really brilliant observational details and intimate relationship with plants reminded me of my own mother and how on our kitchen table we would always have little sherry glasses or egg cups with some exquisite specimen she'd picked from the garden, not an arrangement, but just a sprig of this or that, which was very much Vita's style, too."
- Derry Watkins, owner, Special Plants Nursery, outside Bath. "Unusual plants and a fantastic eye."
- Juliet Glaves, British flower farmer and floral designer
- Melissa Richardson, floral designer, owner of JamJar Flowers, London

Georgina Reid

> "I want to inspire people to fall in love with the world around them through falling in love with plants"

HER WORK Editor and founder, *The Planthunter*, Australia

HER PLANT "I could be any number of things, but today I will be a *Casuarina glauca*. This is a tree endemic to the Hawkesbury River, where I live. They grow in big clumps from root suckers and whisper quiet songs of the earth when the wind blows. We have a stand of them down next to our boat shed, their roots twining together, stabilizing the riverbank. There's an old mother tree in the middle. I imagine she's been there for many hundreds of years, singing her songs. Today I am a *Casuarina glauca* because I'm dwelling next to a river, am good (mostly) at keeping things stable and together, am tall and skinny and sometimes look a bit scrappy and I, too, love to tell stories of the earth."

HER PLANT JOURNEY The premise behind *The Planthunter,* an online magazine launched in Australia in late 2013, and the book *The Planthunter: Truth, Beauty, Chaos, and Plants* (2019), "is the exploration of the notion that gardening is a very powerful act, that it nourishes the human spirit in so many ways, and yet it is often not seen or valued. *The Planthunter* shares stories that illustrate the power engaging with nature can hold for individuals, but also more globally as a species." It asks about different ways we humans might converse with nature, because, for its founder, Georgina Reid, the conversation "is happening all the time in the garden. What better place to be talking about the truth, beauty, and chaos of what it means to be human?"

When Georgina first launched *The Planthunter* online, the early thirty-something touched a nerve with her "invitation to see and connect with the rich, messy, growing, decaying, evolving world around us." She had no idea her "little idea of a website exploring the connections between people and plants would be read, shared, and loved by so many people." But it was. In its first two years, "*The Planthunter* grew from a tiny idea into a rather rampant online publishing venture." It had "eighty contributors, produced nearly 500 stories, and engaged and excited readers from all corners of the world."

Publishing several in-depth stories weekly, *The Planthunter* "is organized around monthly themes, like nostalgia, obsession, and ugliness." The way it "weaves a rich story of connection and respect between humans, culture, plants, and environment—and draws equally from culture and horticulture, from art and science, from beauty and botany," is singular. Its Australian origins, with that country's cultural history and peoples, vast geography, range of climates, and diverse native flora make the project that much more unique. "We are a gardening nation still finding our identity. There are many, many stories of this land and its first people that are yet to be truly heard and reflected in the way we engage with landscape, with place. We have much listening to do."

Born and raised on a farm in central west New South Wales, near a town called Orange (four hours west of Sydney), Georgina recalls, "I grew up in the garden with my mum. I spent school holidays weeding, mulching, and pruning." Her mother "is an incredible green thumb, a nurturer. She studied horticulture when I was in high school and began a native-plant propagation nursery soon after, with which she supplied revegetation projects around our area and for greening our farm." By the time Georgina was in her late twenties and her parents sold the farm, they had, as a family, "planted 50,000 trees on the property, all driven by my mum. She's incredible."

Georgina's grandmother, Olga, "was a gardener and taught my mum a lot. She was incredibly no-fuss. Her garden was beautiful in a very humble way. She always had plenty growing in the vegetable patch, and she saw wonder and beauty everywhere. Each time we'd have a picnic on one of our family properties, we'd go for a

Plants and books— two of Georgina's essential nourishing elements.

walk through the bush or a paddock. She'd always come back with a few rocks she thought were particularly beautiful, or a stick, branch, or leaf. She noticed everything and took genuine pleasure in the world around her." To Georgina, Olga modeled how to "see, celebrate, and be grateful for the simple things we often overlook as not important enough."

The landscape of Georgina's childhood was an "enduring influence. I didn't realize until my parents sold our farm how embedded the place was in my soul. It has shaped me in ways I am only now beginning to understand. I can't remember not gardening. Officially, I began studying horticulture and landscape design in 2002, graduating in 2004."

After school, she started her plant-based career as a landscape designer. She designed gardens for nine years before starting *The Planthunter* "as a way of exploring the questions" that designing gardens brought up for her. Questions like: what makes a garden interesting or engaging? "The gardens I responded to most were not designed—they were loved. Though I think design is hugely important and can be a really important tool to encourage people to engage with plants more, I also felt constrained by the practicalities of pursuing it as a career. I felt like it didn't capture the vastness of what it can mean to engage with the natural world through the act of gardening. I wanted to explore the vastness," she exclaims, especially in the face of the realization that sometimes overly designed gardens left her "cold."

This is the kind of exploratory connection and shaping story that *The Planthunter* seeks to express and share. "Plants have been inspiring, feeding, sustaining, and soothing humans for eons. *The Planthunter* documents and celebrates these connections. It highlights the ties that bind us to our leafy friends in an authentic, unexpected, and creative manner. It gently coerces people to reconnect with plants."

"My hope is that more and more people awaken to the incredible beauty and fragility of this planet we exist on. I would love for the awareness of the interconnectedness of *all* life to grow and become an influencing factor in the ways individuals, businesses, and governments interact with the natural world."

OTHER INSPIRING WOMEN

- Edna Walling (1895–1973), influential Australian landscape designer
- Olive Pink (1884–1975), Australian anthropologist, botanical illustrator, gardener and activist
- Fiona Brockhoff, Australian landscape designer. "Her work challenges the stereotypical perceptions many people have regarding Australian native plants."
- Kate Cullity, Australian landscape architect and environmental artist

Margaret Roach

HER WORK Garden journalist, Copake Falls, Columbia County, New York

HER LANDSCAPE "The view from the windows where I sit, as I have for decades, typing. Those are the intimate pictures of my true home."

HER PLANT JOURNEY "For me, my garden is my life partner. We are one organism—garden and gardener. It is my spiritual home and heartbeat," writes Margaret Roach, one of the leading garden journalists in the United States. Margaret wrote her first book, *A Way to Garden* in 1998, while working as garden editor and then editorial director for *Martha Stewart Living* (*MSL*). During her fifteen years at *MSL*, Margaret's personal and aesthetically rich directing of the gardening content educated, inspired, and influenced millions of people each month.

Since retiring from corporate life in 2007, she's continued to share her knowledge and personal passion for "horticultural how-to and woo-woo" on her gardening blog and weekly public radio program and podcast, both also named *A Way to Garden*. And the book that started it all is still going strong, with a fully updated twenty-first-anniversary edition published in 2019.

Margaret was born and raised in Douglaston, Queens, New York. She had a botanically minded grandmother, and parents who were editor/journalists. While studying at New York University, she enjoyed her practical work placements more than her classes. After one summer of interning at the *New York Times*, she just "kept working more hours, and taking fewer classes." She would work the better part of ten years there, starting off a "copy girl in the newsroom," becoming a copy editor and writing a Sunday "women in sports" column on the side. While she didn't have a deep personal interest in sports, she was game for anything and eager to try new experiences and learn—she credits her early experiences for giving her a solid education in "old-school" journalism.

> "Gardening is the lens through which I make sense of everything"

"I became interested in plants sort of in self-defense, when, in my mid-twenties, I was called home to the house I grew up in to care for my ailing mother." Though just forty-nine years old, Margaret's mother was already a widow, and suddenly also in the early stages of Alzheimer's. "I could only watch so much daytime TV before going to my night shift at the *Times* (when someone else cared for her). Somehow I acquired *Crockett's Victory Garden* (1977) and started ordering bulbs and planting tomatoes and busying—distracting—myself with things more hopeful than her situation." Margaret's "self-prescribed occupational/horticultural therapy in those bleak years" provided her with a passion for life.

Once she started gardening, Margaret wanted to write about it. In 1982, she accepted a position with *Newsday* on Long Island, where she spent her first few years as fashion editor, another subject in which she had no real interest. Several years into her almost ten years there, she was offered the garden column. Her column was twice weekly—one column focused on the how-to, while the second was a "personal essay focusing on the woo-woo," which for Margaret—then and now—refers to the spiritual and philosophical side of *why* people garden. Her writing caught the attention of the team directing early pilot issues of *MSL*, and soon enough she was a contributing writer. When the magazine moved to ten issues a year in 1992, she joined the staff as the first garden editor.

When Margaret first began contributing to *MSL*, it was already known for its glossary-style layouts displaying a whole variety of different types of one thing, for instance white, collectible pottery. "They wanted to do something like that with plants, but they didn't have anyone that really knew gardening." One of Margaret's early suggestions was a layout with pumpkins and winter squash, which met with some skepticism. She assured them: "Wait till you see what my friend, Glenn Drowns of Sandhill Preservation Center, who's been collecting squash germplasm in Iowa for years, has for us." Crates of interesting winter squash from all over the country started arriving at the *MSL* offices, getting "unpacked and all lined up like sculpture, in that very Martha way. It was amazing."

Her years at the *New York Times* and *Newsday* had given her the confidence to call any expert in any field and request an interview (after doing her own extensive research). She had a broad network of fellow gardeners and teachers, "often turned friends," around the globe, and at *MSL*, her "passion for plants, plant knowledge, and connections combined really well with Martha Stewart's presentation style and resources. Her love of gardening and willingness to try everything gave me the freedom to let my cravings and knowledge, creativity, and obsessions out." Margaret recalls, "I was excited to have an opportunity to showcase some of my passion for plants." She was "happy to honor the people doing their life's work, not following trends just because someone said 'Ok, everything's purple this year.'"

After retiring from *MSL* and corporate life to her 2.3-acre home and organic, edible, and ornamental garden in the rural Hudson Valley (in part to have a full-time

Margaret's home garden.

relationship with her garden), Margaret applied her curiosity for learning and her journalistic skills to her blog, then to her weekly public-radio program, which became one of the earliest and best gardening podcasts. Both her blog and her radio work have deepened her spiritual engagement with gardening, while continuing to expand and share how-tos with garden-loving readers and listeners.

"The subject matter I'm most excited about at this point is the interaction of plants and the other organisms in the ecosystem. Teaching people about those—hosting moth nights and bird gardening workshops—is probably my current favorite." Through her twenty years of open gardens, lectures, and workshops, she is more and more enamored with sharing her knowledge. "I like answering questions, in the hope that it demystifies things for people so they don't give up in their own efforts. To me that is the core of what I do—help people (including young children) stay engaged and not give up, whether with some essential how-to detail or telling them about some moment of awe with a bird or snake or caterpillar."

Margaret takes frogs appearing in her home garden as a signifier of its overall health.

In 2018, Margaret was awarded the Massachusetts Horticultural Society's highest award, the George Robert White Medal of Honor, for her "distinguished career" in horticulture, as a garden communicator whose work "makes meaningful connections between people, plants, and their beloved gardens."

OTHER INSPIRING WOMEN

- Margery Fish (1892–1969), English cottage gardener, author of *We Made a Garden* (1956). "She influenced me early on."
- Eleanor Perenyi (1918–2009), American gardener and author of *Green Thoughts: A Writer in the Garden* (1981). "She helped me visualize becoming a garden writer—taking my journalism ability and melding it with my budding 'hobby.'"
- Ruth Bancroft (1908–2017), gardener, creator of the Ruth Bancroft Garden, a succulent and cacti garden in Walnut Creek, California. "It was the first garden incorporated into the US-based Garden Conservancy."
- Elizabeth Farnsworth (1962–2017), research ecologist and educator, New England Wild Flower Society. "Both Ruth Bancroft and Elizabeth made very strong impressions on me for their depth of passion and focus, and their boldness."

Martha Schwartz

HER WORK Founding principal, Martha Schwartz Partners, New York, London, China; professor in practice, landscape architecture, Graduate School of Design, Harvard University

HER LANDSCAPE "Parc de Sceaux, France. While this garden by Le Nôtre is flawed in how it hangs together, the poplar allée is sublime and is my favorite landscape space. It demonstrates how scale and simplicity can create a powerful spatial and emotional experience."

HER PLANT JOURNEY Martha Schwartz loves trees. For close to forty years, she has been designing and directing global landscape architecture projects. "I am focused now on how landscape, specifically afforestation, can play a more aggressive role in helping cities to withstand issues they will be soon facing in regard to global warming." When it comes to the realities of climate change, Martha feels passionately that "as long as we keep topping off architects' buildings with green roofs, we're fiddling while Rome burns. We're seven billion people now—we have to really figure out how to build cities, not just buildings."

As a landscape architect, she sees in trees and urban afforestation—creating a forest where there isn't one—heroic potential for mitigating climate change. This idea is integral to her visionary work seeing and thinking strategically across landscapes as a continuum, from a single residential property to the capital city of a nation. "I am looking at how afforestation, in conjunction with technologies such as automated vehicles can, in the future, be inserted into cities at a scale that can have many benefits for a city's ability to adapt."

Martha was born and raised in and around Philadelphia, Pennsylvania. Her love of trees, "especially good climbing trees, like beech," started early, and she remembers very distinctly one spring day when she was quite small and "a copper beech had just flushed out, and the leaves were so thin and delicate, the sunlight shone through them." When she stood beneath the tree it was "this

"Tree's-eye view or higher"

unbelievable, big red glow. I remember being in awe for days." She also remembers visiting the greenhouses at Longwood Gardens as a girl and thinking, "Why wouldn't anyone just move in here, with trees all around you? Why don't we all just live in such a living environment?"

For Martha, these kinds of "hybrid spaces—somewhere between human-made and natural—are incredible, magical, and seminal." While studying at the University of Michigan, her imagination was captured during a woody-plants systematics course, and she appreciated how different plant groups evolved in relationship to insects, how they changed and moved and adapted to soils and climates. "I've only gotten more and more interested in plants since."

In her design work, trees are often the "framework for everything. I was drawn to large landscape art installations, and the trees set up the spaces—they are the walls, they set the scale, they set the tone, they create the structure, and the rest is secondary. The trees are the skeleton of the spaces." Trees become a primary language of expression, especially as bridges between the ground scale—human scale—and the larger environment.

In a 2012 interview with *Yale Environment 360*, Martha said, "Great landscape design can moderate extreme heat, recycle water, reduce energy use, lower carbon emissions, and attract people to urban areas. Most of our urban environments aren't waterfronts and parks. They're our streets, our sidewalks, our utility corridors and parking lots. It's everything outside the building. And yet there's very little design to what these spaces look like."

The arc of Martha's career charts the importance she sees in redefining, renewing, and re-understanding our cities as critical hubs of sustainability in order to curb and survive climate change. She has also incorporated art, color, whimsy, and humanity. She founded her firm, Martha Schwartz Partners (MSP), now with offices in London, New York, and China, in the late 1970s and earned early recognition for her Bagel Garden home installation in Boston, which featured only items she could purchase in her immediate vicinity—which included bagels, purple gravel, and pink begonias. Its quirky references to pop art as well as insightful expression of the changing reality of "native" urban landscapes remains iconic in the world of landscape architecture.

In MSP's design of such large-scale urban projects as Dublin's Grand Canal Square, Exchange Square in Manchester, England, and Abu Dhabi's Corniche beachfront area, the firm demonstrates the urgent need and potential effectiveness of looking at landscape design with not only human engagement and enjoyment in mind, but also climate change. "We always start a project by asking how can we help a client future-proof their investments. We need to understand how they see water; very soon weather patterns will result in much heavier periods of rain during winter periods, at a much greater volume, with too little rain falling in the dry seasons." In Abu Dhabi, for example, the team analyzed the water use of large trees in an area with little human use. They strategically relocated the trees to an area further inland, where they could be appreciated not only for their aesthetics but also their ability to provide habitat,

An urban design in Beijing, with trees providing shade, shelter, and scale—bridging buildings and humans.

shade, scale, and to ultimately protect the soil from future erosion with rising water impacts.

In her own climate change research education, Martha hit a wall in 2016. "Grasping how deep into it we are, that even with fire alarms going off all around the world, there is very little we can do as landscape architects working with individual clients, working site by site." She decided to use her "small bully pulpit to teach, lecture, and try to persuade." She ran a studio at Harvard with "pretty amazing metrics that demonstrated compelling results from integrating afforestation into the urban landscape—especially integrated with the benefits of automated vehicles and other technologies."

In 2018, Edition Axel Menges edited and published a monograph, *Martha Schwartz Partners: Landscape Art and Urbanism,* documenting MSP projects and masterplans from close to forty years of design in more than forty countries and across six continents. The firm's manifesto places MSP "at the intersection of landscape, art, and urbanism and is committed to the design of urban landscapes and the public realm as the foundation for sustainable cities that are healthy across all aspects and sectors of urban life." The team at MSP understands the urban landscape as the platform upon which human and natural environments can be brought into an artful balance, and sees as fundamental to the practice's process that people are engaged by bringing delight and playfulness to urban life. The creation of humane spaces can, as a result, positively impact sustainability by supporting density and the benefits and efficiencies gained through urban living.

Nouvelle at Natick, MSP's award-winning, almost 35,000-square-foot green roof garden in Natick, Massachusetts.

OTHER INSPIRING WOMEN

- ◆ Kate Orff, American landscape architect and recipient of a 2017 MacArthur Foundation fellowship; founder and principal of SCAPE, New York City
- ◆ Susannah Drake, American landscape architect, founding principal of DLANDstudio, Brooklyn, New York
- ◆ Dr. Kristina Hill, associate professor of landscape architecture and environmental planning and urban design, University of California, Berkeley, California

Jane Scotter

HER WORK Biodynamic farmer, Fern Verrow, Herefordshire, England

HER PLANT "I use the farm organism a great deal when dealing with everyday problems. I have often asked myself 'What plant am I today?' The emerging seedling, fresh, vital with energy and strength for life ahead? The well-rounded, mature lettuce, full of promise and wisdom? The bolting chard, rather ethereal, scatty, creative, and interesting? Or the wilting, tired, not-on-best-form cabbage ready for the compost heap? I can be the compost heap too, reinventing myself, useful and necessary for the farm, not always looking my best, or appreciated, but always present and needed to make things happen. I would like to be a rose—scented, elegant, beautiful, sometimes prickly, but liked by everyone."

HER PLANT JOURNEY "It's about the decisions we make in our lives, isn't it? I am the proof in the pudding. I would rather have really lovely food in my house—really nice olive oil and wine, really nice vegetables, really nice meat all cared for properly by people who make a proper living themselves—than a really nice car, or a monthly subscription to Sky TV. These are the interesting things in life—the cultivated pursuits."

In 1996, Jane Scotter left a high-profile and profitable position as one of the founding partners at Neal's Yard Dairy, a high-end purveyor of fine British-made cheeses in London, to become a farmer on her own small family farm called Fern Verrow, sixteen acres in the foothills of the Black Mountains in Herefordshire, England. More than twenty years later, the organic, biodynamic farm grows beautiful produce year round, and Jane and her husband, co-farmer Harry Astley, care for the soil and land, care for the animals, and cultivate nourishing produce as their living in this world. Since 2015, they have been in a direct farm-to-table collaboration with acclaimed Australian chef Skye Gyngell and her restaurant, Spring, in Somerset House, London.

Fern Verrow's beautiful diversity of pumpkins and gourds.

Fern Verrow and its farmers are models of how to value the land, the farmer, the quality of the food, and the quality of living made. Through her farming, writing, collaborations, and educational outreach, Jane is a forerunner in the United Kingdom as an alternative to an agro-industrial-complex-based food, land, and livelihood ethic.

She grew up in a military family and moved around a good deal throughout England, Germany, and Canada. Her most consistent and happy time was in New Forest, in Hampshire, where her paternal grandparents lived. "I've always loved and had a cultural connection with food," she remarks. Both her parents, but especially her father, brought Jane and her brother up with a love of good food. "It was what they chose to spend money on—going out and enjoying really good food." Likewise, since she was a small girl, land captured her imagination. "The shapes and colors of landscapes—I remember the haze of purple heather and golden bracken of the New Forest in late August, the wheat fields of 1976 (the hottest, longest summer on record) in Dorset; the movement of that golden sea of wheat against a bright blue sky and the rich sunlight of August was truly beautiful."

In the early 1980s, government food-safety regulations were changing the culture of many artisan-style, farm-based traditional foods—from eggs and milk to cheese and meat. Partnered with Randolph Hodgson of Neal's Yard Dairy, Jane "traveled the length and breadth of the British Isles, visiting, learning about, and encouraging" traditional cheesemakers. Jane and Randolph knew the quality of cheese they wanted, which they could sell in London, and they paid their cheesemakers "double what they could get elsewhere in order to keep making their cheeses the way they always had," without starters and without pasteurization. "Neal's Yard Dairy really changed the face of British cheese."

Eventually, when she was ready for a move away from the pace of her city life, Jane relocated with her children to Fern Verrow, a fallow fifteenth-century farm with its own spring, which had only ever previously been used for grazing. "I had no idea of how to grow anything. I had no training but just a lot of will to grow food and live off the land if I could." With experience and insights from neighbors, as well as instinct and "sort of stabbing in the dark, we plowed up a small patch and put in things that seemed good: broad beans, peas, a big patch of potatoes." Two years later, the farm was fully certified as biodynamic.

Biodynamic farming is "based on the teachings of Austrian thinker Rudolf Steiner and conceived as a way of thinking holistically about food, nutrition, and the world of nature, as well as a renewal of agricultural practices—the oldest consciously organic approach to farming and gardening," Biodynamics incorporates the energetic cycles of the seasons and cosmos, especially the cycles of the moon, into when and why you do anything and everything on the farm. "The honest and challenging nature of growing food is central to why we do it. We find that growing vegetables and fruit in good soil, at the right time of year—open to the elements—adds greatly to their character and flavor."

In 2015, Fern Verrow began collaborating with chef Skye Gyngell. Now the vast majority of their crops are planned for and go to supplying her restaurant, Spring. This partnership ensures that Fern Verrow's produce and methods are understood and valued, and it gives them a stable business model from which to think more broadly—to experiment with crops, to help design and consult on other biodynamic gardens, and to begin developing educational forums. The forums provide a venue in which to grapple with obstacles for viable smallholders, such as access to land. Through the forums, Jane and Harry share their knowledge and experience forward in pursuit of a strong and resilient smallholder economy.

The creativity and beauty of the "dark, dark green of the Black Mountains," including what biodynamic practitioners refer to as "the unseen forces and energies of life and growth that permeate all living things," is important to Jane. She found her art, her vocation, and her place "in the fabulous colors and intricate, glorious forms" of the produce and flowers grown and prepared here. "It always surprises me. Twenty-two years on, and I am still thrilled by the sight of the plants—it's fantastic, I love them. They feed me in many ways. I am thankful that I live and work here every day."

OTHER INSPIRING WOMEN

- Tessa Traeger, British photographer
- Skye Gyngell, British chef. "She has truly inspired me in my growing and as a woman doing a so-called man's job."

Summer's soft fruits from Fern Verrow.

Renee Shepherd

HER WORK Founder and owner, Renee's Garden, Felton, California

HER PLANT "The chili peppers. They are fun, hugely colorful and flavorful, diverse, and international."

HER PLANT JOURNEY It's the loveliness of the illustrations—cheery, plump tomatoes, scrambling nasturtiums, a picnic table set with flowers, wine glasses, deep purple eggplants, and succulent melons just cut—that first catch the eye. The romantic images branding the seed packets, website, and other marketing materials of Renee's Garden initially evoke whole narratives of what it means for something to be homegrown, tapping into a growing movement for a meaningful garden-to-table connection.

The appeal of the images is just one aspect of how Renee Shepherd changed the way home garden seeds are sourced, packaged, marketed, and purchased in the United States. As she explains, "My focus has always been to spread and promote the true pleasures of growing from seed and cooking from the garden." She seeks out and makes available seed varieties from growers around the world, both large and small, choosing varieties for superior flavor and easy culture.

Born and raised in Ohio, Renee came to California to pursue a doctorate at the University of California, Santa Cruz. There, her own love of gardening rooted and blossomed. She also met Dutch seedsman Cees Boonman, who gave Renee specialty vegetable seeds for her garden. She credits the taste and beauty of that produce with inspiring her to start her own company.

Shepherd's Garden Seed—founded in 1985—was a print catalogue–based company that specialized in vegetable, fruit, and flower seeds especially for the home gardener looking for taste and beauty. After over a decade of success,

> "My goal is to spread the joy of gardening as a practical, meaningful activity that connects people with each other and the earth"

Renee sold that company and soon after founded the web-based Renee's Garden, which, with the help of twenty-five staff, she still runs today. It now has trial gardens in California and Vermont, and, in addition to selling direct to gardeners on the website, Renee's Garden–brand seeds are sold in more than 1,500 independent garden centers across the country.

Renee knew from her beginnings as a gardener that she wanted to grow more—more organic, more interesting, and more new and heirloom varieties of the vegetables, culinary herbs, and flowers she loved and had yet to meet. She reasoned accurately that she was not alone in wanting something more than what the standard American seed companies at the time were offering. To achieve her interesting selection of seeds, she attended national and international seed growers' conferences, working with seed growers from around the world whose professional standards for seeds met hers.

For home gardeners and plant lovers, Renee scaled up the standards of what to look for and what to expect in home garden seeds and their packaging. San Francisco–based watercolor artist Mimi Osborne has painted the homey watercolor illustrations from the beginning, using photos of each variety taken in the company's trial gardens.

Renee's Garden seed packets and web information aren't just lovely—they include carefully tested and evaluated, step-by-step instructions for successful growing in any major climate zone of the country plus recipes for cooking with the resulting fresh produce. In a gesture that shows both insight and foresight, Renee writes the instructions as though you, the reader/gardener, might not have done this before, but she also encouragingly assumes you are eager, bright, and capable. The direct customer service phone line to Renee's Garden's horticultural advisor, Beth Benjamin, provides the third support that gardeners might need in rearing their young seeds with success.

Renee also sets her company apart with the interesting sampler packets of seed combinations she develops—mixes of braising greens, cottage flowers, carrots, or peppers. To her way of thinking, most home gardens aren't vast enough to use an entire packet of seed—so you end up choosing one variety, or you get three varieties and end up with a lot of seed gathering dust in the garage or shed. Her mixes provide the best

Garden-to-table produce from seed in Renee's own garden.

of both worlds—diversity without waste—and they encourage a home gardener's curiosity and inclination to experiment with success.

A believer in community as much as in the power of passion (for growing) and process (of seed to table or vase), Renee stays attuned to the plants themselves as they teach her how they want to grow, what they need to grow well, and where they want to grow to taste and look their best. Her cookbooks are the best evidence for these lessons, bringing her work in seeds full circle. Coauthored with Fran Raboff, her books include *Recipes from a Kitchen Garden* (1994), *More Recipes from a Kitchen Garden* (1995), and *The Renee's Garden Cookbook* (2014). She owns the rights to all her books and sells them almost exclusively through Renee's Garden.

Looking back on her forty-plus-year career in the seed industry, Renee is most proud of her seed-donation program. It pays the season's leftover packets from Renee's Garden forward to school gardens, prisons, community gardens, and other organizations that teach gardening or provide food for the hungry and disadvantaged.

When she started in this business, few women worked as owners, leaders, or influencers in the seed production and distribution supply chain. "There are more now, but still relatively few in the top positions. When I first started attending conferences and meeting with growers, I would often be the only woman in a group meeting with a seed producer. Where others were mostly concerned with shipping and packing capacity, I was asking to compare varieties for flavor. Fortunately, that is changing now, as consumers are looking for more tasty produce."

A selection of unique Renee's Garden seed packets.

OTHER INSPIRING WOMEN

◆ Elisabeth Sahin, visionary managing director of Dutch flower seed company, K. Sahin Zaden B.V.

◆ Robin Parer, owner of Geraniacaea, a specialty geranium nursery in the San Francisco Bay Area and founder/coleader of a plant-besotted, horticultural, world-traveling adventure group known as the Hortisexuals

◆ Barbara Damrosch, farmer, cook; author of *The Garden Primer* (1988) and *The Four Season Farm Gardener's Cookbook* (2013)

◆ Patty Buskirk, managing partner and seed/plant breeder at Seeds by Design and Terra Organics, the largest USDA Certified Organic seed producers

Midori Shintani

HER WORK Head gardener, Tokachi Millennium Forest, Hokkaido, Japan

HER PLANT "*Miscanthus sinensis*. A field of miscanthus was the first place that as a child, I was overwhelmed by plants and their vigorous strength. At first, I felt a little fear there, and then I realized, 'I actually am living with them.' It's never changed since."

HER PLANT JOURNEY The Tokachi Millennium Forest in Hokkaido, Japan, models for visitors that "the natural environment is an asset worth preserving for future generations for the thousands of years to come." Midori Shintani, its head gardener, explains that she and her garden team strive to "merge" the cultivated landscape and gardens seamlessly into the natural areas surrounding the site. With a goal to tend the connection between nature and humankind, the Millennium Forest serves "a deeply felt sense of beauty in Japanese culture and garden history," where the ancient calendar recognizes seventy-two distinct seasons in which "tiny delicate changes occur," and through which you can feel how "everything is connected, and the importance of taking great care and making close observation of natural processes."

Midori was born and raised in Obama City, of the Fukui Prefecture in central Japan, an area rich with natural areas, including Wakasa Wan Quasi-National Park and its stunning and rugged coastline along Wakasa Bay. This "countryside surrounded by sea and *satoyama*, a harmonious environment (or landscape) between people and nature," was among Midori's earliest influences. She describes how "plants were always by my side; I spent a lot

> An intimate relationship between humankind and the productive agricultural landscape at the boundary of the wild. Deep, important interconnections between people, landscapes, natural habitats, plants, and animals

of time with them through the seasons. I helped my mother to pick artemisia to make rice cakes in spring. In summer, I chased frogs in the rice paddy fields; I often made grass whistles, leaf masks, flower-seed parachutes, and flower crowns. When miscanthus flowers told of the arrival of autumn, I picked its spikes to decorate with at home."

Another of Midori's influences was a grandfather who loved Japanese arts and crafts—ceramics, paintings, Noh drama, kimonos, tea ceremonies, bonsai— "His garden was an inspirational place for me to develop the connection between Japanese traditional culture and modern gardening."

She studied landscape architecture and horticulture at university in Japan at a time when there was a big trend toward English garden styles. After university, she knew she wanted to "think about Japanese horticulture from the outside, by working in another country." In her early thirties, she traveled to Sweden for horticultural internships. In the first year, she learned Swedish and apprenticed at Millesgården, a sculpture garden outside of Stockholm, where she "created a good relationship with art" and began to "think about gardening and how gardens relate to people."

From there, she moved to Rosendals Trädgård, and it was here, one sunny afternoon when "I was weeding in the kitchen garden, as usual, and I suddenly thought 'I want to do this forever.' It was an unforgettable moment—like every separated part of me united into one." Soon after, she made the decision to become a professional gardener in a public place.

Midori at work in the meadow garden of the Tokachi Millennium Forest.

To continue her training in specific areas of professional gardening, she returned home to Japan and studied "garden design and construction, in order to understand the whole process from desk to land—traditional Japanese garden design, construction, and maintenance. I also studied nursery work, including how to grow perennial seedlings, and I learned about regional differences in climate, native vegetation, and correct plant selection. It was the hardest four years of work in my life!"

All the while, she was looking for a garden to which she felt she belonged. In 2008, she "finally met" Tokachi Millennium Forest, and she's been the head gardener of the almost 990-acre garden and forest since.

The Millennium Forest is located at the foot of the Hidaka Mountains on Hokkaido, the northernmost island of Japan, and was originally started in 1990 in order to provide carbon offset in the form of forest for the Tokachi Mainichi Newspaper Company. A good portion of the forest was designed by Japanese landscape architects Takano Landscape Planning and British garden designer Dan Pearson. Pearson contributed to the overall garden design and helped determine the site's distinct gardens—Earth, Forest, Meadow, and Farm—with additional spaces for a kitchen garden, rose garden, orchard, and goat farm. His international expertise and connections have provided Midori with additional mentorship and training.

Midori's work "merging people into wild nature" is reflective of a naturalistic garden movement in Japan, rooted in a deep connection to nature, and a reengagement with the ancient Japanese belief in animism, as illustrated in the expression "plants and trees all have something to say." Japanese believe trees, plants, and even boulders have a soul, and they say humans can sense spirits, or *kami* ("god" in Japanese) within them. She sees these beliefs as central to the existence of the Millennium Forest project, and that her "work in the garden, informed by the local ecosystems of Hokkaido's native forests and fields, serves a deeply felt sense of beauty in Japanese culture and garden history. My personal hope is that the garden helps to evoke everyone's inner 'wild.' Because this, for me, is happiness."

OTHER INSPIRING WOMEN

- Masako Shirasu (1910–1998), Japanese author. "I admire her incredible sense of beauty and her work to create deep relationships between nature and Japanese culture—arts, crafts, religion, history, and literature. I am inspired by her words and actions to relate to the local vernacular and revitalize Japanese culture."

- Yoshiko Tatsumi, Japanese chef and culinary educator. "I am inspired by her works with food and the edible plants that we literally cannot live without. She founded *Daizu Hyakutsubu Undo* (The Group to Support the Planting of 100 Soybean Seeds) to address food self-sufficiency, by teaching children in more than 300 elementary schools across Japan to plant 100 soybean seeds, then to grow and harvest them to make food such as tofu and miso. I respect her teaching us how to live through the most beautiful Japanese language."

Vandana Shiva

HER WORK International environmental health and social justice advocate, Dehradun, India

HER PLANT "Neem (*Azadirachta indica*). The name is derived from the Persian and means 'free tree.' After the Bhopal disaster, when a Union Carbide pesticide factory killed thousands, I started a campaign—No More Bhopals, Plant a Neem—to promote the use of neem in nonviolent pest control. Ten years later, I discovered neem was patented by W. R. Grace and the US Department of Agriculture. For eleven years, we fought against the biopiracy of neem. We won. Neem, the free tree, is free."

HER PLANT JOURNEY Dr. Vandana Shiva is a celebrated international leader in environmentalism, ecofeminism, and agroecology. An internationally known public speaker, writer, educator, and organizer, Vandana is a passionate advocate for the preservation of biodiversity, the importance of traditional agroecological knowledge, and the correlation between the status of women and the future of the planet's environmental health. Vandana is also a well-known critic of agro-industrial complexes and their lack of concern for the environment and human life, especially in their reliance on petrochemical products and genetically modified and/or patented seeds as the dominant model for agriculture and the global food system.

In her 2010 book, *Staying Alive*, Vandana directly correlates current ecological crises, global colonization, and the marginalization of women, especially women of color. She has written more than twenty titles on subjects ranging from third-world agriculture to ecofeminism to the climate crisis. She is a leader in the International Forum on Globalization (IFG) and the Slow Food movement, and the founder of Navdanya, an Indian-based, nongovernmental, conservation, research and teaching farm, and seed bank in her hometown of Dehradun, India. From there, she leads the Diverse Women for Diversity and the Earth University outreach and advocacy movement.

Born in Dehradun, India, in a valley of the Himalayas, Vandana grew up in "forests of oak, rhododendron, pine, the deodar (God's own tree—a Himalayan cedar), wildflowers, and ferns." Her father was a forest officer and her mother was a farmer by choice, after having been a teacher, inspectress of schools, and women's rights advocate in India and Pakistan. Vandana remembers "collecting and making art with forest plants. My mother wrote nursery rhymes on plants for us. We would go into the fields and pick and eat green chickpeas (which are delicious), peas, and sugar cane."

Having begun her higher education in India, Vandana received her master's degree and doctoral degree in philosophy in Ontario, Canada, graduating in 1978. Her environmental advocacy started early, when she would return home from school and see the losses of land and other natural resources to development and damage. Returning to India, she worked for several Indian agencies before founding what is now the Research Foundation for Science, Technology and Ecology in 1982.

Just a few years later, her philosophy and purpose came together around both environmentalism and humanitarianism. "After the economically based Punjab violence of the 1970s and 1980s, and the Bhopal disaster in 1984 (in which thousands of people were killed or critically injured as the result of a disastrous leak at a factory producing chemical pesticides), I turned more deeply to agriculture and seeds, to protecting our biodiversity, and to making peace with the earth through poison-free, chemical-free organic farming. In 1987, in reaction to an agrichemical industry statement in Geneva that they would spread genetically modified plants and seeds and take patents on seeds, I started Navdanya."

> "The idea that we can improve plants is part of human hubris—if anything, plants improve us—we are one part of the earth family"

Navdanya is a conservation, research, and teaching farm and seed bank that has grown slowly and naturally in its scope of work and land in the more than thirty years since it was established. "We now have 2000 varieties of crops growing on the farm, including 750 rice varieties, 200 volunteer native and nonnative beneficial, medicinal, edible species, and 200 species of trees. We have a wide mix of people, including farmers who work the land and who are also experts. I have a deep belief in the principle of diversity in all things—in plants, in seeds, in knowledge."

The Earth University on the farm hosts, at any one time, "twenty-five interns learning about organic farming and how to be earth citizens." On the sesquicentennial of Ghandi's birth, Vandana and Navdanya launched a thirty-year campaign "on our breads as our freedom—our breads can only be our freedom if they are diverse, if they are made according to our cultures and knowledge, if they are free of poisons, and they are free of the control of those who do not care about the earth, biodiversity, or our health. This initiative is working toward poison-free farming around the world by 2050."

A range of seed varieties at Navdanya.

Having won international legal cases against seed patents and the appropriation of traditional cultural knowledge and techniques (such as the attempted patenting of neem oil as an organic insect repellent), Vandana and her coalitions have "defended seed as a commons, created 130 community seed banks, and a global Seed Freedom network. We have created better agriculture food and farming systems and living economies based on biodiversity of food, of natural colors, of fibers and fabrics. We have created the living democracy, Diverse Women for Diversity, and the Earth Democracy movement. As an 'earth family,' we are all equal, and violence against the earth and women is not acceptable. All of us, women and men, are called on by the earth to contribute to the work needed for the well-being of earth and society." Her book *Oneness vs. the 1%* (2019), co-authored with her son, poses to readers the fundamental question: Do you want an interconnected world or one based on separation?

"I believe in the power of each and every garden. There's always something you can do. If you have a small plot of land, start a garden; or, make some small effort to link yourself to someone who is a farmer or gardener by the food you buy, the economic choices you make. And through that, you become part of the garden—whether it's as an eater or as a tender, we are alive only insofar as we are part of a garden. Otherwise we are part of the war against the earth." The future is based, believes Vandana, "on our core intelligence of evolution with the plants."

OTHER INSPIRING WOMEN

- JK Shiva, Vandana's mother
- Rachel Carson (1907–1964), American marine biologist and ecologist; author of *Silent Spring* (1962), which helped to have the chemical DDT banned in the United States and to launch the modern environmental movement
- Kusum Panigrahi, of Balasore, Odisha. "She has saved 1000 rice varieties, including salt-tolerant rice varieties she distributed to coastal farmers after the supercyclone in Odisha in 1999 and after the tsunami in 2004."
- Rukmini, of Tehri Garhwal, "whose valley was destroyed by the Tehri Dam, but who has rejuvenated cooperative organic farming with women and created climate resilience and economic prosperity through native seeds."

Michelle Slatalla

HER WORK Journalist and former editor in chief, *Gardenista*, Mill Valley, California

HER PLANT "Daphnes—very sturdy, evergreen, and every year when you need them most, they give off the most amazing scent. They do not like to be moved."

HER PLANT JOURNEY "The proof is everywhere: treating the outdoors as a natural extension of living space makes you happier. It doesn't matter if you're a neophyte or a master gardener: you can do this," Michelle Slatalla, editor in chief of Gardenista.com from 2012 to 2019, assures readers on the home page of the popular online garden and garden-lifestyle website. "Our secret mission at *Gardenista*," Michelle shares, "is to connect people to the outdoors more. First we want to get them out on the patio reading the paper or looking at something on their phone in the shade, then we want to get them to look up—maybe notice something blooming—then to get out more."

Michelle was born in Chicago and raised in the suburbs in a family in which gardening was just something you did. While both parents gardened and worked together on DIY projects like laying a flagstone path, it was her father who was the more avid, and "family conversations regularly included questions like 'I wonder if there's a variety of gardenia that would overwinter here?' Chicago was a challenging gardening climate." Her father's mother was also a gardener. "She had grapes and made grape jelly, had a wonderful rose arbor and big compost pile in the back that was mysterious to all of us

> " Gardens matter. So does your patio, your porch, your front stoop, or your apartment's sunny windowsill "

growing up, and grew African violets on her radiators." Michelle's father was "determined to have a colorful garden through masses of spring tulips and other bulbs, and there was a lot of heartbreak through the years with April or May snowstorms." Michelle considers herself "a plant person by osmosis."

She studied journalism and English at Indiana University before moving to New York City at the age of twenty-two to attend graduate school in journalism at Columbia University. Throughout grad school, she worked as journalist at *Newsday* on Long Island, then stayed on staff for ten years, covering general news assignments on government, politics, and health care.

While still in New York, Michelle moved from *Newsday* to the *New York Times*, where she wrote regularly about family life and parenting, and the then-novelty of the online world. Having become a dedicated gardener at her first house, she remembers writing a column in the late 1990s/early 2000s about her Felco clippers, how she "loved them so much but they needed some repair work, and how amazing it was that online, you could get Felco repair parts. It was a very popular column." She realized this was a way to personalize the whole gardening experience and have people be interested in reading about it.

Michelle was a fan of several established garden writers, notably Henry Mitchell, whose Earthman columns for the *Washington Post* "illuminated the triumphs and disappointments of the human condition." But she could now envision ways of "tapping into the universal particular and to show that we are part of a bigger whole" in a new online world. This "informed how we created *Gardenista* and our approach to covering the topic. Not as a hardcore gardening/horticulture site, but through a lifestyle approach and in that intersection of indoors/outdoors and how exterior design can help you to get more outdoors into your life."

Gardenista launched in 2012 as a sister-site to Remodelista.com, which was founded by Michelle's good friends Julie Carlson and Josh Groves. While *Gardenista*'s "success and resonance with readers was not a surprise" to Michelle, she also knew launching it was a risk. "At the same we were launching, the general publishing industry was

Michelle with Mollie Katzen, gardener/cook/cookbook author famous for her vegetarian *Moosewood Cookbook*.

killing gardening coverage in magazines and newspapers across the country." But she (and Julie and Josh) believed in her instinct that "gardens matter and people are interested in them."

Gardenista's 1.3 million readers a month include a wide range of ages, geographic locations, and types of gardeners, even people who don't want to garden, but who want to make their outdoor spaces as enjoyable as their indoor spaces. With more than seventeen posts a week, which is about equivalent to "a good, old-fashioned, special garden section of a newspaper," *Gardenista*'s articles and topics include "ways you as a gardener can feel good about your practices without sacrificing the things that make gardening lovely—beauty, your lifestyle, or just a sense of style in the garden." Contributors write about how to improve soil through incorporating natural amendments, how to design a beautiful garden that blooms all year with low-water native plants appropriate for your climate, and how to get along with your surroundings without fighting them. "Part of our mantra is 'Get Along'—plant a hedge instead of a fence. A hedge is better for the environment and a better neighbor than a fence."

The book *Gardenista: The Definitive Guide to Stylish Outdoor Spaces* (2016) codified Gardenista.com's mission into a manifesto: "We believe gardens matter." Michelle explains, "Every single garden in the book is one we feel good about philosophically as well as aesthetically; if someone simply grows a pot of parsley on their kitchen counter, and that's their garden, we respect that and will try to help make it more beautiful and useful and happy-making to them."

And, she hopes, all this encourages more and more people to get outside. "If we run a feature on tiny folding tables for balcony-sized spaces and windproof votives—and even one of these is a hook for someone to eat dinner outside or deciding to do it regularly after seeing that post and trying it once, I would call that a big win for gardening. That's how expansive our definition of gardening and a garden is, because that's how far removed many people are from being outdoors every day."

OTHER INSPIRING WOMEN

- Helen Van Pelt Wilson (1901–2003), American gardener and garden writer. She was a columnist for the *Philadelphia Record*, and her books include *Perennials Preferred* (1950), *The Joy of Geraniums* (1965), and *The Fragrant Year* (1967), cowritten with Leonie Bell.
- Katharine S. White (1892–1977), American writer, editor, and gardener. A longtime editor and contributor to the *New Yorker*, her most well-known work is the posthumous collection of her garden articles, *Onward and Upward in the Garden* (1979).

Janet Sluis

HER WORK Program developer and curator, Sunset Western Garden Collection; West Coast program director, Plant Development Services, Inc., Berkeley, California

HER LANDSCAPE "A Piet Oudolf–designed garden—I like the wildness of his meadow plantings with their highly planned internal structure, but wild appearance and diversity of plantings. It's complex simplicity."

HER PLANT JOURNEY People have been breeding and selecting plants since the beginning of humankind—choosing, planting, saving, sharing, and tending more carefully in their natural and cultivated environments those plants they preferred—often focusing on such traits as vigor, productivity, flavor, color, strength, or ability to store well. Once basic genetics and inheritance became more widely understood, plant selecting became far more targeted toward breeding specific traits into and out of plant lines for human purposes. In our modern world, professional plant-breeding people and processes dictate, in large part, what plants we gardeners and plant buyers have available to us through standard retail suppliers such as independent nurseries, chain nurseries and garden centers, and big box stores.

Janet Sluis is a leader in American plant breeding and selection. She's been in the field since early 1990 and now works as the West Coast program director for Plant Development Services, Inc., curating the Sunset Western Garden Collection and the Southern Living Plant Collection. Hailing from a long line of horticulturists, she proudly explains, "My dad's family has been in the horticultural seed industry in the Netherlands since the early 1800s (Royal Sluis and Sluis & Groot)—I'm the sixth generation in horticulture."

After World War II, her father and mother emigrated to the United States, and Janet was born and raised in Redlands, California. Her earliest memories include lying on the ground in the spring sun watching a crocus take its time to open. She and her siblings were each given a section of the family's land on

> "I want to bring gardeners joy and help them be successful, by introducing regionally appropriate and improved plant varieties to the market"

which to have their own gardens and by the age of five she was cross-pollinating ranunculus and collecting the resulting seeds. Her mother, who had "grown up in an apartment in Rotterdam" was a natural-born plantswoman and, as they say in the trade, "could have rooted a pencil." Janet recalls fondly, "My mom was always getting cuttings from people, and then referred to said plant by that person's name. It wasn't until high school that I discovered haworthia was not actually called Mrs. Battain."

After receiving her master's degree in horticulture and agriculture business from California Polytechnic Institute, San Luis Obispo, Janet worked for many years with large box-store growers. She also served on the Lowe's Perennial Council, helping select which perennials the big-box chain would carry each season. For a time, she was the only woman on the council, but she would soon have a chance to work with like-minded women in the field.

October Magic® Snow™ camellia, a Sunset Western Garden introduction.

The Sunset group was Janet's first experience working directly with home gardeners. *Sunset* magazine's garden editor, Kathleen Brenzel, an organic home gardener herself, had issued the mandate "to not promote thirsty plants, potentially invasive plants, or plants with high pest problems," which really resonated with Janet. From her organic, home-gardening perspective in Northern California, "it was eye-opening to see how inappropriate the plants developed to sell on a national scale were on a regional scale."

One of Janet's personal goals is "to reassure home gardeners that they can be doing the right thing, be ecologically sensitive, and still have the lush, green garden they want. I want people to have beautiful gardens—we in the horticultural industry have often failed them by not giving them the right tools, information, support, or knowledge to be successful in their gardens. That's at the root for me—how can I find plants on a global scale that are appropriate regionally and will be better choices than what the big garden centers are offering?"

For the Sunset Collection, Janet selects plants for the thirteen Western states. She works with a small group of "wonderful women," who are gardeners, garden writers, and garden designers in other markets and climates. These women trial potential plants and send her input from their locales—and their information is vital to the success of Janet's plant introductions across the region.

Genetically modified (GMO) plants and pesticides are high on Janet's mind in her work. She doesn't object to GMO plants on principle, "but it's a mixed bag—some have potential good (salt water infiltration resistance, for example), as well as the potential to cause real damage to larger environments." For her, it depends on how companies are using these technologies and why. "We spend a lot of time talking about the negatives of GMOs, which are very real, but there are positives as well, worth controlling for."

As an organic grower, her position is, "I don't grow or select plants that tend toward pest issues. I look for plants that aren't troublesome and meet our mission for this western collection." Introductions under Janet's direction include Chef's Choice® rosemary (*Rosemary officinalis* PP18192), Clarity Blue™ dianella (*Dianella revoluta* 'Allyn-Citation' PP22965), and Platinum Beauty™ lomandra (*Lomandra longifolia* 'Roma13' PP25962).

Almost all plants in Janet's collections are patented or trademarked. Personally and professionally, she believes in plant patents. "I see firsthand how hard a lot of these plant breeders (who are often backyard gardeners with a passion and who do this on the side) work, and how much money they invest to do it. And there's just no way to protect and monetize their investment without a patent. You can't get a patent unless you can prove the plant's history of being bred and selected and that it's truly unique and different from a species plant. But in order to support innovation and develop plants for evolving circumstances like disease, pests, and drought, we need to be able to protect breeders' work."

After more than twenty-five years in the business, Janet still considers herself a plant geek at heart. She still gets a thrill when she sees a new plant that intrigues her, and she still loves working with fellow plant-geek breeders whose work is often deeply personal.

OTHER INSPIRING WOMEN

◆ Kathleen Norris Brenzel, American plantswoman, garden writer, and editor; garden editor at *Sunset* magazine from 1982 to 2015. "My mother referred to *Sunset* all the time and it was always in the house. She learned about California gardening from those pages. Kathy had a strong ethos on the gardening complement in the magazine and was always on the forefront of trends we see widely embraced now: drip irrigation, succulents, summer-dry plants, mulching. While these all seem rudimentary now, Kathy was writing about and promoting these best practices in *Sunset* way before they were popular. She changed the way we garden in the West for the better."

Lauren
Springer

HER WORK Plantswoman, garden designer, author, Fort Collins, Colorado

HER PLANT "Eastern pasqueflower (*Pulsatilla patens*). It's slender yet tenacious, a pioneer in harsh places. It's the first to bloom and looks vulnerable and soft but survives difficult conditions and manages to grow and thrive. It will be gloriously full of furry flowers and pollen all there by itself, helping hungry ants and bees at the crossroads between winter and spring, with maybe a few of its seedlings alongside for company, on a hillside with no one watching but grass and rocks."

HER PLANT JOURNEY In the United States, plant research, design, and communication can feel very bicoastal and urban, as though everything is coming down to the rest of us from San Francisco, Los Angeles, Seattle, Philadelphia, or New York. But plants are beautifully served locally and regionally as well. In any region, you can find plantspeople of all levels working to address the needs of their region very specifically.

Lauren Springer is one such regionally based, globally knowledgeable plantswoman. Her plant research, plant introductions, garden writing, and design across the Intermountain West continue to bring attention to the tough, resilient, and beautiful plants of her climate and the need for regionally adapted gardening and designs. Through the course of her more than thirty-year career, Lauren has introduced between fifty and sixty new plants to the trade in the Rocky Mountains and at least six to the wider nursery world, including *Salvia* 'Ultra Violet' and *Oenothera* 'Shimmer'.

Her books address and expand on possibilities for beautiful, year-round, ornamental gardens in high elevations with cold winters and dry summers. Integral to Lauren's design philosophy was her early awareness and responsiveness to climate change, ecological gardening, and the increasing importance of native and regionally adapted plants for gardens and landscapes.

> **My email address says it all, I'm plantmom. Family and friends, home and land, hometown and state, region and country, they are my support and I would protect them with my life, but what makes me *me* is my work with plants**

Born and raised near Philadelphia, Lauren has been a plant and nature person since birth. These aspects of her person are "by and large innate. My first memory, preverbal, is of warm sun on my back, damp earth on hands and knees, and a sea of blue, starry flowers at eye level." She spent her formative childhood years "in the Philadelphia woods, around the patches and washes of naturalized bulbs in the old neighborhoods, parks, and graveyards where I grew up, and the meadows and alpine fell-fields of my Austrian summer vacations." Her parents were central European, and the family spent many summers exploring the wild landscapes of the Alps. They also spoke German at home—Lauren's first word was "doodie," an attempt to say *blume*, which is German for flower.

After receiving her master's degree in horticulture at Pennsylvania State University, Lauren worked as a propagator, cut-flower grower, and professional gardener on the East Coast, including "three years at Chanticleer, as one of the first trained horticulturists hired to help the once-private estate transition into a public garden." Her work took her to New York City, Ireland, England, and finally to Colorado's Front Range in the late 1980s. There, she became involved with the Denver Botanic Garden (DBG) and began writing a garden column for the *Denver Post*. In 1994, she published her first book, *The Undaunted Garden*, which highlighted in lush photographs her planting style, climate attunement, and extensive plant knowledge.

While continuing to teach, design residential gardens, and write, Lauren invested a great deal of time into her own home gardens in the Fort Collins area. Each of her zone 4–5, 5000- to 6500-foot-elevation home gardens were laboratories for her plant trials and introductions—their layouts, layered planting palettes, and sublime native and regionally adapted herbaceous perennials, woody shrubs, bulbs, and grass combinations showed the rich and beautiful potential of gardens in such challenging environments. The success of *The Undaunted Garden* surprised both Lauren and her publisher—success due, in part, to the public's hunger for regional information and amazement at her home gardens showcased in the photography. "I made gardens like no one had seen or thought possible in this climate, and with plants that no one was growing. So I was a pioneer without knowing it."

After *The Undaunted Garden*, she became more involved in public garden design, collaborating on plant selections and designs for High Country Gardens in Santa Fe, New Mexico, designing five garden spaces at the DBG, and creating the cottage garden at Hudson Gardens, a public garden in Littleton, Colorado. She also gained experience in propagating while working for Laporte Avenue Nursery, a specialty native and alpine plant nursery in Fort Collins.

In 2013, Michelle Provaznik, director of the Gardens on Spring Creek in Fort Collins, hired Lauren to create and manage a .75-acre garden space along with propagation and other design work. It is named The Undaunted Garden, "same as my flagship book, to call to mind the challenges of our climate and soils and how beautiful, sustainable, and wildlife-friendly gardens can be made with the right plants, design, and approaches."

Though she's had a long, successful career, the Spring Creek project holds a special place in Lauren's heart. She explains, "I've designed several public garden spaces over the years, but I've never been hired to also care for them, edit them, help them change and develop over time. I'm a physical person who likes to do and make things and be outside and experience nature and the elements. So now I get to do what I do best and love best and share it with people in the town I've loved and called home since my twenties."

In addition to *The Undaunted Garden,* Lauren's books include *Passionate Gardening* (2000), cowritten with plantsman Rob Proctor, and her most recent titles, *Plant-Driven Design* (2008) and *Waterwise Plants for Sustainable Gardens* (2011), both cowritten with her husband, plantsman Scott Ogden.

OTHER INSPIRING WOMEN

- Beth Chatto (1923–2018), English plantswoman and gardener. "In her book *The Dry Garden,* her 'right plant in right place and soil' mantra spoke loud and clear to me as a young woman, and her attraction to the flora of dry places parallels mine."
- Joellyn Duesberry (1944–2016), American-landscape oil painter. "Joly was a close friend and influenced me and my work on a deep level. We connected through our singular drive and shared finding our inspiration in nature and living most of our lives outdoors."
- Nurserywomen. "Karen Lehrer, Deborah Whigham, Katherine Tracey, Gail Haggard, Annie Hayes, Kim Hawks, and Ellen Hornig stand out for me. Their work is hard, and pay often scant, and they are, for the most part, barely known. They live their passion."

Lauren's native prairie garden design at the DBG's Chatfield site is full of drought-tolerant, colorful native and climate-adapted prairie perennials.

Gwen Stauffer

HER WORK CEO, Ganna Walska Lotusland, Montecito, California

HER LANDSCAPE "Lotusland. I know that sounds too easy, but I fell in love with this garden when I saw it for the first time in the 1990s. I dreamed of it after that—always wanted to work here. Now I do—a dream come true! I am in as much love with it now as I was then. I am constantly inspired by it. It feeds my soul. And, there is something very spiritual about this garden—visitors who are open to that receive it unquestionably."

HER PLANT JOURNEY Ganna Walska Lotusland is a thirty-seven–acre garden with a 130-year history. Private for most of those years, Lotusland opened to the public in 1993, and it was conceived in something close to its current form by the dashing and idiosyncratic Madame Ganna Walska, who was born in Poland in 1887. Ganna, who had studied singing and performed and lived as a socialite around the world, was looking for her purpose in life when she purchased the estate in 1941 with her sixth and final husband, Theos Bernard. They named the house and garden Tibetland, and when they were divorced in 1946, Ganna renamed it Lotusland and spent the remaining forty years of her life designing, building, and working in her very personal and layered garden.

Currently, Lotusland is comprised of twenty-one individual gardens, including a newly renovated Japanese Garden, Succulent Garden, the famed Blue Garden, Cactus Garden, and Insectary Garden. In total, Lotusland is home to more than 3000 different plants from around the world, including 208 different plant families and 3286 distinct taxa. Ganna Walska died in 1984, leaving the estate to the Ganna Walska Foundation. In 1990, the Garden Conservancy Advisory Committee voted to accept Lotusland as their "second sponsored garden," the first having been the Ruth Bancroft Garden in Walnut Creek,

California. In 1993, after receiving a conditional use permit from Santa Barbara County, Lotusland opened to the public.

Today, Gwen Stauffer serves as the garden's CEO, and in her words, public gardens of all kinds "need to be leaders—aside from being sanctuaries for communities, we have a role to play in the advocacy of larger issues. Just by virtue of having important plant collections, we need to play a role in their conservation, to have a position on climate change, collaborate with community and research science with our talents, skills, and shared germplasm. We have a role to play in teaching and inspiring our communities."

A woman-created and now woman-directed garden, Lotusland illustrates some of the many intricacies and variations on what it means to be a public garden in the twenty-first century. Gwen's position daily navigates and illustrates the conundrums and joys of public garden administration. Encompassing the artistry and heartfelt personal intent of a private garden, accessibility throughout the gardens is slowly being brought up to ADA standards.

The historic garden has been successfully conserved, but has to operate within tight restrictions of the county's conditional use permit. The garden can only be open for nine months a year, four days a week, with a maximum of 200 visitors or 35 cars a day, whichever comes first. It has to work to sustain funding as a nonprofit without full endowment for the kinds of upgrades, repairs, and maintenance that are needed. With only 15,000 visitors allowed each year, Gwen is constantly trying to balance being of community service, funding the work, and not lapsing into being exclusive to a wealthy few. One of the hopes of Lotusland is to be "renowned globally, treasured locally."

Gwen came to Lotusland in 2008 with a background that seemed almost custom made for its challenges. She was born in Fleetwood, Pennsylvania, a small, rural town. Her earliest childhood memories include plants, such as "red tulips with black-star centers. Bleeding hearts that looked just like the name, but when pulled apart looked like fairy slippers. Bridal wreath—looking just like that in spring, when brides married. Climbing a big Baldwin apple tree—best apples ever. A lilac by the dining room window, blooming just about the time it was nice enough to open the windows, and then the fragrance wafted into the house. My father loved to garden—we had a huge vegetable garden that fed our large family, and we all had to work in it every day." They gardened organically and lived "a stone's throw from the Rodale research farms" and many other gardens and farms, including Longwood Gardens—"like magic to me, especially the conservatories."

As a teen, Gwen realized she "wanted to be in a job outdoors, in nature," so she worked toward degrees in everything from ornamental horticulture and landscape design to public horticulture leadership and administration. She worked as a professional gardener in commercial and public gardens and later served as a director of several public outdoor spaces, including the historic Hillwood Museum and Gardens in Washington, DC, and Callaway in Pine Mountain, Georgia, where she "learned a lot about ecological management, prescribed burns, stream-bank restoration, and deer management." Gwen became the New England Wild Flower Society's executive director in 2005, but when she was recruited by Lotusland, it was a dream realized.

> I love the science of conservation, I love the culture of plants, I love garden history, but I really love the combination of art and science that makes gardening so fulfilling

She started in 2008 and was immediately faced with the Great Recession and, soon after, the garden gaining its not-for-profit status. Of her dream job, Gwen says, "The specific duties of my current daily work as CEO of Ganna Walska Lotusland generally are not plant related. That said, my entire purpose is plant related, in that my work is to ensure that this amazing garden and its plant collections are sustained in perpetuity. The complexities of layers exist all over Lotusland, but I love the whole mess of it—the research, planning, strategy, design, layout in the field, construction, weekly progress meetings, fundraising, leadership." It may not be what she envisioned as a teen, but Gwen is very clear: "This is where I have the most joy, the most to give, and the most to grow from."

The Lotus Garden with its pool house in the background.

OTHER INSPIRING WOMEN

◆ Rachel Carson (1907–1964), American biologist and ecological writer and advocate. "She was a keen observer, and there is so much to be learned from just observing. To be a good plantsperson and gardener, one must be observant and wondering. And, to my philosophy, plants and gardens are to be shared. I also admire how Rachel Carson, as a woman in a field dominated by men, gracefully became a strong advocate for Earth and made a call to action to save it—she was unafraid of controversy because her convictions were more powerful."

◆ Marian Cruger Coffin (1876–1957), American landscape architect. "She was persistent in her desire to seek a career in landscape architecture, despite it being a male-dominated field and deeply prejudiced against women, forcing her to set up her own practice. She was one of the first American women to work as a professional landscape architect and created some of the most famous historic landscapes in the United States. She was a true pioneer for women in the field of gardening and garden design."

Amy Stewart

HER WORK Writer, author, and artist, Portland, Oregon

HER LANDSCAPE "The plants as they change through the seasons in Portland's Washington Park, where I have appointed myself artist-in-residence."

HER PLANT JOURNEY We don't always expand our terrain intellectually or physically from within—sometimes it takes the insight and perspective of an outsider to see beyond our preconceived horizons. Not everyone expanding the plant world will identify as a gardener, plantsperson, or botanist. Amy Stewart is a writer. She loves plants, but she says, "My thing is not gardening—my thing is books, and six of them just happen to be about plants and natural science, and also about global commerce and poisons and cocktails and whatever else I can sneak in there." She writes about people and their interesting human stories, but her writing has intersected meaningfully with the plant world during her eighteen-year writing, teaching, and public-speaking career. Beyond her books, she has helped catalyze change in the horticultural world through the energetically irreverent *GardenRant* blog platform, which injected the field with some much needed (often female) sarcasm and deep critique of its precious and often-elitist posture.

In her twenties, with a master's degree in urban planning, Amy, a fifth-generation Texan living in Austin, thought there must be more to the world. After she and her husband moved to Santa Cruz, California, she discovered what it was—the lush garden climate captured Amy's imagination, and she took on creating her own garden around their house. Her first book, *From the Ground Up* (2001), started as a weekly column in a feminist newspaper in Santa Cruz. At that point in her life, gardening was what she loved, so that's what she wrote about.

Her second book, *The Earth Moved* (2004), completed after she and her husband moved to Eureka, California, on the remote Northern California coast,

showcased Amy's research skills and personal-interview reporting style, integrating complex ideas about earthworms across narrative nonfiction storylines, a skill that would really shine in her third book, *Flower Confidential* (2007).

In *Flower Confidential*, Amy tells the stories of several interesting flower breeders, growers, and suppliers around the world. Through these stories, she brings to light the detrimental economic, cultural, and environmental costs of the industry. The book raised the bar on what the public expected out of garden writers. The resulting cultural conversation opened the door for changes in how flowers are bought and grown in the United States. *Flower Confidential* bolstered organic gardening and supported the introduction and success of the subsequent Slow Flowers and Flower Farming movements.

In 2006, Amy cofounded *GardenRant* with garden writers Susan Harris and Michele Owens and later, Elizabeth Licata. For its tenth anniversary, Amy describes the new undertaking as "a modest little idea we had to stage as a horticultural revolt. We were tired of what the mainstream gardening media had to offer—warmed-over garden tips, repurposed press releases about the ten thousandth new coleus on the market, dull little essays about the wonders of spring—and we were convinced that bloggers could overthrow the gardening establishment. Like all good revolutionaries, we began by writing a manifesto."

The manifesto began "We are convinced that gardening *matters*." To Amy, it was critical that for gardening to matter, gardeners had to "get out of the lifestyle section and as far away from home decorating as possible. We're talking about how we interact with the plant kingdom, not how to choose a throw pillow. This shit is important! We're flabbergasted at the idea of 'no maintenance' gardens. Gardening is something you *do*. It's not something you buy and arrange around the exterior of your home in between fluffing the aforementioned throw pillows."

GardenRant was a compelling twist in gardening conversations that leveraged the new powers of the socially connected digital world to disrupt the gardening-as-consumerism model. Amy describes the beginning, recalling, "You could not say things critical of a company, or anything like 'I f***ing hate nandinas and they should be banned.' It was so boring." *GardenRant* opened doors in garden communication and addressed a blindspot for plantspeople that needed attention.

Amy followed up *Flower Confidential* with the best-selling *Wicked Plants: The Weed that Killed Lincoln's Mother and Other Botanical Atrocities* (2009), *Wicked Bugs: The Louse that Conquered Napolean's Army and Other Diabolical Insects* (2011), and *The Drunken Botanist: The Plants that Create the World's Great Drinks*, (2013).

She and her husband moved to Portland, Oregon, and, in 2018, she tapped into her background as a visual artist and took up a botanically themed project. "I live just a block from Portland's magnificent 410-acre Washington Park, and I've decided to appoint myself Washington Park's artist-in-residence for the year. A self-appointed artist's residency turns out to be the best kind: there's no application process, and my only duties are to walk through the park when the mood hits me, and to sketch and watercolor what I see."

> "Get us out of the lifestyle section and as far away from home decorating as possible. We're talking about how we interact with the plant kingdom, not how to choose a throw pillow"

"I've always thought of myself as telling human stories that just happen to intersect with the natural world. We in the plant world have important contributions to make, and it's not just breeding a prettier flower. Climate change, agriculture, and the development of new medicines are all fundamentally plant-related problems that we can solve if we put aside our differences and work together."

OTHER INSPIRING WOMEN

- Sue Hubbell (1935–2018), American writer. "Sue was the nature writer I admired most when I started. Her books *A Country Year: Living the Questions* (1986) and *A Book of Bees: And How to Keep Them* (1988) were so inspirational to me. I still use passages from those books when I teach writing."
- Hope Jahren, American geochemist and geobiologist, University of Oslo, Norway. "I admire her for writing about plant science in such an honest, funny way."
- Debra Prinzing, founder of the Slow Flowers movement. "She's really devoted herself to the cause of American-grown flowers and a more seasonal approach to flowers, and I think it's amazing what one woman can accomplish when she puts her mind to it!"

Claire Takacs

HER WORK Photographer, Victoria, Australia

HER LANDSCAPE "The garden that has beautiful landscape behind it and transitions into it."

HER PLANT JOURNEY Light and its qualities vary with geography, geology, climate, and surrounding elements, natural or built, and each place in this world has its own quality of light—London is very different than Santa Fe, Kyoto very different than the Austrian Alps. The light off the Northern California coast is, to the trained eye, different than that of the Maine coast.

All photographers rely on light—the quality, intensity, and angle—to see and create their images. And the different ways in which photographers use light is often unique to them. Claire Takacs (pronounced tac-ash), an Australian garden photographer who grew up "surrounded by tall eucalyptus forests and lush gardens" in the Dandenongs, a set of low mountain ranges in Victoria, Australia, writes, "I use light to help capture the beauty in gardens. I was initially drawn to painting landscapes, then later to photographing landscapes and travel scenes. This brought my attention to light and the difference it makes to the atmosphere of a place,"

Raised immersed in the native flora and gardened environments of southeastern Australia, Claire's visual sensitivities evolved to create bright, light-filled works, which have expanded the viewing audience for what were once outlying regions and climates, where great gardens are created and tended with their unique plant palettes, vistas, and specific qualities of light.

After starting her garden photography career in Australia in the early 2000s, Claire traveled the world photographing gardens for international publications, including magazines in Australia, the United Kingdom (she is a

"Gardens are works of art with ever-increasing importance and potential in our daily lives"

regular contributor to *Gardens Illustrated*), and the United States. Her books include *Dreamscapes* (2017), which chronicles seventy of her favorite gardens around the world, including fifteen Australian and three New Zealand gardens; *Australian Dreamscapes* (2018), with its in-depth images of Australian gardens and designers; and the upcoming *The Gardens at Windcliff*, for which she spent a year documenting plantsman Dan Hinkley's Washington State garden.

When she was growing up, Claire's family valued the outdoors and their own one-acre garden, "with old azaleas and tall eucalyptus trees." Her Hungarian father and English mother took her and her brothers camping and traveling to see countryside and gardens in Australia and England. Family trips to England and Europe between the ages of nine and fifteen introduced Claire to

Hilldale, New South Wales, Australia—bright light and layered plantings.

very different environments than in Australia. "Touring and visiting beautiful English gardens really opened my eyes to the world and also to gardens at a young age." Her combined travels left her "blown away by all I'd seen, and this planted the seed for wanting to explore the world."

Even as a teenager, Claire knew she wanted to work outdoors and with nature, but she couldn't see her path for some time. She began instead by earning her bachelor of science in environmental science, and after graduation she "bought a one-way ticket to London" and spent two years exploring Europe with a great sense of freedom. She was very interested in painting and took art courses throughout her education, but became increasingly interested in photography on her travels. Inspired, she returned to Australia at twenty-six and enrolled in a two-year photography course. Around this time, she also had her own garden and "became obsessed with plants, loading up my car almost every weekend with a new haul from the local market or nursery and taking great pleasure in planting them and watching them grow." She would often work "late hours, in the rain, and all weather," which, these days, helps her empathize with the gardeners whose creations she photographs.

She knew she'd found her place in life when, during her photography course, she had the opportunity to photograph Cloudehill, "a stunning garden in The Dandenongs. This garden was ten minutes from where I'd grown up, but I'd never seen it. Garden owner and creator Jeremy Francis had two long double borders, with tall eucalyptus stands at the rear. It blew me away." The next morning, with permission, Claire jumped the fence at 5 a.m. to photograph the garden. "I had a definite realization that there was great and fleeting beauty here and no one capturing it. It was my first experience of having a garden all to myself. Watching the light come up into it and pass through it at sunrise, I was so inspired by the beauty I saw. It completely changed my life, and I became very determined. Jeremy Francis's openness and willingness to share his garden was also formative."

Upon completing her photography course, Claire returned to the United Kingdom for another year or two to give herself "something of a practical education in gardens by traveling across the UK, stopping to see as many National Trust properties as I could." At that time, "I could just walk onto most properties at sunrise and have the garden to myself," cementing "the compelling immediacy of photography" and the power of light in the landscape.

"I often see gardens as works of art, and they're constantly changing. So, their beauty and moments are ephemeral. I love this, and I think it's worth capturing the best gardens as moments in time, to record these extraordinary places to which people devote so much of themselves and their lives. Gardens are hugely inspirational, especially when they are created from the heart and show excellence in design and a sensitivity to place. They connect us to nature and ourselves. Most gardeners I meet care deeply about their environment and want to do as much as they can, not only to beautify, but also to create habitats for all the life they support."

Hummelo, Piet Oudolf's famous garden and nursery in the Netherlands.

OTHER INSPIRING WOMEN

- Marianne Majerus, garden photographer, 2018 European Garden Photographer of the Year. "I love Marianne's use of light and admire her massive body of work over many years."
- Georgina Reid, Australian gardener and garden writer; founder of *The Planthunter*, an online garden forum based in Australia
- Carolyn Robinson, Australian garden designer. "Her New South Wales home garden, Eagles Bluff, celebrates the climate and natural aesthetic. Her plantings include a remarkably wide range of the native flora of her region."
- Sarah Ryan, Australian garden designer and nurserywoman; owner of Hillandale Garden and Nursery, Yetholme, New South Wales
- Sally Johansson, Tasmanian gardener and nursery owner. "Hugely inspirational and beautiful garden in the foothills of Mount Wellington, just outside Hobart. Sally was initially a florist, and has that magic touch with plants, so her garden is completely alive with a highly biodiverse selection of interesting and rare perennials and native species, all happily intermingling in a gorgeous setting."

Tessa Traeger

HER WORK Photographer, North Devon and London, England

HER LANDSCAPE "Our own twenty-five acres bordering on the River Torridge in North Devon. A large part of this is woodland and the rest is grazing and wild-flower meadows. We treasure all our trees, and I spend much time photographing them and getting to know them. There is a great mixture of rare Victorian hero trees and local classic trees such as groups of ash trees 100 feet high, huge horse chestnuts, sycamores, and beeches, all about 200 years old, and then the ancient oak trees, much older. We've created an uninterrupted sheet of bluebells in one of our woods by cutting back brambles and scrub. There we have built a little hut where we can sit and enjoy their sweet scent and the buzzing of the wild bees."

HER PLANT JOURNEY Among garden, landscape, and landscape architecture photographers, Tessa Traeger represents a line of photography that focuses as much on plantspeople as on their plants and created spaces. She is known for her in-depth photographic monographs on individual regions or landscapes. Her career reached a new height at the turn of the millennium when she was commissioned by England's National Portrait Gallery to make portraits of the United Kingdom's fifty leading horticulturists and their gardens. The resulting book and touring exhibition is called *A Gardener's Labyrinth*. This group of portraits is the first in the British National Portrait Gallery collection specifically commissioned to honor horticulturists and plantspeople.

> "Photographing a garden is a form of contemplation. It requires total concentration, observation, and waiting. It takes you into the essence of the place before you"

Tessa's subsequent work includes the books *Voices of the Vivarais* (2010), which highlights the traditions of the farmers of the Ardèche region of France; *Fern Verrow* (2015), an in-depth history and cookbook of the working biodynamic farm; and *The Loveliest Valley* (2016), a monograph of a private garden in Sussex.

Tessa grew up in a small country village near Guildford, Surrey. The first seven years of her life were dominated by the realities of World War II. Nevertheless, she was brought up with an early love of plants and science. "My uncle, who was a teacher, told my mother I had a natural affinity for plants and should be given a plot in the garden to experiment with. She gave me a shady part of the garden, which was bare, and to her astonishment, I brought it all alive with shade-loving plants begged or borrowed from the neighbors. At my girls' school in Guildford we had an annual all-school competition called 'First Finds' and we competed fiercely to find the first primrose or coltsfoot to appear, sometimes as early as January. I was familiar with plant names from an early age."

Her family history is rich with fine artists—"My grandmother was a painter, my mother was a painter, my sister went to school to be a painter and a fabric designer, and my brother studied architecture"—but Tessa decided at age thirteen that she wasn't going to be a painter. Instead, she was going to combine her love of art, science, and math by pursuing photography (at that point still a highly technical profession, because of the expertise it took to operate the large-format cameras and printing equipment and develop the images in a darkroom). She followed her older sister to the Guildford School of Art and Photography, and it was here she started making the collages of plant images that would help to launch her career. She started as a freelance photographer, and in 1962, one of her plant collages was used as the cover image of Britain's popular *Tatler* magazine. From 1975 to 1991, Tessa worked on a food series for *Vogue* magazine, for which she "made many collages of vegetables and flowers." Her

Landscape portrait of wisteria and historic garden folly.

well-known "vegetable collage of Monet's Bridge," from 1989, was on exhibit in London in 2018 "to celebrate fifty years of the Association of Photographers."

During her training and early freelance years, Tessa spent a lot of her free time photographing open National Garden Scheme gardens for pleasure, while most of her early professional work was of food. As she deepened into her plant work and collaborated on book projects like *Voices of the Vivarais*, her portraits of landscapes and people working the land took on strength of character. She became known for her sharply detailed, monochromatic, and black-and-white portraits of proudly weatherworn, calloused land-working hands and faces.

When the National Portrait Gallery commissioned Tessa to take portraits of horticulturists, they also commissioned her husband, Patrick Kinmonth, to write the accompanying text. Tessa and Patrick were provided with a starter list of horticulturists, garden owners, and high-end designers, but their additions expanded those represented to include plantspeople from all the British Isles, including Ireland, Scotland, and Wales, and they added artists such as Ian Hamilton Finlay and Charles Jencks, as well as working head gardeners. From 2000 to 2003, Tessa and Patrick "went from one sensational garden to the next, meeting and photographing legendary figures in the plant world." For Tessa, "This confirmed our gardens are among the most important parts of our culture."

In 2005, she began to work in digital photography. She has always kept an organized and catalogued library of her analog and digital work, as well as prints, from her long career. After all she has accomplished in the medium, she describes photography simply as "a way of catching a memory of the things we love, which enhances our lives."

The equipment of a career photographer.

OTHER INSPIRING WOMEN

- Valerie Finnis (1924–2006), English gardener and garden photographer
- Miriam Rothschild (1908–2005), British natural scientist. "For her work on wildflowers."
- Isabel Bannerman, British garden designer
- Carol Klein, British gardener and garden writer
- Alys Fowler, English gardener and garden writer. "Her study of and focus on the less-obvious, unnoticed, close-up world of plants and fungus all around us in everyday life is important."

Beth
Tuttle

HER WORK President and CEO, American Horticultural Society, Alexandria, Virginia

HER PLANT "Hollies (*Ilex*) represent foresight and forward thinking, which is the way most people would characterize me. They can be a little prickly, too! On an emotional level, however, the violet remains a symbol of everything I love—beauty, persistence, simplicity, honesty—and its emergence each spring inspires hope and memories of loved ones."

HER PLANT LANDSCAPE The American Horticultural Society (AHS), founded in 1922, is among the longest-standing American organizations dedicated to horticulture. A membership organization, the AHS engages gardeners nationwide through online resources, events, and programs, publishes the bimonthly *American Gardener* magazine, and maintains its headquarters at River Farm, a twenty-five–acre historic site along the Potomac River. River Farm has been the headquarters since 1973 and comprises several distinct gardens, including a creative children's garden, perennial borders, a meadow garden, and more.

After a twenty-five-year career in issues advocacy and the arts, Beth Tuttle took on the role of president of AHS in 2017, "because of the potential for enormous societal benefits if we are able to instill deeper and more diverse kinds of engagement with the plant world and nature all around us. As a national organization that has remained committed to presenting trusted, scientifically based information to educate and inspire gardeners of all kinds, at every life stage and level of ability, AHS is fulfilling an important need." With AHS entering its second century, Beth is "looking forward to transforming the ways in which we communicate with and engage a much broader range of individuals, in order to meet them where they are, with the resources they need, so our vision of America as a nation of gardeners and a land of gardens becomes a reality."

Beth is keenly aware of and actively grappling with issues of diversity and inclusion in the mainstream garden world. The urgent responsibility—and great opportunity—of the AHS right now, as she sees it, is to listen to and learn from all potential audiences, then "to create pathways and inviting experiences to welcome, nurture, and support unleashing the latent power of younger, nonwhite, culturally diverse, and less economically, socially, and physically advantaged people into the realm of active gardening and earth stewardship."

Though she's been at AHS just a short time, Beth engaged in these same concepts in the art world and has learned to always consider the bigger picture. "The questions of whose garden and horticultural narrative/story it is, who is empowered to tell that story, how is that story told, and how does it get acknowledged and then accepted into the canon—who decides it's part of the canon for that matter!?—these are fundamental questions. Gardening is an expressive activity, like art. How we arrive at these questions and answers is being redefined right in front of us, right now, for the better of us all."

Born Mary Elizabeth Tuttle, in Atlanta, Georgia, Beth recalls going, as a young girl with her mother, "into the backyard in search of common spring-blooming dog violets (*Viola riviniana*), which we candied and put on top of 'fairy cakes' for my classmates. The intersection of beauty, flowers, food, wonder, and magic (who knew you could eat flowers?) was incredible. From that time onward, I was hooked."

After graduating from Brown University, Beth went on to work as a nonprofit leader and consultant in the arts and culture sector, including at the Smithsonian's Hirshhorn Museum and Sculpture Garden. She is coauthor of *Magnetic: The Art and Science of Engagement* (2013), which explores the practices of high-performance museums. Throughout her life and career, "being a gardener has been a huge aspect of my personal identity and my primary personal outlet and passion."

As time went on, she "became much more interested in the science and practices that underpin successful gardening." Interested in growing healthy food for her family, she learned about soil pH and pest control. When she and her husband started a big food garden on shared property in the Shenandoah Valley, it fed her "interest in learning about successful varieties, planting times, and techniques. We also began to learn more about the environmental impacts of fertilizers, insecticides, the need to restore riparian buffers and habitats, and other common problems."

> "Every time we're able to create a garden and engage people with some aspect of gardening and plant growing, a host of social and public goods emerge from that"

In her early forties, Beth had two life-changing experiences, both of which inform her leadership of AHS in important ways. With an opportunity to take a year off work, she "seized on that time to take on the considerable task of the Master Gardener training program. At that same time, I had the opportunity to spend three years immersing myself in the work of the TKF Foundation (now known as Nature Sacred). This nonprofit is dedicated to advancing understanding of nature's power to help individuals and communities heal, thrive, and unite in profound ways by supporting the creation of public green spaces that offer a temporary place of sanctuary, encourage reflection, provide solace, and engender peace and well-being. This work marked the first significant time my personal passion for gardening and my professional life were aligned." Her leadership at the AHS marks the second time.

As she helps AHS, and tangentially other mainstream gardening institutions and membership organizations, reinvent themselves for a brighter future, she

sees AHS positively affecting "people at any number of places that are highly relevant to their lives. We are, and need to continue, moving our cultural understanding of gardening and our relationship to plants from nice to necessary. Particularly when we think about the demographic we're striving to represent and reflect right now—gardening is fundamentally an expression of cultural heritage—the way we grow food, what foods, the way we interact with plants."

OTHER INSPIRING WOMEN

- Elizabeth Murray, American artist, author, and photographer. "From twenty-five years working in and photographing Monet's Giverny, she shares her philosophy on plants, nature, spirit, creativity, and connection."
- Holly Shimizu, American horticulturist and educator, executive director of the United States Botanic Garden 2000–2014; AHS board of directors
- Kaifa Anderson-Hall, founder, Inspired Horticultural Services; former program director for Washington Youth Garden
- Katie Stagliano, founder, at age nine, in 2008, of Katie's Krops, in Summerville, South Carolina. "Katie's Krops empowers kids around the country to create vegetable gardens in their communities. The food grown in the gardens is then donated to shelters and people in need."

Facilitating changing environments in horticulture in the United States.

Mégan Twilegar

HER WORK Nurserywoman and designer; owner and founder, Pistils Nursery, Mercantile, and Landscape Design, Portland, Oregon

HER PLANT "Wild onion. There are many species native to our region, and I have fallen in love with all of them. Being bulbs, they have the ability to grow in the leanest, grittiest, and heaviest of soil and, depending on the species, push through the toughest mats of grass to return year after year for eons. For me, they represent flexibility, perseverance, and longevity. As a woman, I aspire to embody these qualities, as I feel they are needed to navigate life. Also, wild onions are caretakers offering us sustenance, as many are medicinal and edible."

HER PLANT JOURNEY "There has been a renaissance of cultivating and collecting houseplants. Folks today want to surround themselves with indoor tropical, semisucculent, and succulent houseplants, creating their own urban jungle within their homes. It is very much an extension of interior design as an expression of living a healthy lifestyle," writes Mégan Twilegar.

Started at the turn of the twenty-first century, Pistils is known as "Portland's specialty plant shop and mercantile." Its founding, iterations, and growth reflect urban nurseries across the country trying to meet the shifting needs of city dwellers who want to connect to nature in an ever-more digitally and technologically connected world. According to statistics, from 2000 to 2018, the percent of the United States population living in urban areas moved from approximately 80 percent to 83 percent. In 1990, the population of Portland was 486,000, and according to the US Census, in 2016 it was just over 632,000. Simultaneously, a wide variety of international research has reported on the importance of time spent in or with nature and plants for quality of life, mental and physical health, and well-being.

> Hands-on, living art

Mégan was born and raised in Boise, Idaho, where she and her family lived in the same house for her first eighteen years of life. She moved to Portland to attend Lewis & Clark College, where she received her bachelor's degree with an emphasis in photography. While in college, she rented an old Victorian farmhouse that she would later go on to buy, and it was this farmhouse, its history, and its quarter acre of land where Mégan became "tied to the soil, and the awareness of plant life and its cyclical nature. It was a very romantic place—a rambling house painted soft purple with pink accents. Cherry, pear, and apple trees and all kinds of dated-yet-dear shrubs planted decades prior adorned the property. It was that humble homestead that grew me into the plantperson I am today." While Mégan had many interests, she wasn't sure of her direction and followed her instinct to work with what she loved and derived satisfaction from—her hands in the soil, growing plants.

She founded Pistils in 2001 with her sister, Amy, who transitioned to other endeavors after being instrumental to the launch. Mégan knew she was in it for the long haul, despite being on the steep side of the learning curve for how to be a businesswoman. As it evolved, Pistils became known as an urban farm store and nursery. It had a large outdoor nursery, for which much of the plant material was propagated organically at a nearby grow site and brought over when it was ready to retail. Mégan recalls, "When we began, I wanted as much soil area as we could get." The business was her life and saw many successes. For example, "We were the catalyst for the backyard chicken movement that hit Portland and many urban cities for a spell."

However, after taking a break from full-time work to have her two children, Mégan realized that Pistils had stagnated slightly in her absence, and she needed to refocus and "breathe new life" into it or get out. She notes this as the turning point when Pistils grew from being not just a personal passion but also a successful business, attuned to people's needs and desires for plants. With the help of a business consultant, she brought in "new people with skills to fill roles that had never been filled before—a retail manager, brand manager, and office administrator. We developed a social media and e-commerce presence," and evaluated every square inch of indoor and outdoor space for functionality and profitability.

Pistils Nursery,
Portland, Oregon

Pistils' staff is now at fifteen and growing. Mégan is proud to offer "good pay, with benefits and raises," and the company is "now known for the plants we carry and curate in the shop." She describes the process of choosing and presenting the specialized wares as making "a lot of sculpture with plants." Pistils offers a wide range of "exotic specimen indoor and outdoor plants, everyday plants, terrariums, urban farm supplies, botanically inspired goods for the home, and locally made wares."

For Mégan, "The dependence on and rampant use of chemicals in the horticulture and floriculture industry" is one of the biggest challenges in her business today. She laments, "While there has been a growing awareness to support a growing organic food movement, there still appears to be a chasm in other areas of plant culture. To me, you cannot separate them." Pistils is conscientious about where they source their plants, and while not all growers are 100 percent organic, once a plant reaches the shop, it's a whole new life for them. Every care is taken to avoid chemical intervention. Mégan's awareness of plant life is deepening in whatever environment surrounds her, "whether it's my garden full of cultivated plants in the city, stumbling upon another native gem I didn't know inhabiting our farm in the Columbia Gorge, or the tropical environs of a trip abroad. This awareness makes my life feel so rich in the sense of belonging to this earth. I feel like the more we are glued to a glass screen, the more we become divorced from ourselves and the natural world around us. We miss so much—I so want folks to find a moment to pause in their day, set aside their Instagram posts, to be present in the now, to connect with something green that actually does need water and care to thrive. And I feel that being the steward of plants affords this opportunity."

The lush solarium at Pistils Nursery.

OTHER INSPIRING WOMEN

- Laura Ingalls Wilder (1867–1957), American writer. "Laura represents someone in touch with the land that raised her, yet ultimately kept her in a state of poverty much of her life. She was very tied to the plants of the Plains—the wild roses, the bluebells, the wildflowers—that came forth each season. It was something she could rely on year after year that gave her life meaning."
- Rachel Carson (1907–1964), American marine biologist and ecologist. "Reading *Silent Spring* in my late twenties had a profound impact. So progressive for her time—advocating for and ultimately seeing through the banning of DDT use in the United States was an enormous victory for our country."

Edwina von Gal

HER WORK Landscape designer; founder, Edwina von Gal + Co; founder, Perfect Earth Project, East Hampton, New York

HER LANDSCAPE "The view of Accabonac Harbor from my house. It's a protected salt marsh so I can't—and wouldn't want to—change a thing. It is incredibly peaceful and beautiful every day, just as it is."

HER PLANT JOURNEY In her long career as a landscape designer, Edwina von Gal has founded two companies: Edwina von Gal + Co, which works around the world designing chemical-free and sustainable landscapes, and the Perfect Earth Project, a nonprofit organization that "seeks to free the world" of chemically-dependent landscapes by raising awareness and educating homeowners and professionals.

While Edwina's personal gardening experiences have always been organically based, it was somewhere mid-career that, as landscape designer to an elite audience, she underwent a revelation about the impact of the gardens she was designing for others—negatively or positively—on the wider natural environment. She then began to ask her clients to think about what chemicals were being used on their plants and to consider switching to toxic-free landscapes.

Born and raised in Brewster, New York, "in an old farmhouse, surrounded by cow pastures and abandoned successional woodlands," her early gardening education was based on "obsessively reading garden catalogues," weeding her father's vegetable garden, and playing in her grandmother's flower borders, as well as "spending endless hours in the sandbox laying out neighborhoods with roads and houses and little gardens."

She spent several college years pursuing biological sciences before marrying and starting a family, when she also "started gardening like a maniac." She grew all the food she could for her daughter, worked at a garden center, "and kept gardening, not knowing that it would become the basis of my future

> "On all of my jobs, one member of the client team is Nature"

281

career." After getting divorced, Edwina was raising her daughter on her own and decided to pursue her love of gardening. She took classes at various places (including the New York Botanical Garden) in garden design, horticulture, and architecture, while earning her living working for a well-known Manhattan real estate developer, Peter Jay Sharp. Her job gave her an incredible "education on the go," including a lot of experience in complex project management and interior and exterior design, and she became known in the company as the "woman to go to for anything related to plants and plantings."

In the late 1980s, Edwina went on an American Society of Landscape Architects tour of New York City's Channel Gardens at Rockefeller Center, and after asking a lot of questions about the site and the plants, she landed a job designing the gardens' rotating, seasonal installations. Her designs, featuring everything from topiaries to gardens planted exclusively with grass, received a lot of press, and she met many gardeners with whom she would later collaborate. In 1984, she launched her own landscape design firm, Edwina von Gal + Co. She grew her portfolio and clientele, from upstate New York to the Hamptons and beyond, through her signature aesthetic of seamless connection between architecture and nature with subtle, plant-based designs.

Awareness of the environmental impacts of gardening came and went and came back again for Edwina. She recalls, "as a young hippie mom, I wouldn't have dreamed of using chemicals on my vegetable garden." But as she transitioned into the world of professional landscapes, and the world moved away from the "hippie organic approach," she focused on design more than maintenance and didn't stop to ask what was happening once she moved on to the next project.

However, the importance of creating totally sustainable landscapes was inevitable. In 2002, Frank Gehry hired her to design a park for the Museum of Biodiversity (Biomuseo) in Panama City, Panama. Immersion in that project, working with the scientists from the Smithsonian Tropical Research Institute, inspired a deep commitment in her to protecting Panama's biodiversity. This led to her cofounding the Azuero Earth Project, an environmental nonprofit devoted to sustainable land use, native-species reforestation, and conservation of the dry forest of Panama's Azuero Peninsula—all without chemical inputs.

Edwina among the flowers.

Soon after, Edwina had what she calls her "dental chair epiphany," when her Long Island dentist asked, "How do I get information on managing my own waterfront property without chemicals?" Water-quality issues were just becoming a big area of concern, and it clicked that her passion for and knowledge of these practices (good ones and bad ones) was just as needed in her own (figurative) backyard as it was in places like Panama.

She began asking her clients if they'd agree to let her look into making their properties chemical free, while keeping them beautiful. After going through contracts and invoices, she realized massive amounts of chemicals were being dumped on her clients' properties without their knowledge or understanding. When she identified the chemicals and their effects on people, pets, and the planet, she realized, "This is *really, really* bad." In 2013, on her sixty-fifth birthday, she officially launched the Perfect Earth Project.

Edwina understands she began her mission by speaking to a highly privileged group of people, but also that they were people in positions to make a real difference. "They are the trendsetters"—if they do it, others will follow. All of her clients were happy to have her explore a sustainable approach, and she reports "their landscapes look more vibrant with the nature-based maintenance." She can't overstate the results and how happy her clients are to know they are chemical free. "The biggest lesson was that it really is not all that difficult, and it doesn't have to cost more."

"My landscape projects have become increasingly focused on native plants and plant communities, and my work with Perfect Earth encourages people to become involved with the care of their properties in a way that changes their connection to nature. I am excited so many people are now interested in learning about the role they can play and how I can help them to do so. I am ever less afraid to let nature and plants make decisions for me."

OTHER INSPIRING WOMEN

- Betsy Barlow Rogers, American landscape designer, preservationist, and city planner. She served as the first administrator for New York City's Central Park and is credited with its revitalization in the 1980s and '90s.
- Lynden Miller, American landscape designer, responsible for the restoration of the public garden spaces in New York's Central Park in the 1980s and '90s under Betsy Barlow Rogers
- Claudia West, American landscape architect
- Penny Lewis, executive director, Ecological Landscape Alliance, Sandown, New Hampshire

Ira
Wallace

HER WORK Worker and owner, Southern Exposure Seed Exchange; cofounder, Harvest Heritage Festival, Monticello, Charlottesville, Virginia

HER LANDSCAPE "The seed garden, my home garden at Acorn Community Farm."

HER PLANT JOURNEY "Heirloom plant varieties allow us to carry the story of the past into the future rather than just throwing away everything and then having to dig around when you run into troubles," says Ira Wallace, gardener, heirloom seed advocate, and educator based in rural Louisa County, Virginia. "I think of my job as introducing gardeners and cooks to the more than 700 varieties of heirloom seeds we offer. Should they then want to join the proud ranks of home-garden and small-farm seed savers, I also teach them how to save their own seeds."

Just like plants, seeds have historic associations, with different climatic, geological, and cultural regions of this world, by virtue of having evolved there or by virtue of having been acculturated and acclimated there over a time. In the world of organic, open-source (nonpatented), heirloom seed research, education, and advocacy, the Southern Exposure Seed Exchange Cooperative (SESE) is a leader. Officially founded in 1982 near Charlottesville, Virginia, by Jeff McCormack and Patty Wallens, SESE was purchased by and moved to the Acorn Community Farm in Mineral, Virginia, in 1999.

Ira Wallace is a founding owner and worker of Acorn Community Farm, a sixty-acre organic farm and intentional community. In many ways, she is the public face of SESE and its seed work. "I work with our network of more than fifty contracted small family farmers who produce much of the seed we offer in the SESE catalogue. I grow and do trials of our vegetable, herb, and flower varieties, evaluate possible new additions to our catalogue, and coordinate our outreach and education."

Ira grew up gardening with her grandmother in Tampa, Florida. "She was an avid home gardener, and I expected to follow in her footsteps, but I never expected it

> "Saving the past for the future"

to become my life's work. She died the year I graduated from high school and my first year at New College. These were the days of desegregation, and New College was virtually all white. I wanted to fit in, so I got together with the 'organic' kids. Together with a couple of other students, we started a small student garden. It felt right, and I knew that gardening was going to have a big role in my life."

After college, Ira and her husband helped found an intentional community in Cedar Grove, North Carolina. "We grew vegetables for ourselves and to sell at the newly organized Carrboro Farmers' Market, where I was first introduced to heirloom vegetables." She also had the opportunity to volunteer at the North Carolina Botanical Garden in Chapel Hill, where she "learned about herb gardening and native plant rescue. The plant rescue and propagation area there was my first real introduction to seed saving." Between North Carolina and Virginia, Ira spent a year living and working on a kibbutz in Israel, and a summer on the largest organic farm in Scandinavia, both experiences solidified her appreciation for community living with shared work and life goals.

In 1984, Ira settled outside of Charlottesville, Virginia, at Twin Oaks Community, and in 1993 she helped found Acorn Community Farm. When the community decided to take on the management of SESE, Ira stepped up "to become a better writer and public speaker, to better tell the stories of the heirloom vegetables and why preserving their seeds and the genetic diversity they represent is important." Her new-and-improved writing skills helped her author *The Timber Press Guide to Vegetable Gardening in the Southeast* (2005), as well as its forthcoming state-specific follow-up guides. And her voice as an advocate for SESE brought her to serve on the boards of several organizations, including the Organic Seed Alliance, Open Source Seed Initiative, and the Virginia Association for Biological Farming, working to support heirloom varieties, breeding of open pollinated varieties, and the use of organic methods in agriculture.

In 2006, inspired by a harvest festival she attended on the West Coast, Ira cofounded the Heritage Harvest Festival at Monticello. She regularly presents at the festival as well as helping organize each year. In 2018, the twelfth annual festival, "hosted by the

Acorn Community Farm seed gardens.

Thomas Jefferson Foundation in partnership with SESE and Seed Savers Exchange, celebrated Jefferson's legacy and the contributions to American cuisine by enslaved workers, while promoting gardening, sustainability, local food, and the preservation of heritage plants."

In the course of her research on seed-saving methods in the American South, she read *Collards: a Southern Tradition from Seed to Table* (2015) by Ed Davis and John Morgan, which galvanized her to help make the most of Davis and Morgan's conservation efforts. Since reading the book, she has "been working to evaluate and make available to gardeners many of the ninety-plus varieties Davis and Morgan collected and deposited in the USDA Seed Bank. Southern Exposure, the Seed Savers Exchange, and Sow True Seeds have set up a website, heirloomcollards.org, to let gardeners know about all these great varieties."

Corn seed for Southern Exposure Seeds.

Among Ira's cultural seed interests are those of the African diaspora—seed collected and saved and shared among people of African descent, many of whom descend from enslaved peoples. Along these lines, Ira is finding, documenting, and collecting "edible gourds, moschato squashes, unusual peanuts grown as vegetables or used in sauces, unusual edible amaranth, and edible celosias." When she has twenty different seeds of the African diaspora, she will develop an identifying indicator for them in the SESE catalogue.

OTHER INSPIRING WOMEN

◆ Diane Ott Whealy, cofounder of Seed Savers Exchange, Decorah, Iowa

◆ Dr. Elaine Solowey, desert ecologist, international expert on arid land agriculture, Kibbutz Ketura, Israel

◆ Rozzana Medina, manager of in vitro culture at Bolivia's National Institute for Agricultural Innovation and Forestry (INIAF) for almost ten years. Her lab stores the entire collection of Bolivian Andean tubers for the Potato Park project, dedicated to the genetic origins of potatoes.

◆ Dr. Jeanine Davis, horticulture extension specialist and researcher with North Carolina State University; author of *Growing and Marketing Ginseng, Goldenseal, and Other Woodland Medicinals* (2014)

Françoise Weeks

HER WORK Floral designer, woodland and botanical couture, Portland, Oregon

HER LANDSCAPE The woodlands of her home neighborhood (and the world)—full of old trees, lichens, mosses, ferns, berries, cones, and other often-overlooked surprising beauty.

HER PLANT JOURNEY Some people teach us how to look, how to really see the natural world, through their photography, their landscape design, their articulation of concepts. Some people, like floral designer Françoise Weeks, teach us to see plants differently. Françoise and her woodland botanical couture tap into a broader—shifting—narrative about what we see as beautiful and valuable. With her often unexpected decorative designs and arrangements, Françoise teaches us to see beyond florals in floral design and appreciate materials such as wood, bark, seedpods, moss, foliage, and anything else naturally textural. Her designs draw a direct line to the natural woodland places of the planet that inspire her.

Born and raised in Belgium, Françoise has always loved flowers because they feed her soul. She came "from a country where flowers are part of everyday life." When her older sister moved to the Pacific Northwest, Françoise visited and fell in love with the beauty of Oregon, relocating to Portland herself at the age of twenty-five.

While she didn't feel herself to be a creative person, she did work part-time at a local family florist in her hometown for a short time before she moved to the United States. Getting to work at 2 a.m. and working until 8 p.m., and with kind guidance by her employers, Françoise learned a great deal about working with flowers and design styles. However, when she arrived in Portland in 1977, floral design culture was not what it was in Europe, and she found red roses, baby's breath, carnations, chrysanthemums, and gladiolus. She decided to wait on working in floral design. For the next twenty years, she worked in a medical lab.

> Designing with the woodlands as my inspiration gave me new eyes for the gifts of Mother Nature all around us

In 1996, she was ready for a new direction, and she started the flower business she'd dreamed of when she first moved to Portland. For seventeen years, she designed flowers for weddings and events. In 2003, she started to teach some classes in her home studio. Then, "a big shift happened in 2007." While working on a photo shoot with a team, "a memory popped in my head: from the time I was six until I was ten, my family would spend a one-month hiking vacation in Switzerland. Every year my parents chose to stay in a different region of the Alps. We'd hike all day, and after lunch, my siblings and I often went to look for a piece of bark, we'd scrape some moss, and pick some wildflowers. We'd place the moss on the bark, and somehow secure the flowers—and give the arrangement to my mom."

The creative director of the shoot told her to "run with the idea." She couldn't find bark at the flower market, but bought a log and decorated it with textures. Photographer Joni Shimabukuro documented the design, and Françoise added some of the photos to her portfolio. Two months later, she had a client—a bride who was getting married at Timberline Lodge on Mount Hood, and her fiancé's name was Woods. "She asked me if I could make 'log arrangements' for the buffet table, and if I could interpret that style for centerpieces." Francoise's woodland design style focused on "textures," which she defines "as anything but flowers: seedpods, buds, succulents, grasses, foliage, bark, acorns, and anything from the forest floor or meadow."

A second shift happened a couple years later, when she saw a picture of a beautiful Parisian dining table, and "each plate was set with a small gift from the hostess, which was a small flower purse. They were all different, and they very much struck my fancy." She experimented "to figure out how to make very light botanical purses for flower girls," until they were part of her regular repertoire and she'd expanded the idea to "bridesmaids and centerpieces for bistro tables." This idea of botanical accessories would quickly snowball to become a signature.

The idea to decorate stiletto heels (something she herself has never worn, she says laughing), was born when she discovered the "fabulous book, *Shoe Fleurs* (2007), by Michel Tcherevkoff, with the most incredible selection of virtual images of botanical shoes and purses." And when photographer Ted Mishima contacted her about a collaboration, "he was interested in botanical headpieces." Botanical jewelry followed, thanks to a student in one of her workshops who showed her a floral ring. Botanical dresses came soon after.

Françoise is very aware her woodland aesthetic, while exquisitely beautiful and interesting to her eye, is not for everyone. But, "when I started to do this style of design, I got new eyes. It allowed me to see things in my surroundings that had been there forever, but I had never noticed. Old trees in my neighborhood—I had never looked at them—I had always been much more interested in looking at flowers in gardens. When I looked beyond flowers and gardens—when I looked up—I saw the ferns, the trees, lichens on the branches. Mosses. All these gifts of Mother Nature that I hadn't noticed."

By 2013, Françoise was teaching workshops around the country as well as at home in Portland. "I had no idea the concept would take off the way it did. Explaining mechanics and techniques to create projects, letting students choose the plant material that 'speaks' to them, and watching how they all interpret what they just learned, makes my heart sing every single time."

She designed her first woodland botanical dress in 2015, "for a bridal shop in Portland. The skirt was overlapping evergreen branches and the top was decorated with hundreds of tiny succulents, tiny pinecones, tiny berries. It looked great in the shop window for a whole month. People in Europe also do fashion shows and botanical couture as art. Like a painting, you don't ask 'What's it for?' It's about creating beauty." Her beautiful arrangements are also featured in the keepsake book, *The Herbal Recipe Keeper* (2019), where they help inspire home herbalists to harness the full healing power of their herbs.

Françoise's curiosity is not ebbing. "The options to design are endless. Discovering new plants and flowers always fuels creativity, and when I go to places where the flora is so vastly different than here in the Pacific Northwest, it is super exciting to make those discoveries and design with a totally different set of plant materials."

OTHER INSPIRING WOMEN

◆ Paula Pryke and Jane Packer, British floral designers. "These two designers and their books were incredibly inspiring to me when I first started my business."

◆ Natasha Lisitsa, American floral designer, Waterlily Pond Design, San Francisco, California. "She is an extraordinary designer who creates magnificent structures and decorates them with botanicals."

◆ Elly Lin, Taiwanese floral designer. "She combines traditional ikebana with international floral design philosophies."

Françoise's woodland couture shoes and handbag.

Claudia West

HER WORK Landscape designer; principal, Phyto Studio, Arlington, Virginia

HER LANDSCAPE "I'm inspired by plants that thrive in sidewalk cracks or on highly contaminated brownfields. I can't help but admire *Solidago canadensis* and *Andropogon virginicus* for their beauty, resilience, adaptability, and function. These are plants that don't need us. I use many of these types of plants in my designs, because I want them to form populations that survive us and our clients."

HER PLANT JOURNEY Claudia West is a passionate advocate for functional and ecological planting design. In the book she coauthored, *Planting in a Post-Wild World* (2015), she wrote, "I don't consider myself a person that fits into one box. By experience and by training, I'm a hybrid of naturalist, horticulturist, plant grower, designer, and land manager. . . . Bringing on board and learning from the ecological sciences, from traditional horticulture, being closely aligned with architecture and plant community science—these all form an understanding of where we fit in and what we need to be thinking about."

Claudia believes that cultivated plantings of all kinds "must be beautiful, inspire, have emotional content, *and* provide high ecological value and function. They must feed and provide habitat for wildlife, clean our air, soak up and purify polluted stormwater runoff, sequester carbon, treat soil contamination, and reduce noise in our cities."

Born and raised on her family's farm in Germany, in the small town of Meerane in Saxony, she grew up planting and "cultivating vegetable gardens, orchard meadows, and species-rich pastures. After the wall that divided East and West Germany came down, my parents started a florist business as well as a design-build landscape firm and niche perennial nursery." She

> Every planting is an opportunity for us to reintroduce more beauty, function, and diversity to our cities to rebuild abundance

The full Phyto Studio team, including landscape architects Thomas and Melissa Rainer.

was surrounded by farmers, planting designers, plant breeders, and nursery growers, who provided her with the foundations of horticulture, planting design, and land management. When, as a young teen, Claudia met family friend Wolfgang Oehme (founding partner of the award-winning firm Oehme, van Sweden Associates in Washington, DC), he became a mentor and helped her secure an internship at Blue Mount Nursery, which specialized in "beautiful and resilient perennials" in Monkton, Maryland.

Throughout her internships and travels, she saw what the American landscape looked like on a large scale. "It was disillusioning—with oceans of mulch and plants placed in solitary confinement, planted from huge container sizes"—a waste of time and resources. She saw how the horticulture industry was making *money*—not better, lusher, denser planting systems. Though she started out "maintaining purely ornamental plantings," including regular "weeding, remulching, dividing, transplanting, enhancement planting, hoeing, and treating planting edges with herbicides," she grew "increasingly uncomfortable with traditional horticulture" and its blind acceptance of using a lot of resources for a "few moments of spectacular color—it just didn't seem ethical." This realization inspired her "to be part of a landscape revolution, to change boring lawns and oceans of mulch into thriving and inspiring plantings humming with life."

She was interested in how plants grow in nature versus how we cultivate them. "East Germany was full of old industrial wastelands, sand quarries, soft coal mines, and mountains of overburden from uranium mines," where she saw "plants pop up on even the most contaminated sites. They had a kind of beauty and resilience seen only in very few gardens. In nature, without any human care at all, plants often grew better than in our gardens. They create lusher and more functional plant communities."

To succeed, Claudia knew she had to understand the field from both the plant and design sides. She returned to Germany and the Technical University of Munich for her master's degree in landscape architecture and regional planning. "Because landscape architecture and environmental planning were taught in the same building, we quickly understood that ecology must be a part of every landscape architecture project. Incorporating principles of wild plant communities into design seemed to be the solution to creating better planting."

After completing the six-year program, Claudia returned to the United States in 2008. She took a position as an ecological sales manager at North Creek Nurseries, which focuses on growing "ecological plants in very small container sizes and plugs. My role was to bridge the gap between the worlds of design, installation, and land management, and grow the market for landscape plugs." She understood that homeowners, landowners, and consumers needed a reeducation on what is beautiful, functional, and emotionally powerful. They needed to be part of "an environmental solution that added beauty, habitat, and ecological function with less cost, less waste, a smaller carbon footprint, and more carbon sequestration."

Having met and worked with landscape architect Thomas Rainer, the two began work in 2013 on writing *Planting in a Post-Wild World*, as a preliminary introduction to, overview of, and plea for more-ecological landscape designs. After the book received critical acclaim, Claudia, Thomas, and his wife and fellow landscape architect, Melissa Rainer, formed Phyto Studio, outside Washington, DC. Their landscape architecture firm has expanded the kinds of projects they take, and with each one they introduce plant-community-based technologies. Claudia truly believes "these are technologies, not a style," and equally useful in "formal, casual, or any other landscape design in between."

"We're on the front lines now—the linking educational and motivational piece that brings together the right nursery source, the right installer, and the right land manager." The team collects observations, outcomes, and a lot of data, such as "species compositions, soil health, water-retaining capability, and cost over time" from each project to understand what's working and what's not working. They're on the road a lot, each "speaking several times a month, trying to inspire other people, from professionals to hobby gardeners, to give this a shot, to continue to change the way we treat land on a much larger scale—and to make this goal mainstream."

Claudia is clear that in the work Phyto Studio is doing, "we are not alone. A whole international team of professionals and hardy gardeners are out there working on different pieces. It's an amazing opportunity to be part of this team trying to contribute to the general knowledge. It can only succeed collectively, and we need more young people and more intelligent brains on board to get this to the next level."

OTHER INSPIRING WOMEN

+ "The most inspiring women in my life are my mother and grandmother—both incredibly strong women who taught me strength, confidence, never to give up smiling, and to be aware of the world around me."
+ Kate Kennen, American landscape architect, Massachusetts. "Her book *Phyto* (2017) is one of the best books about phyto technologies. Her company, Offshoots, specializes in using plants to clean up our environment. Brilliant!"
+ Emma Marris, American environmental journalist. "Her book *Rambunctious Garden: Saving Nature in a Post-Wild World* (2015) is a book everybody should read, emphasizing the importance of urban nature."

Rowen White

HER WORK Seed keeper; founder, Sierra Seeds, Nevada County, California

HER PLANT "Corn Mother. She has been with my people since our creation story, she has helped nourish our people, and she has a very healing spirit that will help us through these times. Sometimes I ask, 'Am I growing the corn, or is she growing me?'"

HER PLANT JOURNEY Seeds "are intimately connected and intertwined with story and lineage, place and people; they illuminate this beautiful coevolutionary dance that humans and plants have been engaged in for millennia," writes Rowen White, a Mohawk woman, mother, and seed keeper.

Rowen's deepest calling and interest lies in "empowering and growing confident seed stewards. Locally adapted seeds are at the foundation of any durable and resilient food system. By growing a network of capable seed stewards, we are making a lasting contribution to seed and food sovereignty," and furthering "true seed literacy" in the world. She fulfills her calling as founder of Sierra Seeds in Nevada County, California, a locally grown seed cooperative and educational resource, as chair of the Seed Savers Exchange, and as a member of the Indigenous Seed Keepers Network (ISKN).

Rowen was born within Akwesasne, a Mohawk community along the St. Lawrence River, "straddling the border between upstate New York and Canada." She "grew up in the embrace of the indigenous community," and her parents "work on legal issues defending indigenous sovereignty, such as land and water rights, including for the Native American Rights Fund and other associated law firms in Colorado."

When she attended Hampshire College in western Massachusetts, Rowen explored ethnobotany, culture, and agriculture at the school's organic farm. "Natural science classes were held on the farm, which functioned as a living

> "Seeds are only the beginning. Every single seed we plant is a tiny, loving prayer in action"

laboratory and classroom." The farm manager, Nancy Hanson, gifted Rowen the responsibility of an heirloom tomato trial project and collection created by a past student. "There were fifty different varieties planted out from all over the world."

Before planting the saved trial seeds, Rowen "read through the seed packets and the Seed Savers Exchange annual yearbook describing the growth, the stories, the places they'd come from," and she had a "cornerstone experience" around seeds as holders of important cultural history and identity. This comprehension was not without inherent conflict. "I think equal to my joy and enthusiasm in learning and opening this new doorway of understanding was this palpable sense of grief and longing. Understanding that as a Mohawk woman, as someone who understands who I am and where I come from, that we are and continue to be agricultural people, and that I had no idea of the foods that fed my ancestors, and no sense of intimacy with or responsibility to them." She made a commitment in both that joy and grief that she "was going to set out on a path to discover the foods of my ancestors and really begin to renew what I eventually found out were the *original agreements* that we had with these plants to take care of them. It is through these relationships with plants and seeds that I'm finding my way home to a deeper understanding of being human."

When Rowen, her husband, and their two young children relocated to Northern California, she was "deeply inspired by the vibrant food and farmer network working to ensure a sense of food security and food sovereignty" in her new region. But after hosting a seed swap and subsequently founding Sierra Seeds, she saw that few people followed that passion "all the way back to the seed and knowing who is taking care of the seed and stewarding it."

With this epiphany, Rowen shifted her direction toward "education around seed literacy and why local seeds are important." As a mentor, educator, and writer, Rowen draws on her deeply "personal perspective, beyond the biological and scientific aspects of seeds—it's imperative for me to talk about the cultural and spiritual and emotional elements of seed." Rowen has seen time and again in her work that when she gets people to "engage the heart, and engage the layers of that spiritual and emotional and cultural connection, it rehydrates their cellular memory, like a dormant seed. We are all bound in a reciprocal relationship with plants and seeds, and that reconnection builds true sustainability into the system." She sees hope in "a great resurgence of indigenous tribes building healthy and resilient food systems as a cornerstone to cultural and ecological renewal programs, as well as a means to reclaim indigenous economies and true economic and political sovereignty."

ISKN is "a formal intertribal group coming together in solidarity around food and seed sovereignty and history," in order to more effectively find funding, share skills, and set priorities. As a group, they "leverage resources for indigenous communities cultivating culturally appropriate solutions to restoring seed stewardship of traditional foods." A 2018 initiative was a "seed sovereignty assessment toolkit to help communities develop a blueprint for creating a seed bank or seed library and training mentors to help guide the process."

ISKN is also involved in seed rematriation. "This is an intentional shift of word choice from repatriation of objects to their tribal origins, because seeds are traditionally the responsibility of women, and it speaks as well of seeds returning to the Mother Earth." The group works with a whole matrix of networks and organizations to see where "seed important to tribal communities might exist outside of their mother communities and to get them back into those communities. As indigenous cultures, we see these seeds as relatives, and new ceremonies have been developed to welcome them back home into the rich soil of our everyday lives."

For the people involved in this work, rematriation is helping to heal "intergenerational trauma and rage." Rowen explains, "When we as indigenous peoples, who continue to be deeply affected by the negative consequences of colonization and acculturation, cultivate trusting relationships with people who have historically been our adversaries, when we lay down those differences and look to the seeds and this work with the seeds, they become a means of reconciliation and reparation."

Selections of heritage seed corn in Rowen's care.

In all of this, Rowen sees a "deeper revolution," one that has capacity to "compost our current food, economic, and justice system. In the long-game approach, staring down industrial food systems and GMOs will take us all reclaiming our responsibilities for our relationships with seeds, plants, food. That reclaiming can be healing—it can be glorious and healing and beautiful and flavorful."

The last of Rowen's family to farm were her "great-great-grandparents. My great-grandparents and grandparents were of the forced boarding school era for indigenous people, who quite literally had their culture and language beaten out of them. I make my life a love poem and an honoring song to them for all they endured, and I make my work a recommitment to not forget them and all they did to make sure that these seeds and foods were still here for me."

OTHER INSPIRING WOMEN

- Mary Arquette, Mohawk seed keeper and mentor
- Vandana Shiva, scientist, ecofeminist, and leader of the seed sovereignty movement in India
- Jessika Greendeer, Ho-Chunk Nation woman and Army veteran, researching connections between post traumatic stress disorder and food, Wisconsin
- Winona LaDuke, environmentalist, activist; executive director of Honor the Earth, an indigenous environmental advocacy organization

Kristen Wickert

HER WORK PhD in plant pathology

HER LANDSCAPE "If I were a landscape, I'd be a desert—able to withstand hard times then be amazingly beautiful and powerful when the going is good."

HER PLANT JOURNEY Doctor Kristen Wickert (Kaydubs to her fans) believes in the power of plant science to help humans navigate toward a future where we know, appreciate, and steward our planet far better than currently. She has felt the magnetic power of plants in her own life and education. She feels called to share this passion, as well as her specific knowledge base, with others. And she sees discrepancies in how most science is valued, and how it's ultimately communicated (or not communicated at all) to the general public.

Bridging this communication gap is as much a part of her passion as is her expertise in forest health and mycology. She has earned thousands of engaged and interested social media "students" with her affable and very informative social media account, @kaydubsthehikingscientist, (featuring her hiking cat, Tabitha), on Instagram. Her dual identity as an academic and a social media communicator makes for a powerful bridge, illustrating how science can be mesmerizingly beautiful and applicable to the quality of people's everyday lives—improving efficacy, economics, and environmental stewardship.

Kristen was born in Lehigh Valley, Pennsylvania, in a "standard suburban home." Her stepfather was a lifelong mentor, and the two spent a lot of time gardening together. At a local community college, she enrolled in a biology course, where they dissected an onion and looked at the onion cells under the microscope. "Something clicked." The onion cells made sense to her, where her previous college courses never got her excited or invoked passion. She knew she had to make a change in her career path but didn't know to what, except that she wanted to be outside interacting with the natural world. Finally, she joined the

> "With adequate knowledge and a lack of ignorance, we can figure anything out and make it better"

@kaydubsthehiking-scientist on the trail with her cat, Tabitha.

Pennsylvania State University forestry program. She recalls being "put on a bus, dropped off at a forest, given a compass, and instructed to find this or that tree, and then complete data sheets about the trees." She loved it.

At Penn State, Kristen unknowingly jump-started her science career by working in an entomology lab. "If I agreed to count insects in a basement for three months, I could go to Greenland for three months, expenses paid. So the adventurous part of me said 'deal.' This experience gave me street cred in the science world." When she returned from Greenland she was offered a position in a plant pathology lab, where she became the "lab jockey who made media, maintained cultures, and did the hard manual labor in the field, like chain-sawing trees and hacking paths through greenbrier."

After graduation, Kristen got a job with the Texas A&M Forest Service out of Houston, doing "traditional timber management, water-resources planning, and urban forestry." In Texas, she took every opportunity she could and "spent a lot of time by myself in the wilderness, doing research and teaching jobs other people didn't want to take." She loved every new habitat, especially Big Bend, a landscape of which she'd had a National Geographic poster on her bedroom wall as a girl, and she went into adventure mode—hiking every trail, "treasure hunting" for all the plants in her field guide, and learning to appreciate all the "wonderful things you can find when you learn to read the landscape." As she got better and better at observing and identifying plants, she realized she "had a special talent and love for little growing things," becoming fully aware of "how much plants mean to me and how that deep love always existed in me without a label."

Ultimately, she got restless for science again and looked into graduate school, working with Dr. Matthew Kasson, a teaching assistant at Penn State when she was an undergraduate student there. He had just been offered a professorship at West Virginia University and wanted her as his first student. Kristen completed her master's degree on the hemlock woolly adelgid, then, based on her experience in controlling tree-of-heaven at Penn State, she accepted a doctoral student position at WVU and completed her PhD in 2019.

Between earning her degrees, Kristen continued her treasure hunting and hiking adventures, covering more than 1000 miles of the Appalachian Trail (AT). She goes long-distance hiking any chance she gets and has nearly completed the AT through long section hikes, aiming to do the same next on the Pacific Crest Trail.

Her doctoral work is mainly focused on a native fungal biocontrol for the invasive tree-of-heaven (*Ailanthus altissima*). She also works intimately with chestnut blight, ambrosia beetles, fungivorous millipedes, and many other insects and plant pathogens. She sees widely applicable prospects in the approaches of this world, and she loves being "able to inspire people to care about nature through sharing results. I love thinking about how, by being a good role model, I can inspire young people to be scientists and care about protecting and respecting nature." She encourages home gardeners, corporate growers, and foresters to be open to ways of managing land without using chemicals and interfering with the land's own processes.

Kristen sees genetic modification as a powerful tool in the quest to manage land sustainably, and believes it will benefit the world in the long run. Though she sees them as the future, she emphasizes that the ethics around GMOS are critical. "It's the job of science to ask the questions: What if X? And if X, what is and why is Y? It's the job of humanity," she believes, "to ask if, or what, we do with what science demonstrates."

Her perspective comes from being both a hard research lab scientist and an educational ecologist addressing a broad audience from the hiking trail on social media. She believes the plant world can help meet the challenges of environmental degradation and has great hope in more and a greater diversity of people "being able to understand how plants and other organisms work together, and how we can harness our intelligence to be proactive."

OTHER INSPIRING WOMEN

- Jane Goodall, researcher who worked with chimpanzees as she studied their habitat and ecology. "She is a great conservationist of botanical habitat."
- Rachel Carson (1907–1964), marine biologist, conservationist, author of *Silent Spring* (1962). "Her efforts to open the everyday person's eyes to the effects of DDT on the ecosystem are truly inspiring."
- Dr. Mary Beth Adams, research soil scientist, US Forest Service. "She studies ecosystem impacts from nutrient deficiencies and clear-cutting tactics. She has more than 150 published scientific articles! As a woman in the male-dominated forestry field, I look up to her determination and expertise."
- Dr. Elizabeth Brantley, associate teaching professor, Pennsylvania State University, Mont Alto. "She is a tough and well-respected professor but a collegial collaborator. She teaches plant pathology, wildfire ecology, and silviculture at an extremely male-dominated, forestry-school branch campus."

Sue Wynn-Jones

HER WORK Plantswoman and plantseeker; cofounder and owner of Crûg Farm Plants, near Caernarfon, Wales

HER LANDSCAPE "I travel between two and four months every year for plant-collecting expeditions, and I love traveling to unusual places, but Crûg Farm and its 200 acres in north Wales is home."

HER PLANT JOURNEY Traditional plant hunting is an area of the plant world that is both historically and currently interesting and controversial, with growing concerns about ethically conserving biodiversity, controlling invasive plants, and cultural appropriation. Sue Wynn-Jones is a notable plant seeker and collector for both passion and purpose. She has been involved in the work since 1990, when she and her husband, Bleddyn Wynn-Jones, founded Crûg Farm Plants.

Over the course of her career, Sue has been party to more than fifty international plant-collecting trips, on which she and Bleddyn collect only for seed or mother-plant propagation material, never for direct commercial sale. Beyond collecting for the nursery's stock, in order to introduce new plants to the horticultural world, Crûg Farm Plants works in partnership with experts from governments as well as botanic gardens in the United Kingdom, Poland, Germany, France, Italy, and Georgia, among others. The specimens Sue helps locate, identify, and grow assist scientific collections to conserve biodiversity, collect data, and establish plants' original locations in the wild. Sue and Bleddyn's work helps answer questions and untangle histories for collections whose provenance has been poorly tracked or lost through crossing/hybridization and many name changes over the past 150 years of global plant collecting and exchange. Increasingly, their collections are instrumental in research and restoration.

Sue was born and raised in Caernarfon, where she and Bleddyn were childhood friends. Her grandmother was a passionate gardener, and Sue spent a lot of time "pottering about in the garden with her." She trained in London for fashion design, then began traveling. On a trip home in 1975, she and Bleddyn met again, and within four days they were living together at Crûg, then a working 200-acre farm.

> "Life is a very rich tapestry"

Bleddyn already had a greater passion for interesting plants than he did for farming. After starting to develop the garden around their home at Crûg, Sue and Bleddyn realized how lacking in interesting plant diversity most nurseries were. They both loved international travel, "going backpacking in India and the like," and they started to look for plants on their journeys. When Bleddyn first suggested starting their own nursery, Sue was reluctant, but they forged ahead, and for the first year, they ran the nursery hand in hand with farming—then the nursery took off, and they "haven't looked back since." Twenty-five acres at Crûg are dedicated to the nursery, trial beds, propagation beds, sales, and the government-sanctioned quarantine unit. Early on, the Wynn-Joneses applied for and received an official ongoing scientific license from the Animal and Plant Health Agency (APHA), of which there are only two such licenses currently held in England and Wales, the other being with the Royal Botanic Gardens, Kew.

When they first began, they did no mail order and were open on-site for only seven months of the year. During the closed winter months, they would travel and collect. "There was no internet, no mobile phone, no GPS, and no ATM! We were in remote and often challenging areas," Sue recalls. Her stories from this time are full of clambering up mountains, traversing large rivers, and avoiding armed people of dubious intention, with no room for being "squeamish about bugs or snakes, and prepared to eat everything from anteater to grasshoppers. All for the love of plants." With the advent of the digital age, they now travel much lighter, with reliable ATMs, cell service, and lightweight polypropylene gear, enjoying the luxury of "searching the internet for information." They now offer on-site sales as well as mail order throughout Europe all year, so Sue especially travels for shorter periods of time.

When describing an expedition, Sue says, "In the main, we go to a spot looking for something quite specific, but are always open to finding new and interesting things as well." They generally collect seed but only enough to grow out from plants with a strong chance of surviving in their climate and propagation-house conditions. "The country in which we're collecting gives all the permissions to collect seed or plants. When we find something new, we write up a paper about the plant and the collection. And everything, seed and knowledge, is shared with the host country."

Any live plants collected in the wild are eventually given to botanic gardens or kept as mother-plant material, but first they go into a period of government-mandated quarantine at the nursery to ensure biosecurity. Any plant deemed to show signs of pests, disease, or invasive tendencies is destroyed. While seeds do not have to be quarantined, they must be washed thoroughly before they are brought into Wales, and they have to be transported separately from any live plants to avoid any cross-contamination.

Sue and Bleddyn have "a devoted following of regular plant-collector buyers," as well as long-term relationships with botanic gardens. They are fully self-financing, and they've never taken on sponsors in order to pay for their collecting, preferring to maintain full control of their collections. They work in a complementary, collaborative partnership. "My strengths are often noticing the less-flashy plants for collection, as well as cleaning of the seed, wrapping of the plants, and a very good artistic eye for putting plants together in combination," says Sue. Over the years "it's been so beneficial to see plants in the wild, getting just what they want in terms of soil, light, community, etc., so we can replicate those conditions. One hosta we collected from Korea grew on very exposed cliffs above the sea, and it was well adapted to this exposure. Most plant people would assume that as a hosta, it would need shelter, but this one needed the exposure to thrive. Going out and collecting, you are always learning. Always."

This happy *Gunnera killipiana* in the Crûg Farm collection originates from Sue and Bleddyn's first trip to Guatemala in 2001.

Sue's early training in fashion has been instrumental in her work with presenting plants at the nursery and in display gardens. She first brought her love of combining colors and textures to the RHS Chelsea Flower Show in 2011, winning a gold medal and a President's Best in Show award. "It was the first time at Chelsea that someone had created a display using entirely plants grown by them, from seed collected by them, in the wild." She has continued to create innovative designs for Chelsea to great effect.

Sue and Bleddyn invest time and plants to help younger plantspeople coming up in the world and believe this succession of knowledge and passion is very important. "My greatest joy is finding something new in the plant world, and the many people we meet in the amazing places we go. We will never be financially rich, but with all my experiences over the years in the plant world, I am rich in many other ways."

OTHER INSPIRING WOMEN

- Ellen Willmott (1858–1934), British horticulturist, gardener, plant collector, and plant collecting patron and sponsor; recipient of a Victoria Medal of Honour from the Royal Horticultural Society, 1897
- Elizabeth Strangman, British plantswoman; owner and founder of the now-closed specialty Washfield Nursery, Kent, known for introducing remarkable hellebores
- Sophie Walker, British garden designer; author of *The Japanese Garden* (2017). In 2014, Walker became the youngest person to design a garden at the RHS Chelsea Flower Show.

Ayana Young

HER WORK Cofounder, executive director, and host, *For the Wild* podcast and projects, coastal redwood mountains near Lost Coast in Northern California

HER LANDSCAPE "It was life changing to be in the temperate rainforest, and the plants that spoke loudest were the bigleaf maple, the cedar, the Doug fir, and one of my closest lovers, devil's club (*Oplopanax horridus*). The scent of devil's club is pure vibrance and strength—it is willpower. It is the magic that the temperate rainforest community makes when it comes together that feeds my spirit. Without the trees, the understory wouldn't survive, without the understory, it would be barren. We need it all."

HER PLANT JOURNEY Ayana Young is cofounder of *For the Wild,* "an anthology of the Anthropocene, focused on land-based protection, coliberation, and intersectional storytelling rooted in a paradigm shift from human supremacy toward deep ecology." She hosts the nonprofit organization's podcast and oversees a team of like-minded individuals engaging in ecological restoration projects, advocacy, and education. Born of grief and hope regarding humanity's relationship with the earth, the *For the Wild* podcast was launched in 2014, and in 2018, the one-hour, weekly production celebrated its hundreth episode.

Ayana grew up in Orange County, California. Her father was a lawyer and her mother was an industrial real estate broker who was proud of her rose garden, gladiolus bulbs, jacaranda tree, and fruit trees she planted on a sloped section of their suburban property. Her mother spoke of her own great-grandmother being able to take a cutting and grow just about anything, and in these histories, Ayana sees the seeds of her own plant love.

By the time Ayana was nine months old, her mother had dedicated herself to Ayana's career as a child actress, working her way from advertising and modeling to television and movies. At the age of eighteen, "disgusted with the entertainment industry's treatment of women and its overall cultural message,"

> "Stand where you love and fight like hell"

Ayana went to college to study art history, religion, and the humanities. She went on to Columbia University in New York City for graduate work in environmental studies, but ultimately dropped out to become an organizer for Occupy Wall Street, a movement started in 2011 and focused on the excesses of the United States stock market and the environmental and human suffering caused by global economic disparity. This was the pivotal moment in Ayana's life, when her own personal definition of success became more clearly centered on being of service to the earth.

In New York, Ayana met March Young, a "homeless artist with blue hair" with whom she spent the next few years unlearning much of what she had believed. The two backpacked around Peru, living in a tent. The experience fed her "hunger for adventure and wild places." Returning to the United States, Ayana and March moved to a "cedar cabin on ten acres of old-growth, redwood forest, which was surrounded by thousands of acres of logging land, in Oregon's Cascadia bioregion."

While in Oregon, Ayana attended the Portland Plant Medicine gathering, where she heard the teachings of herbalist Cascade Anderson Geller. "She was so fierce and fiery and she was talking about protecting the plants. She lit the path that I, too, could actually speak with plants. She was a mentor and elder who opened that door."

Ayana "fell in love with the temperate rain forest." She and March decided to traverse the forests of Oregon, Washington, and British Columbia, collecting mushrooms to sell commercially. Although commercial mushroom hunting opened up its own set of environmental and ethical questions, Ayana "learned more during this time than any other time" in her life. She observed many different forests in different successions and "witnessed immense plant diversity and, likewise, painful lack of diversity; what happens to a river or creek when logging has clear-cut the riparian corridors." All the terms she would later "learn in school for restoration ecology," she was learning in her body.

After the 2011 nuclear disaster at Fukishima, Japan, Ayana was so worried about the "toxification of my beloved places and the earth," that she and March retreated to his parents' Pennsylvania home to sit with their "grief and incubate" next steps. In time, she heard a clear message saying, "Stand where you love and fight like hell." She returned to Cascadia, and the idea of the podcast began "as a way of seeking mentorship and conversing with elders who understood the realities of the world, but were not giving up." She bought a piece of land in the coastal redwoods and mountains near the Lost Coast of Northern California and returned to school for restoration ecology, which, while not a cure-all, was "exciting and a relief to discover a toolbox for beginning tangible work."

The more she studied, though, the more she understood that mainstream "reforestation ecology" is often based on "logging methodology and an extractive industrialization and commercialization of wood, of forests, of timber." Instead, she wants to restore forests "biomimetically, with integrity, in a way that is healing," not in a way that "justifies using oil, poisons, and other destructive techniques in order to plant as many straight, girthy conifers as possible. That's not what's valuable about the forest, and that's not the way to do this work."

Today, Ayana lives on the land with several teammates, and "every day we wake up, research, work with the soil, talk to our community, do the podcast, work on projects like the 1 Million Redwoods, and keep chugging along, really wanting to walk lightly with integrity in this project."

At work on the *For the Wild* podcast.

While she once looked to her academic education for direction, what directs her now is the joy of "watching the creeks and rivers swell in a big rainstorm and rush with force and vigor; watching the leaves turn in autumn and seeing that incredibly colorful transition into winter; smelling the manzanita and mountain jasmine blossoms and picking off the cream-colored flowers and eating them."

At the heart of *For the Wild* are the critically important questions Ayana asks herself and her community, her guests (ranging from philosophers and indigenous elders to writers and artists and environmental thinkers), and her listeners to ask of themselves, "How did I/we get here? How am I complicit in the system?" She recognizes that "complicity is what makes my life's work harder. Only in seeing my complicity can I creatively figure a way out, in community with people from different backgrounds and perspectives."

OTHER INSPIRING WOMEN

- M. Kat Anderson, researcher, Department of Plant Sciences, University of California, Davis; author of *Tending the Wild: Native American Knowledge and the Management of California's Natural Resources* (2013). "Reading her work changed my whole concept of humans; learning we could be ecosystem engineers toward more biodiversity and abundance."

- Diana Beresford-Kroeger, Irish botanist, medical biochemist, and writer; author of *Arboretum America: A Philosophy of the Forest* (2003). "She was able to give away 750,000 seedlings. It inspired me to know that I could do that, too. She really was a catalyst for me to know I could do large-scale reforestation."

Resources

Leslie Bennett: pinehouseediblegardens.com

Erin Benzakein: floretflowers.com

Eliza Blank: thesill.com

Jinny Blom: jinnyblom.com

Carol Bornstein:

- carolbornstein.com
- nhm.org/nature/visit/nature-gardens

Marion Brenner: marionbrenner.com

Cindy Brown: gardens.si.edu

Yolanda Burrell: pollinatefarm.com

Ariella Chezar: ariellaflowers.com

Marina Christopher:

- greatdixter.co.uk/learning/tutors/
  marina-christopher

Peggy Cornett:

- monticello.org/site/house-and-gardens/
  historic-gardens

Philippa Craddock: philippacraddock.com

Karen Daubmann: nybg.org

Andrea DeLong-Amaya: wildflower.org

Sasha Duerr: sashaduerr.com

Fionnuala Fallon:

- irishtimes.com/profile/fionnuala-
  fallon-7.1837454
- flowerfarmersofireland.ie

Severine von Tscharner Fleming

- greenhorns.org

Lorene Edwards Forkner:

- ahandmadegarden.com/about

Alys Fowler: guardian.com/profile/alys-fowler

Tiffany Freeman: tiffanyfreemanwellness.org

Kate Frey: freygardens.com

Christin Geall: cultivatedbychristin.com

Flora Grubb: floragrubb.com

Annie Hayes: anniesannuals.com

Elizabeth Hoover:

- gardenwarriorsgoodseeds.com/about
- brown.edu/academics/native-american-
  and-indigenous-studies/faculty

Elaine Ingham: soilfoodweb.com

Robin Wall Kimmerer: esf.edu/faculty/kimmerer

Jamaica Kincaid:

- aaas.fas.harvard.edu/people/jamaica-
  kincaid

Lauri Kranz: ediblegardensla.com

Barbara Kreski:

- chicagobotanic.org/therapy/staff

Mia Lehrer: studio-mla.com

Arabella Lennox-Boyd:

- arabellalennoxboyd.com

Cara Loriz: seedalliance.org

Clare Cooper Marcus:

- ced.berkeley.edu/ced/faculty-staff/clare-
  cooper-marcus

Mary Pat Matheson:

- atlantabg.org/about-the-garden/
  administration-partners/mary-pat-
  matheson

Marta McDowell: martamcdowell.com

Jekka McVicar: jekkasherbfarm.com

Amy Merrick: amymerrick.com

Julie Moir Messervy: jmmds.com

Julie Nelson:

- backcountrypress.com/authors/julie-
  kierstead-nelson

Ngoc Minh Ngo: ngocminhngo.com

Anna Pavord:

- bloomsbury.com/author/anna-pavord

Frances Palmer: francespalmerpottery.com

Susan Pell: usbg.gov/staff/susan-pell-phd

Leah Penniman: soulfirefarm.org

Hemlata Pradhan:

- serindiagallery.com/hemlata-pradhan

Sarah Price: sarahpricelandscapes.com

Milla Prince: thewomanwhomarriedabear.com

Debra Prinzing:

- slowflowers.com
- slowflowerssociety.com

Sarah Raven: sarahraven.com

Georgina Reid: theplanthunter.com.au

Margaret Roach: awaytogarden.com

Martha Schwartz: marthaschwartz.com

Jane Scotter: fernverrow.com

Renee Shepherd: reneesgarden.com

Michelle Slatalla: gardenista.com

Janet Sluis: plantdevelopment.com

Lauren Springer:

- houzz.com/pro/bestplantmom/lauren-
  springer

Gwen Stauffer: lotusland.org

Amy Stewart: amystewart.com

Claire Takacs: takacsphoto.com

Tessa Traeger: tessatraeger.com

Beth Tuttle: ahsgardening.org

Mégan Twilegar: pistilsnursery.com

Edwina von Gal: perfectearthproject.org

Ira Wallace: southernexposure.com

Françoise Weeks: francoiseweeks.com

Claudia West: phytostudio.com

Rowen White:

- sierraseeds.org
- iskn.org

Kristen Wickert:

- plantandsoil.wvu.edu/spotlights/kristen-
  wickert

Sue Wynn-Jones: crug-farm.co.uk

Ayana Young: forthewild.world

Acknowledgments

The seventy-five women whose stories and work comprise this book are the real writers of it, although any errors or unseen biases are mine alone. Their unlimited creativity, heart, and perseverance stand as powerful testament to what really being human and interdependent with plants and with one another means. Their patient and expansive sharing and teaching throughout this process cannot be overstated. Thank you as well to Timber Press who put forth the invitation and opened this door to me. Stacee Lawrence, Sarah Milhollin, Jacoba Lawson, and Besse Lynch, your patience, persistence, grace, and humor have made this a better book and me a better writer. Thank you.

To my sisters, Sabrina and Flora, my Aunt Di, my stepmother Isabel, my friends Mary and Nancy, and other family, friends, and colleagues who've so long supported me and my vision for the radio program and podcast *Cultivating Place* and this new book: thank you from the depths of my heart.

To my lively, lovely, bright daughters, Delaney and Flannery, who are on their paths and already making the world a better place: your dreams are big and your hearts and minds are even bigger. Thank you both for your love and support.

To Sheila Blackford, my deeply literate and kind cousin, who painstakingly pre-edited every word of this book.

Finally, to John who walked with me every step of this way—listening, curious, encouraging, insightful—with loving kindness, cookies, dinners, coffee, wine, and understanding. You made the whole process more fun and fully celebrated.

Photography Credits

Jonah Vitale-Wolff, Courtesy of Soul Fire Farms, 9 (top)

Jonathan Buckley, 2 (first column, bottom), 213, 214

Jordan Kinley, 82

Judy Pak, 9 (second down)

Julian Wass, 176

Julie Hassett Sutton, 225

Kara Pearson Photography, 252

Kate Frey, 99

Kate Garlock, 273

Ken Burns, 169

Kevin McConnell, 277

Kiichi Noro, 237

Lauren Springer Ogden, 255

Laurie McKenzie, 146

Lindsay Morris, 280

Lorene Edwards Forkner, 87

Courtesy of Lotusland, 257, 259

Marina Christopher, 54

Marion Brenner, 34, 35, 41, 43, 109, 149, 245

Margaret Roach, 222, 223

Marta McDowell, 159

Martha Schwartz, 226, 227

Martin Pope, 140

Mary Grace Long Photography, 211

Meghan Spiro, 47

Melissa Ozawa, 179

Micaela Colley, 144

Michael G. Davis, 121

Michelle Slatalla, 2 (fourth column, fourth down)

Milla Prince, 205, 206

Ming de Nasty, 89, 90

Missy Palacol Photography, 2 (third column, fourth down), 10 (bottom), 85, 208, 210

Molly Leebove, Courtesy of For The Wild, 311

Neshima Vitale-Penniman, Courtesy of Soul Fire Farms, 194

Ngoc Minh Ngo, 178

peganum, Flickr CC BY-SA 2.0, 55

Courtesy of Peggy Cornett, 59, 65, 66, 67

Philippa Craddock, 62, 63

Rachel Warne, 25

Raleigh Latham, Soil Foodweb Inc., 117

Ray Mims, Courtesy of the United States Botanic Garden, Smithsonian Gardens, 39

Richard Johnston, 2 (first column, fourth down), 76, 78, 79

Rivkah Beth Medow, 72

Rob Cardillo Photography, 2 (second column, bottom), 292, 294

Rob Woolmington, 125

Courtesy of Robin Kimmerer, 122

Rumplefarm, LLC, 118

Sarah Milhollin, 2 (fourth column, third down), 261, 263, 265

Sarah Price Landscape Design, 202

Sasha Duerr, 74, 75

Sera Lindsey, Courtesy of For The Wild, 2 (first column, second down), 309

The Seeds of Vandana Shiva, vandanshivamovie.com, 241, 243

Shogo Oizumi, 2 (third column, third down), 238

Courtesy of The Sill, 2 (third column, second down), 20, 22, 23

Siri Thorson, 165

Courtesy of STUDIO MLA, 9 (third down), 138

Susan Teare, 171

Tessa Traeger, 229, 230, 231, 270, 271

Theresa Bear Photography, 288

Thomas Baldwin, 81

Udai C Pradhan, 197

United States Botanic Garden, 189, 190

Virginia Weiler, 170

Yolanda V. Fundora, 157

Index

Jennifer Jewell is a gardener, garden writer, and gardening educator and advocate. Since 2016, she has written and hosted the national award-winning, weekly public radio program and podcast, *Cultivating Place: Conversations on Natural History & the Human Impulse to Garden*, a coproduction of North State Public Radio in Chico, California. Particularly interested in the intersections between gardens, the native plant environments around them, and human culture, she is the daughter of a garden- and floral-designing mother and a wildlife biologist father. Jennifer has been writing about gardening professionally since 1998, and her work has appeared in *Gardens Illustrated*, *House & Garden*, *Natural Home*, *Old House Journal*, *Colorado Homes & Lifestyles*, and *Pacific Horticulture*. She worked as native plant garden curator for the Gateway Science Museum on the campus of California State University, Chico, from 2009–2018. She lives, gardens, and hikes in the rich biodiversity of interior Northern California, on traditional lands of the Mechoopda Maidu people, in the company of her daughters and her partner, John Whittlesey, whenever possible.